DEMOCRACY AT WORK IN AN
INDIAN INDUSTRIAL COOPERATIVE

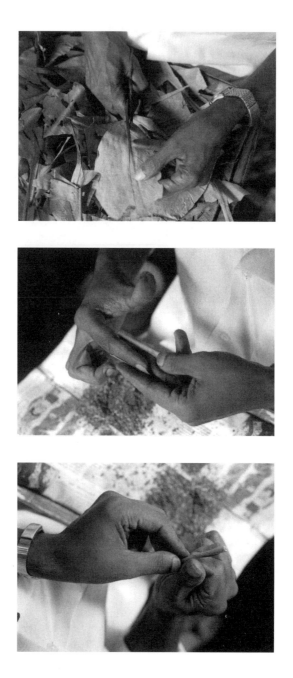

Democracy at Work in an Indian Industrial Cooperative

The Story of Kerala Dinesh Beedi

T. M. Thomas Isaac

Richard W. Franke and

Pyaralal Raghavan

ILR Press an imprint of

Cornell University Press

Ithaca and London

Cornell University Press gratefully acknowledges a subvention from Montclair State University, which has aided in publication of this book.

Photographs on the title page by T. Rajesh.

First published 1998 by Cornell University Press
First printing, Cornell Paperbacks, 1998

Number 34 in the Cornell International Industrial and Labor Relations Report series

Printed in the United States of America

Library of Congress Cataloging-in-Publication Data

Thomas Isaac, T. M., b. 1952
    Democracy at work in an Indian industrial cooperative : the story of Kerala Dinesh Beedi / T. M. Thomas Isaac, Richard W. Franke, and Pyaralal Raghavan.
        p.   cm.
    Includes bibliographical references and index.
    ISBN 0-8014-3384-3 (cloth : alk. paper). — ISBN 0-8014-8415-4 (pbk. : alk. paper)
    1. Kerala Dinesh Beedi (Firm) 2. Tobacco industry—India—Kerala.
3. Cooperation—India—Kerala.   I. Franke, Richard W.   II. Raghavan, Pyaralal.
III. Title.
HD9146.I44K477   1998
334'.68371'095483—dc21   97-52189

Cloth printing   10   9   8   7   6   5   4   3   2   1
Paperback printing   10   9   8   7   6   5   4   3   2   1

To

G. K. Panikkar (1922–1996), Chairman of KDB Cooperative, an administrator whose commitment to the cause of workers' cooperatives was exemplary, and whose individual contribution was one of the most important factors in the success of KDB,

and to

C. Kannan, General Secretary of the Kannur Tobacco Workers' Union, who has been involved with the beedi trade union movement from its inception and who personifies the best traditions of the radical movement in North Malabar.

Contents

Preface   ix

Note on the Spelling of Indian Place-Names   xv

CHAPTER ONE
Beedi Workers and the Kerala Model   1

CHAPTER TWO
The Making of the Beedi Working Class   22

CHAPTER THREE
Solidarity versus Retrenchment: The Birth of KDB   54

CHAPTER FOUR
From Mobilization to Efficiency: The Role of the Central Society   86

CHAPTER FIVE
The Dynamics of Shop Floor Democracy: Empowerment versus
Supervision in the Beedi Primary Cooperatives   118

CHAPTER SIX
Efficiency and Profit in the Primary Societies:
KDB's Market Dilemma   156

CHAPTER SEVEN
KDB and the International Movement for Workers' Cooperatives   182

AFTERWORD:
Tobacco Production and Diversification at KDB   217

Notes   225

Bibliography   233

Index

Preface

The Indian state of Kerala has come to international attention in recent years because of its success in achieving a high quality of life despite severe economic underdevelopment. This phenomenon, referred to as the "Kerala Model," provides the background for our study of the Kerala Dinesh Beedi workers' cooperative (KDB), which manufactures beedis, small cigarettes known in India as "the poor man's smoke."

The current book grew out of the three authors' varying experiences with the Kerala Model. T. M. Thomas Isaac has worked for many years as an academic and a political activist within Kerala's radical movements helping to create egalitarian and participatory development strategies. His interest in Kerala Dinesh Beedi arose as he sought local models of democracy that could inspire and offer examples for the larger society. The idea of bringing KDB to an international audience came after he read *Making Mondragón* by William and Kathleen Whyte (1988), which describes the most well known of all worker-owned cooperatives. Thomas Isaac wondered whether people outside Kerala would also be interested in the dramatic genesis, overall success, and shortcomings of Kerala Dinesh Beedi.

In the 1980s, Richard W. Franke had become interested in Kerala's achievements in raising the material quality of life of its people despite low overall economic growth. Having seen in other societies that growth without equity often leads to persistent poverty, he carried out research in Kerala in 1986–87 to attempt an evaluation of the state's radical redistribution programs at the village level (Franke 1996; Franke and Chasin 1994). His data showed that redistribution has a positive, measurable effect on levels of living. Thomas Isaac's suggestion for collaboration on a study of KDB meant the possibility

ix

of extending the Kerala research into the arena of local democracy, a key element in Kerala's overall development story.

Pyaralal Raghavan is himself a product of Kerala's development history. His father was a trade union and independence activist in the town of Kannur, where the beedi workers were usually in the forefront of anticolonial and proworker struggles. Raghavan decided to study the history of Kerala Dinesh Beedi as part of the history of the working class in Malabar (northern Kerala), part of his own family's history, but with the larger goal of analyzing KDB's general relevance for the cooperative movement in Kerala.

After some preliminary interviews with beedi workers and KDB directors, we held an all-day meeting in January 1993 to consider whether such a study could be done. We laid out the research methods we would use, divided the tasks, planned some timetables, and decided to go forward. Working in two languages, communicating across thousands of miles, sharing ideas and text mostly via air mail and telephone until e-mail services recently became available in Kerala, we found the project took much longer than we had initially estimated. We have simultaneously prepared a version of the text in Malayalam—the language spoken and read by virtually all people in Kerala, including KDB's workers. Beedi workers will thus have as much access to our account of their struggles, achievements, and current challenges as do international readers.

We thank Cornell University Press for publishing this book, and we hope it will make a useful contribution to the international community of academics and activists who share our interest in and commitment to democracy in the workplace.

A number of published and unpublished accounts exist in English concerning the history and structure of KDB (Mohandas 1980; Mohanan 1982, 1983, and 1984; Panikkar 1982 and 1985; Seetharam and Mohanan 1982; Raghavan 1986 and 1995; Kannan 1988; and Mohandas and Kumar 1992). We supplement these sources with printed documents such as trade union remembrance volumes and other local historical materials available only in Malayalam and often only in local union offices. We also collected news reports on beedi workers around northern Malabar from the 1934 to 1969 volumes of the Malayalam daily newspaper *Mathrubhumi*. Founded in 1923 by supporters of India's national independence movement, *Mathrubhumi* (Motherland) was the only newspaper published from Kozhikode

(Calicut) in the Malabar region of Kerala. *Mathrubhumi* is thus the newspaper of record for the time and place that includes the beedi industry and the associated rise of the beedi working class that created Kerala Dinesh Beedi (Jeffrey 1997). Much of the history in chapter 2 derives from *Mathrubhumi* accounts as well as from union remembrance volumes, which we cite to give the workers' own perspectives on the events.

We conducted and recorded sixty extensive interviews with the directors, staff, workers, and trade union activists of KDB between 6 January 1993 and 24 June 1994. More than forty hours of interviews cover topics from the historical background to current worker and management grievances at KDB. English transcripts of many of these interviews—most of which were conducted in Malayalam—have been deposited at the Centre for Development Studies and AKG Research Centre libraries in Thiruvananthapuram, Kerala. We also met for three hours with the worker-elected director board, the chairman and the first secretary of the central cooperative in Kannur, at which time we reported some initial findings and received detailed, articulate, and animated reactions. Follow-up discussions took place with several officers, union activists, and board members over a three-day period.

The financial records of the twenty-two primary societies for the bookkeeping year ending 31 March 1993 were kindly made available to us by the central society director and secretary of KDB in October 1993. We focus our attention on them in chapter 6.

In a written survey distributed to the 154 members of the twenty-two director boards of the primary societies, we asked questions about their experience as beedi workers, their sources of income within and outside the cooperative, their trade union and political affiliations, and their views on important problems and issues facing KDB. Much of the information from this survey appears in chapter 5.

Chapter 1 introduces Kerala, the Kerala Model of development, the beedi industry, and Kerala Dinesh Beedi. We explain why KDB is important to the Kerala Model, to Indian industrial workers, and to the international movement for workers' cooperatives. Chapters 2 through 6 examine particular elements of the KDB experience in the context of one or more major conceptual comparative issues that have appeared in the international literature on workers' cooperatives. We begin our analysis of Kerala Dinesh Beedi with an analysis of the social and political milieu of northern Kerala, where the beedi cooperative originated and functions today. Specifically we focus in chapter 2 on the making of the beedi working class in Kannur. We attempt to uncover the main sources for the origin of the strong radical democratic consciousness in Malabar that is considered essential to the success of cooperatives. In chapter 3 we look into the specific conditions in which the cooperative came to be formed, emphasizing the initiative of the workers themselves rather than government actions. The mobilized atmosphere of the late 1960s in Kerala reflected nearly a century of struggle for changes in the lives of colonial subjects, agricultural tenants and laborers, and workers in many economic sectors. KDB's close ties with the larger social movement that produced the Kerala Model led in part to the cooperative's own success, consistent with observations by other writers that cooperatives benefit from participation in broader social movements.

In chapter 4 we consider the problems of raw material purchase, marketing, and quality control that bind together the smaller units into the central society. Here we refer to the literature citing small size and the hostile market environment that doom many cooperatives to failure. KDB's constant creativity in finding shelter mechanisms such as the thrift fund with which to compete with capitalist production has helped it survive, but difficult times may lie ahead. We also show how the structure of central cooperative and federated local cooperatives helps KDB solve the problem of investment for the future versus immediate distribution to the worker-owners that some theorists have cited as the main cause for failure of workers' cooperatives. Chapter 5 looks at the management of the cooperative in terms of workplace democracy, focusing on the primary societies and work centers. We examine these features in the context of the degeneration hypothesis in economics and its counterpart in sociology, the "iron law of oligarchy." We show that KDB's mix of empowerment and supervision has led to the remarkable achievement of preventing degeneration while maintaining market competitiveness. In chapter 6 we return to the problem of efficiency in a hostile market environment. Chapter 6 contains a mostly statistical analysis of the factors that determine the relative efficiency of the primary societies at Kerala Dinesh Beedi. In chapter 7 we try to bring all the themes together to consider KDB's experience in light of the general literature on workers' cooperatives, including the debate over whether they are practical, and the substantial literature on the psychological and political consequences of worker ownership and control of the workplace. We show how KDB's egalitarianism fits the Rawlsian philosophical principle that any divergence from pure equality should benefit everyone more than pure equality would. We also show how Malabar's radical, activist worker culture combines with the several sound business structures built up by KDB to create a workers' cooperative that appears able to survive both degeneration tendencies and the fierce competition of the capitalist market. We then draw what we believe are the lessons from the Kerala Dinesh Beedi experience for the cooperative and workers' movements internationally. The afterword takes up the problem of workers' producing a tobacco product and considers KDB's recent first steps toward diversification—a process that offers the potential to deepen the cooperative's democracy while broadening its impact on Malabar and contributing to a renewal of the Kerala model.

Many individuals and organizations provided assistance in making this book possible. Some are named in the text or appear in the list of interviews. Others deserve special mention. In the United States, Stephen P. Borgatti offered many helpful suggestions in the statistical section of chapter 6. Barbara H. Chasin and Stephen Rosskamm Shalom read early versions of the manuscript and made thoughtful critiques. Cornell's two anonymous reviewers gave invaluable advice. Cornell University Press Editor-in-Chief Frances Benson assisted us at every stage of review and evaluation to improve the content and style of the original manuscript. We also thank editors Jamie Fuller, Teresa Jesionowski, and Lisa Turner for their many ideas for clarifying and tightening our arguments. We also thank Lou Robinson, the designer, who also designed the jacket and cover. Part of the research for this book was funded by the Global Education Center at Montclair State University. Gregory Waters of Montclair State also gave support in the preparation of the manuscript. Charles Fraser of Academic Computing helped frequently in solving technical problems.
In Kerala, Pookkadan Chandran, union activist, retired president of Chirakkal primary society, and former member of the board of directors of the central society, spent several days guiding us from one interview site to the next, making introductions, and facilitating our research. He was instrumental in bringing us into contact with shop floor workers. KDB's central society secretary, E. Radha Madhavan,

and chairman G. K. Panikkar tirelessly responded to a barrage of faxes to clarify and update information in the last months of preparing the manuscript. N. P. Gopalakrishnan, secretary of KDB from 1982 until his retirement in 1994, gave much of his time and substantial knowledge. Chandan Mukherjee, director of the Centre for Development Studies, was generous in permitting use of the center's research facilities and granting an adequate leave of absence to faculty member T. M. Thomas Isaac. Members of KDB's central society board of directors took a keen interest in our progress, in particular, N. P. Pavithran. C. Kannan, and his colleagues at the Tobacco Workers' Union in Kannur granted us the privilege of describing their half century of struggle on behalf of beedi workers. We also acknowledge the cooperation of the Tellicherry and Payyanur beedi workers' unions, whose officers and members often went out of their way to meet our research needs. Thayath Raghavan, beedi trade union activist, inspired his son, Pyaralal Raghavan, to write about beedi workers and their struggles. Srikumar Chattopadhyay of Kerala's Centre for Earth Science Studies designed and produced the map of Kannur with the locations of the KDB primary cooperatives.

Our fieldwork in Malabar coincided with involvement of one of the authors in an experiment in participatory planning for sustainable development in Kalliasseri Panchayat, which has now become a model for all of Kerala. This experience constantly brought home the importance of studying initiatives such as Kerala Dinesh Beedi from below. Activists of the Kerala People's Science Movement in Kannur and Kalliasseri, especially T. Gangadharan and T. P. Sudhakaran, helped us in many ways to think about the issues in this book.

T. M. THOMAS ISAAC
RICHARD W. FRANKE
PYARALAL RAGHAVAN

Note on the Spelling of Indian Place-Names

In recent years, Indian place-names have been undergoing modifications so that the spellings reflect their pre-British pronunciations. These changes may confuse some readers since few of the new names are yet on maps in the United States. Bombay has become Mumbai; Madras was renamed Chennai. Malayalam, the language of Kerala, has about twenty sounds not heard in English and uses an entirely different alphabet. The new spellings are intended to systematize the English versions. In Kerala, the capital city of Trivandrum is now Thiruvananthapuram; Quilon is Kollam; Trichur is Thrissur. With regard to the beedi-producing areas most often referred to in the text, most names on the map are spelled in the most recent way, but we have kept the older spellings in the text since those are used in the references and were in use at the times described. Some readers are also likely to be familiar with Calicut (now Kozhikode) for its historical importance and with Tellicherry (now Thalassery), which is the brand name of a pepper sold in Western spice shops. Other changes from the text presentations are Alleppey (now Allapuzha), Badagara (now Vadakara), and Cannanore (now Kannur).

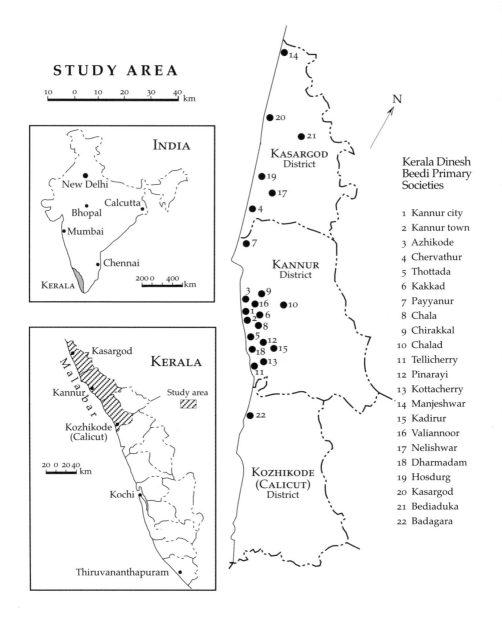

STUDY AREA

INDIA

New Delhi

Calcutta
Bhopal
Mumbai

Chennai

KERALA

KERALA

Kasargod

Malabar

Kannur

Kozhikode
(Calicut)

Study area

Kochi

Thiruvananthapuram

14

20

21

KASARGOD
District

19
17

4

7

KANNUR
District

3 9
16
1 6
2
8
5
12
18 15
13
11

10

22

KOZHIKODE
(CALICUT)
District

N

Kerala Dinesh
Beedi Primary
Societies

1 Kannur city
2 Kannur town
3 Azhikode
4 Chervathur
5 Thottada
6 Kakkad
7 Payyanur
8 Chala
9 Chirakkal
10 Chalad
11 Tellicherry
12 Pinarayi
13 Kottacherry
14 Manjeshwar
15 Kadirur
16 Valiannoor
17 Nelishwar
18 Dharmadam
19 Hosdurg
20 Kasargod
21 Bediaduka
22 Badagara

Kerala Dinesh Beedi Primary Societies

CHAPTER ONE

Beedi Workers and the Kerala Model

Kerala state is located in the far southwest corner of India. It is a subtropical land of coconut gardens, rice fields, and rubber and tea plantations. Because of its great distance from Europe and North America, Kerala's beautiful beaches and spectacular mountains have yet to attract large numbers of Western tourists. But with just 3.5 percent of India's population on an area the size of Switzerland, Kerala has drawn the attention of scholars worldwide. Despite one of the world's lowest per capita incomes, Kerala has achieved levels of literacy, life expectancy, infant mortality, and birth rates nearly as high as those in developed countries. So unusual are the state's material quality-of-life indicators that in recent years academics have come to speak of the "Kerala Model" of development. A large literature has grown up around Kerala's radical land reform, its peasant and farm labor unions, its system of food distribution to the poor, its agricultural workers' protection acts, and other progressive features that we shall describe in more detail later in this chapter. Kerala has given development specialists much to think about and debate.

Because of its rural, agricultural character, Kerala is rarely thought of in connection with industrial workers. The state has had one of the lowest rates of industrial growth in all of India, and it remains economically and technologically more backward than the developed nations and many parts of India itself. Indeed, much of the fascination with the Kerala Model results precisely from the combination of economic underdevelopment with advanced quality-of-life indicators.

1

Kerala has an unexpected contribution to make on a topic usually restricted to the most economically developed countries. In Malabar, the northern part of Kerala, is found the Kerala Dinesh Beedi Workers' Cooperative Society Ltd. KDB, as we shall call it in this book, currently represents one of the world's largest and most successful experiments in industrial democracy. From a few hundred desperate workers in 1969 among twelve thousand who had been locked out by their employers, KDB grew to employ over thirty-three thousand worker-owners in 1993, when we collected most of the data for this study. These workers rolled the poor people's cigarettes called *beedis* at KDB, where they elect their own management from among their own ranks. The shop floor workers elect the day-to-day management of the local cooperatives; these elected directors elect the twenty-two-member general body that has ultimate authority to set policy. From its ranks are elected the five worker-directors who serve on the seven-member board. At the annual general body meetings, workers review the conduct of their management and can directly influence its policies. As trade union members, workers elect local watchdog committees intended to protect them on a day-to-day basis. KDB's workers are *empowered* at their workplace.

How did Kerala Dinesh Beedi come about? How successful has the cooperative been? How did industrially backward Kerala produce such an advanced experiment in industrial democracy? What does Kerala Dinesh Beedi have to do with the Kerala Model? Does KDB have any relevance for the development issues facing India or other third world countries? These and related questions provide the framework for our discussion.

This book is about the origin and survival of a democratic workers' cooperative in the unorganized sector of a fiercely competitive capitalist economy. Despite its apparently strange placement in an underdeveloped, largely agricultural setting, KDB has experienced many of the tensions and dynamics of workplace democracy in industries throughout the world, including the developed capitalist and former and present socialist countries. We will try to show that the KDB experience carries implications for the study of social movements, third world development, and the role of the state in promoting alternatives to capitalist development. But mostly KDB's story offers an inspiring example to the international movement for workers' cooperatives through its combination of formal, structural features and its high level of worker consciousness and activism, both of which have contributed to KDB's remarkable success in overcoming the problems commonly faced by cooperatives worldwide. What happens when workers fully own and manage a large industrial enterprise? Do they award themselves better pay and working conditions? Can they make a profit? Will they invest for the future? How do they boss themselves? What kinds of decision-making procedures do they set up to manage the long-term needs of the company? What kinds of conflict arise between workers and their elected managers and among workers themselves? Can unions continue to function meaningfully in a worker-owned business? These questions have been repeatedly examined in the literature on workplace democracy. We shall consider them, too, in order to suggest to the reader what contributions the KDB experience so far may be able to make to the international movement for workers' cooperatives.

MALABAR, KANNUR, AND KDB

Kerala Dinesh Beedi has its headquarters in the northern Kerala town of Kannur. Northern Kerala is also known as Malabar. Kannur, previously known as Cannanore, is Kerala's fourth largest city with a 1991 population of 464,000 (Bose et al. 1994: 187).[1] Despite its large population, Kannur is a pleasant, bustling municipality with a small-town atmosphere. The packed center of town includes the usual Indian railway station, streets jammed with small three-wheeled cabs called "autoricks" (motorized rickshaws), taxis, buses, bicycles, pedestrians, cows, and hawkers' carts. Everywhere are the smells of fresh jasmine and other flowers, incense, curries and foods of all kinds, and rotting garbage—in the daytime covered with crows who compete with the ever-present Indian cows and underfed dogs for the tidbits of food, decaying banana and palm leaves, and other assorted rubbish heaped here and there. On the whole, Kannur is a clean town, and even the railway station, like most in Kerala, has but an occasional beggar.

From Kannur's busy business district it is less than a kilometer to the quiet, tree-lined lane on which stands a former princely palace that is now the headquarters of the KDB. Across from the palace is a hotel that once housed and fed British military officers—for Kannur was a small base in colonial times. Farther down the lane one reaches a row of fancy homes, inhabited at one time by British officers but now by officers of the Indian army and some of the town elite. KDB's offices are modest; most of the former palace is used to pack and store finished beedis.

Traveling on from Kannur, we quickly reach the Kerala countryside of rice fields broken up by stands of coconut trees behind which most Malayalis have their houses. Speaking Malayalam, of the Dravidian group of languages that have no known connections to other world languages, Kerala's villagers organize their lives around their rice fields, their coconut gardens, and whatever employment they can find in their increasingly difficult job market. Unemployment in Kerala is by far the highest in India.

Within a few kilometers, we arrive at a small, dingy office building inside which a clerk is typing and a "peon," or helper, is carrying around a tray filled with glasses of tea with milk. Next to the office we see a building somewhat like a barn. Inside, KDB workers are rolling beedis. Across Malabar, in all directions from Kannur, are KDB's 326 work centers, in which workers produce and package beedis for the twenty-two worker-owned primary cooperatives that make up the company. The finished and packed beedis are sent to Kannur town, where the central cooperative registers them and prepares them for marketing. The central cooperative is also owned by the workers.

For centuries, the entire region now known as Kerala was called Malabar. It was known to the Greeks and Romans as a source of pepper, cardamom, cinnamon, ginger, and other spices as well as teak wood. Kerala legends claim that the Jewish community at Cochin along the Malabar coast was founded by refugees from the struggles against Nebuchadnezzar in the sixth century B.C. Similar legends claim that St. Thomas founded seven Christian churches in Malabar in A.D. 52. Whatever the truth of these stories, we can say that Malabar played a role in international trade from very ancient times and was influenced over many centuries by cultures from China to Europe.

Malabar became prominent in European eyes after 1498, when

Vasco da Gama sailed to the port of Calicut on its north-central coast. Calicut resisted the Portuguese domination, was brutally assaulted by da Gama and other Portuguese military commanders, and eventually succumbed after its Zamorin, or ruler, lost his alliances with the overlords of Cochin to the south and Kannur to the north. Calicut's brightly colored printed cloth so delighted Europeans that they demanded it for their own garments and for household uses. We still know it today by the name "calico," from the town where Vasco da Gama and his rapacious sailors first laid eyes on it in 1498.[2]

Malabar came under Portuguese influence. The Portuguese built a series of forts at the beginning of the sixteenth century. Kannur's St. Angelo battlements date from 1505 and are remarkably well preserved. The view from the ramparts extends far into the Arabian Sea. Just below the fort, one comes to a stunning mosque, with Persian-style inlaid marble reminiscent of the Taj Mahal. Here today much of Kannur's substantial Muslim population answers the muezzin's call to prayer. Arab and East African merchants and traders had called at Kannur and Calicut for centuries before the Portuguese. Through these peaceful traders Islam entered Malabar.

Following the Portuguese, Dutch colonialists dominated Malabar, but British control, exercised after 1792, had the greatest effect on Kannur and its surrounding areas. The British ruled India directly in some areas, through local princes or nobility in others. Malabar now came to designate a district of the "Madras Presidency," which was under direct British rule. The southern region—the Kingdom of Travancore—and the central region—the Kingdom of Cochin—ostensibly continued to be ruled by their local princes, but in reality they were indirectly governed by a British colonial appointee called a "Resident." When the independent Indian state of Kerala was formed in 1956, Malabar, Cochin, and Travancore were all united on the basis of their common language, Malayalam. The districts had strong cultural similarities but somewhat different colonial histories.

By the 1950s, the old Malabar coast of early colonial days had thus been segmented into three colonial regions and then reunited into a single state within the Indian federation. Malabar became northern Kerala, the most Muslim and the most directly colonized part of the new state. Malabar had also become the main area of Kerala where beedis were produced.

The Technical Process

Beedis are known in India as "the poor man's smoke." About 6 centimeters (2.3 inches) long, of smaller diameter than American cigarettes, and tapered from a small opening at the mouth to a larger end, beedis offer to millions of Indians a mildly intoxicating, relaxing escape from everyday life.

By the mid-1980s a total of 250 million Indians lit up a combined 1 million beedis per minute (Raghavan 1986: 1). Despite this phenomenal demand, India's equally phenomenal poverty makes it possible for the 1.4 billion beedis required per day to be manufactured with no equipment other than scissors, a bamboo tray, and the skilled hands and concentration of a beedi roller: the workers are paid so little that replacing them with machinery would not increase profits.

First, support workers prepare the tobacco by powdering it and pushing it through a sieve. The tobacco flakes are then dried in the sun and later given to the rollers. In the meantime, the beedi rollers

KDB workers witnessing the distribution of the first pension funds in Kannur 1987. The first funds were distributed by K. R. Gowri, the then minister of industries and a key author of Kerala's famous land reform act. Photo supplied by KDB.

A worker rolls a wrapper leaf around the tobacco. The workers who founded KDB in 1969 were nearly all men, but by 1995 60 percent of the workers were women. Photo by Richard W. Franke.

KDB workers enjoy clean, spacious surroundings, in contrast to those of private-sector rollers. Photo by T. Rajesh

are preparing the wrapper leaves from what Indians call *tendu* leaf. These wrapper leaves have been soaked in water to make them easier to shape and cut; the wet leaves give off a strong odor. Each tendu leaf yields from two to four wrapper leaves.

As the worker cuts the leaf, he or she also removes the thick veins of the leaf to make it easier to roll around the pinch of tobacco that will be inserted later. Some workers use a metal form to cut the leaves; the more skilled and experienced can sight in an instant the best layout of wrappers from a particular leaf. Leaves are more valuable than workers' time; broken or wasted leaves cost money.

After about two hours of wrapper cutting, the beedi roller reaches into the bamboo tray, picking up a small handful of tobacco flakes. These are spread evenly down the six-centimeter length of the wrapper leaf. Then, in a swift motion of the fingers and palm, the wrapper leaf is rolled around the tobacco, making a conical shape. The worker closes off the top end with a push of the fingertip and ties the lower end with a piece of thread drawn up from the bamboo tray. The finished beedi is added to the other beedis in a neat pile on the tray.

Rolled beedis are tied into bundles and then dried in the sun or in charcoal ovens. The dried beedis are packed into hanks or bundles, which are wrapped in packages, put into larger containers and wrapped again for marketing. It was estimated in 1997 that, when part-time workers are included (those working fewer than 150 days per year), up to six million Indians made beedis (Srinivasulu 1997: 515).

The Dismal Life of the Beedi Maker

Beedi rolling is skilled work. Rollers depending on their skill, can make from six hundred to two thousand beedis in a day. But beedi making is one of the most exploitative industries in India. Workers in many areas are paid starvation wages. To increase their output, many hire child assistants. The children are paid from the adults' wages. Many appear to be in ill health "with yellowish eyes and haggard cheeks," according to one government report (Raghavan 1986: 25). Work sites are poorly lit, poorly ventilated, and dirty, with torn mats, aluminum, glass, brass tumblers, and other odds and ends strewn all over. Workers frequently cough up blood; many beedi workers are thought to suffer from tuberculosis, but no official statistics are available. Asthma and bronchitis are also widely reported (Government of India 1988: xxvi; Government of India 1981b: 141–45).[3] Workers roll beedis while crowded together on shop floors with less than a meter-by-meter (three feet by three feet) area for each. Women roll beedis with infants on their laps, both mother and child smeared with traces of tobacco and breathing in tobacco fumes (Beedi workers of Sinnar 1974: 947). Basic amenities are lacking. In 88 percent of private-sector beedi shops in Kerala in the 1970s, there was no latrine; 83 percent provided no drinking water (Mohandas 1980: 1520). Thousands of workers roll beedis in their homes, where they can control the environment a little better. But the smell of tobacco permeates their small huts, and children and infants are constantly exposed to the leaves and flakes that cover everything.

Whether working at home or in the small shops, most of India's more than 1.6 million full time beedi workers in 1980 (Government of India 1981a) do "putting out" labor. The immediate boss is a contractor for the larger manufacturer. The manufacturer arranges the purchase of raw materials to prepare the blend of tobacco for the contractors and also organizes the marketing of the finished beedis. The contractor supplies the pieceworkers with specified amounts of tobacco flakes and wrapper leaves each day. The workers cut the leaves, roll and tie the beedis, and deliver them back to the contractor at the end of the day. Fifty-six percent are women; they must tend to household chores and most child-rearing tasks in addition to rolling or labeling beedis.

Abuses are rampant. Contractors typically charge the worker for one kilogram of leaves but deliver only 750 grams. When the worker delivers fewer than the expected number of beedis, the contractor deducts 20 percent from the wages (Government of India 1988: xxi). Another 10 percent may be deducted for "defective" beedis— whether the contractor checks for them or not. Workers typically end up with only about 50 percent of the legal minimum wage. Their arrangements with the contractor are verbal. Most beedi workers in India have little or no land. In a mostly agricultural economy, this means they have no independent sources of income. They cannot afford to be cut off from the beedi work; hundreds of other people are nearby to take their place. They are powerless to complain.

In addition to being denied the legal minimum wage, beedi workers are regularly cheated by their bosses out of the benefits written into the 1966 all-India Beedi and Cigar Workers' Act and the later Beedi Workers' Welfare Fund Act. Contractors also often steal the contributions the workers make to a welfare fund by signing false papers with fictitious names. With such power over their female workers, male contractors often engage in sexual abuse. Women who flirt with their contractors can sometimes reduce the deductions; those who invite them for a liaison may get full pay for the day (Dharmalingam 1993: 1463). In the Nippani region of Karnataka State, a major beedi-producing area, reports indicate that contractors frequently "handle" the women workers during beedi and raw materials deliveries (Avachat 1978: 1178).

Beedi workers are often in debt to local moneylenders. In some areas the loans carry interest charges of up to 10 percent per day. Some workers find it necessary to rent out one or more of their children, who become "bonded laborers," often to the beedi contractors. These children work from 6:00 A.M. until late in the evening, folding the corners of beedi wrappers (Government of India 1988: xxii). In Sinnar in Maharashtra State, workers cut the leaves at night and roll the beedis the following day. They have no family life separate from their work drudgery except for eight days a month, which they are too exhausted to enjoy (Beedi workers of Sinnar 1974: 945). Impoverished, exploited, abused, and desperate, beedi rollers cut and roll and tie until their fingers lose the roughness of skin and dexterity of muscles necessary to produce the required quality. Worked out and useless to the contractors, many end up as beggars (Avachat 1978: 1177).

Why don't beedi workers organize and fight back? Besides being desperately poor, they are rendered effectively powerless by the nature of the production process. Beedi manufacturing requires no machinery, only scissors and a bamboo tray. There are thus no expensive pieces of capital investment that the workers could occupy and threaten to destroy. There is no need to centralize production in large centers where the workers might come to sense their potential organized strength. The bosses seem to hold all the cards.

Despite the odds, beedi workers have struck. In 1980 in Bombay forty thousand workers struck for forty-three days. Eventually they attracted so much attention that the prime minister of India visited the site. High state government officials joined in the negotiations—whether to help the workers or the owners was not clear. In the end, the strikers won almost nothing; the manufacturers easily bypassed laws and agreements because the workers were so dispersed and so poor. Whenever the workers gained strength, the contractors could threaten to move to another location.

The contractors can also manipulate almost every part of the production process—from the price at which they sell wrapper leaves and tobacco to the workers, to the price they pay for the finished beedis, to the weighing of the leaves, to the "quality checks" and rejection rates (Abraham 1980). Despite the odds against them, a few beedi workers have made gains. In Ahmedabad they raised wages through a partially successful union. In Mangalore (Karnataka), many of the welfare benefits are actually paid, especially in the larger work centers where worker organizations can exert some power over the owners and the contractor structure has been replaced by direct employment. But these limited gains are now threatened by the tendency of beedi producers to move out of factories and spread production into the homes, thus reintroducing or reinforcing the contractor institution. Beyond this, contractors in some parts of North India have initiated the "sale-purchase system." Workers actually buy the raw materials from the contractor, then sell the beedis back to him. The contractor rejects up to 30 percent as defective but keeps and sells them. The advantage to the contractor is that he is legally not involved in hiring labor and therefore can escape even the minimal enforcement possible under labor laws. India's poor man's smoke, produced in one of the country's largest employment sectors after agriculture and handloom, comes at a heavy price for those whose hands actually manufacture it. One beedi worker said it for all of them, referring to the contractors, manufacturers, and corrupt labor officials: "How can we ever deal with them?" (Government of India 1988: xxvii).

THE BENEFITS OF KDB

At Kerala Dinesh Beedi, workers also roll and package beedis. They cut wrapper leaves for two or three hours in the morning, then shift to rolling and tying. KDB workers can work from 7:00 to 4:00 or from 9:00 to 6:00. Lunch and tea breaks are guaranteed. Unlike workers at most other beedi establishments, they sit on bamboo benches with cement backrests. Their work sites are clean and recently painted, fluorescent lamps light the work area fairly well, and the workers have more free space to move around without bumping other employees. Outside the work shed are water-sealed latrines, sanitary if not quite as comfortable as flush toilets. At the end of the day, KDB workers can wash up at faucets located at the work sites, cleaning themselves of the smell of tobacco and putting on fresh clothes before greeting their children. The children have been in school, not assisting beedi rollers.

The beedi rollers at KDB do not suffer from unethical deductions. The "maistry," or immediate supervisor, cannot falsify the amount of tobacco, nor can he or she deduct from alleged defective beedis. If defects are claimed, the maistry must show them to the worker and assign another worker to help him or her upgrade skills. If the worker is not satisfied with the procedures, he or she can take the matter up with the trade union committee. This committee has real power and influence to prevent abuses. KDB's workers are much less likely to be in debt to moneylenders than are other beedi workers in India. At KDB, workers can borrow from the cooperative's own "thrift fund" at no interest, with repayment automatically deducted from their pay over a fairly long period.

KDB workers get Sunday off with pay and can take an additional

Table 1.1. Wages and Benefits on 31 March 1993

	Home Workers in the Karnataka-Kerala Border Region	Workers at Kerala Dinesh Beedi in Kannur
1. Wages for rolling[a] 1,000 beedis: Basic wage	Rs 14.50	Rs 14.50
Dearness allowance[b]	Rs 14.50	Rs 18.90
2. Sunday wage	None	All Sundays
3. Holiday Wage	None	14 Days
4. Casual leave wage[c]	None	15 (1 per 20 days)
5. Medical allowance	None	Rs 50
6. Maternity benefit	None	Rs 400+ and 3 months' leave
7. Bonus	11.75%	16.5%
8. Gratuity[d]	?	15 days' wages
9. Provident fund[e]	6.25%	6.25% of wages
10. Retirement benefit	None	Rs 3,000
11. Death benefit	None	Rs 5,000
12. Pension	None	Rs 150 per month
13. Thrift loan	None	Rs 600

[a] Wages for other workers and for management at KDB are given in chapter 5.
[b] Dearness allowance is a cost-of-living component of wages. See chapter 5 for a detailed discussion.
[c] Casual leave wage is the same as personal days in the United States.
[d] Gratuity is a lump sum paid on retirement only to workers with at least five years' service.
[e] Provident fund is a fund to which both employer and employee contribute in equal amounts; it is distributed as a lump-sum payment on retirement.

paid personal leave day for each twenty days of work. They also have fifteen paid national and local holidays. KDB workers and their families are protected by a death benefit of Rs 5,000 to be paid to the family if the worker dies while still at working age. If the worker works on to age fifty-eight and has twelve years employment, he or she can take a lump-sum pension of Rs 3,000. Otherwise, the worker can choose to retire at age fifty-five and receive a lifetime monthly pension of Rs 150. KDB's female workers can be pregnant without fear of loss of employment. They are entitled to three months' leave with a one-time payment of Rs 400 to Rs 600 and the right to return to their jobs after taking pregnancy leave. KDB workers do not, however, have day care centers at their work sites. Table 1.1 compares wages and benefits between KDB workers and home-based beedi workers in the Karnataka-Kerala border region. Pay and benefits in this border region, influenced by KDB's policies, are probably the best in India except for those offered by KDB; the comparison with other areas would be even more striking.

Just being a cooperative does not make KDB stand out within India or the third world. Cooperatives have long been seen as part of the answer to the failure of the market to raise productive levels and protect wages and employment in the underdeveloped countries. According to a commonly accepted view, economic development requires institutional supports that cannot be left to the free play of market forces. Since the 1950s, both development theorists and policy makers have assigned cooperative institutions a vital role in supplying credit and essential goods and services to the many farmers and petty producers who lack sufficient market entitlements, and in revitalizing traditional cottage industries. As a result, governments became active promoters of cooperatives in the third world. Even the colonial governments that were normally indifferent toward the cooperative movement in their home countries often actively encouraged cooperative movements in selected sectors of their colonies. With the attainment of independence, state intervention to accelerate economic development became the hallmark of third world government policies. In Asia and Africa especially, cooperatives rapidly expanded as development devices. Cooperatives provided important policy avenues for third world states to intervene in the product and credit markets, influence income distribution, and protect and encourage local production and employment. Third world governments provided legal frameworks, monitored and supervised the functioning of the cooperatives, contributed to their share capital, and provided substantial financial, marketing, and managerial assistance. The extensive role played by the state in their promotion is perhaps the most distinctive feature of third world cooperatives—so much so that authors like Malyarov (1983) argued that the cooperative movement in India is a part of the state capitalist structure.

Cooperatives and Economic Development in India

With 306,242 cooperatives and 146 million members in 1991, India has one of the largest cooperative networks in the world. Credit cooperatives account for a third of the cooperative units and two-thirds of the total membership—about 98 million. Industrial cooperatives rank next in importance with 42,732 units and 41.6 million members (Raghavan 1995: 55). This amounts to nearly 15 percent of the work force in India's manufacturing sector (Raghavan 1995: 58). The role of cooperative enterprises in the cottage sector began with the first industrial policy adopted after independence. A rapid growth of heavy and basic industries laid the basis for further industrialization. Until the growth of the modern capital-intensive sector gained enough momentum to fully absorb the growing workforce, the traditional and cottage industries played a crucial role in generating and protecting employment. This implied social regulation of technology in these sectors. But at the same time it was considered important to reorganize these industries to withstand the competitive pressures in the input and output markets, improve and diversify products, hold down trader margins, and guarantee a better return to producers. Cooperatives were seen to be the ideal framework for India's initial development.

The extensive state help that other workers' cooperatives in India received did not prevent the majority of them from degenerating into economically nonviable units. The available data suggest that on average 40 to 45 percent of Indian industrial cooperatives in any recent year have been inactive. The normal state strategy to revitalize the cooperative sector has been to periodically liquidate or amalgamate the nonviable ones. Yet less than a third of the cooperatives have been working at a profit. Available data indicate a decline in overall employment generation and in real returns to labor. The expansion of industrial cooperatives has significantly slowed during the last decade (Raghavan 1995: chap. 2).

Trade Unions and Cooperatives in Kerala's Traditional Industries

One aspect of Kerala's economic backwardness is that most industry remains small-scale, handicraft-based, low-tech and low-capitalized, and scattered in small production establishments rather than large factories. Even when these handicraft-based industries are concentrated in large-scale facilities, there is no technical barrier to breaking them into smaller-scale units, since the concentration is not dictated by machinery or other technical factors. Because of the lack of machinery and the use of traditional production techniques, these industries are known in the Indian economic literature as "traditional industries." A striking feature of Kerala's recent history is the development of powerful trade unions in these traditional industries.

A common response by owners to the growth of the unions has been to shift production to areas where unions don't exist (Imam Beevi 1978; Oommen 1984; Kannan 1988: 201–2) or close down the large establishments and subcontract production to smaller units (Thomas Isaac 1984; Rajagopalan 1986) or, in rare instances, to introduce machinery to replace the militant workers (Thomas Isaac et al. 1992). The trade union response to this multipronged attack by owners was to demand cooperative reorganization of these traditional industries. Cooperatives were thought to enable more centralized production systems, eliminate middlemen who were appropriating a large share of the surplus, and regulate the introduction of new technology. The pressure from the trade unions was an important factor in the evolution of government policies toward traditional industries. It also suited the overall interests of the Indian central government, which officially encouraged industrial cooperatives for rural industries.

While Kerala has an exemplary record in the performance of its agricultural credit cooperatives, the industrial cooperatives have generally not been very successful. Handloom, cashew processing, and tile manufacturing cooperatives are found in Kerala. They have been undermined by a series of severe crises that have hit their respective industries: raw material scarcity, market competition from modern products, and failure to introduce appropriate technological modernization. The few studies that have been done on industrial cooperatives in Kerala indicate that worker participation rates are low and that some so-called cooperatives are actually exploitative private companies registered as cooperatives in order to benefit from low interest loans and other government services (Raghavan 1995).

Mismanagement and corruption are not uncommon. The lack of worker participation combines in some cases with the recruitment of management from the educated—thus elite—groups to create conditions that allow the use of cooperative funds for executive privileges not justified by the cooperative's performance (Raghavan 1995). By contrast, KDB illustrates how management can adopt practices conducive to competitive performance. Unlike many cooperatives in Kerala, at KDB managers start work promptly every day at 9:30 A.M., and the working hours often go into the late evening, even on holidays. Daily business decisions have to be made, and KDB has no time for leisurely executive lunches and excessive bureaucratic regulations. Despite its huge output, the management staff is kept to a minimum and ostentatious spending is carefully avoided. Apart from their salaries, the top management, including the chairman and the secretary, enjoy hardly any perks: the chairman and directors ride to necessary functions in a large van that is put to many other uses as well. This is in sharp contrast to a Kerala state government-run industrial cooperative immediately next door. With less than one-tenth of KDB's output, it flaunts four cars for the use of its executives.

In the context of widespread shortcomings of many industrial cooperatives, an analysis of Kerala Dinesh Beedi Cooperative's successes may provide valuable lessons within Kerala toward strengthening the cooperative movement. In addition, the experience of KDB assumes special relevance in the ongoing development debates within Kerala and internationally regarding the Kerala Model.

KDB AND THE KERALA MODEL

The empowerment, the high wages, and the benefits achieved by so many of Kerala's beedi workers are related to what has come to be called "The Kerala Model." The Kerala Model refers to unexpectedly high quality-of-life indicators for a relatively backward economy. Despite a 1993 per capita income of only Rs 6,009 ($189), 60 percent of the all-India average (Government of Kerala 1995: 3, 21), Kerala in 1993 had a literacy rate of nearly 100 percent versus the all-India average of 52 percent (World Bank 1995: 162–63). Kerala's infant mortality in 1993 dropped to just thirteen per one thousand live births while India's overall rate was eighty. The birth rate in Kerala was seventeen per thousand females of child-bearing age compared with twenty-nine for all-India (Government of Kerala 1995: 3, 21). Kerala's child tuberculosis, polio, and DPT (diphtheria-pertussis-tetanus) vaccination rates in 1992 were 100 percent.[4] For measles the rate was 92 percent. These figures are all above the Indian average (Government of Kerala 1994: 119).

Beyond these indicators that have attracted so much academic interest, Kerala is characterized by extensive roads, hospitals, educational institutions, and public food distribution shops, which tend to redistribute services to the poorest groups, who are ordinarily cut off from the benefits of the market, owing to their lack of purchasing power. In the absence of industrialization, these institutional supports appear to be wise policies for the general population. To see the Kerala Model as an outgrowth only of "wise policies," however, is to miss its most significant feature: the organization, mobilization, and active participation of millions of the state's ordinary people in struggles to bring about those policies.

More than in any other part of India in the early and mid-twentieth century, Kerala experienced the development of caste reform associations with extensive grassroots participation and later of class-based organizations such as trade unions and peasant movements. By the early 1950s, tens of thousands of rural and urban workers as well as tenant farmers and farm laborers were experienced participants in petition and letter-writing campaigns, street processions, strikes, and self-help programs such as reading rooms and village libraries.

A key moment was the 1957 election victory of the Communist Party of India, which won control of the state assembly. Since 1957, left-wing governments have held power several times, but even when out of power, forces on the left have been able to exert considerable influence on right-wing administrations. These powerful social movements acted as pressure groups on the successive governments, right or left, to maintain and expand the social infrastructure and social security schemes. These movements were instrumental in redistributing rural wealth through the 1971 land reform abolishing tenancy, the most successful land reform in India. The trade unions were successful in improving the wages of workers in the small-scale and cottage industrial sectors that, in the rest of India, are largely unorganized. Above all, these social movements gave ordinary people a sense of dignity, self-respect, and consciousness unparalleled in most parts of India.[5]

THE CRISIS OF THE KERALA MODEL

Part of the apparent success of the Kerala Model results from comparison with the dismal failure of so many third world countries to raise the standard of living for the majority of their populations despite impressive statistical growth of their economies. But within Kerala, the outsiders' admiration is not so widely shared as one might expect. Numerous problems have developed—to the extent that many Kerala experts speak of the "Crisis of the Kerala Model." The crisis includes many elements. At least 15 percent of Kerala's people have probably been left out of the model altogether: these may include fishing people, female stonecutters, female domestic servants, some female agricultural laborers, some tribal people, migrant laborers from nearby Tamil Nadu state, and some other categories of casual laborers (Franke and Chasin 1996: 625; Kurien 1995). Since the latter half of the 1970s, Kerala's economy has suffered from a generalized economic stagnation resulting from low productivity of crops, including the all-essential rice harvest (Kannan and Pushpangadan 1988; Radhakrishnan et al. 1994), from weak industrial growth (Subrahmanian 1990; Mohan 1994), and from the decline of traditional industries that had employed many workers, such as the *coir* (coconut fiber), cashew, and handloom industries (Thampy 1994). This economic stagnation has exacerbated Kerala's already severe unemployment, estimated at three times the all-India average (Mukherjee and Thomas Isaac 1991). Ironically, among the unemployed are hundreds of thousands of workers who benefited from the widespread increase in literacy under the Kerala Model. As one could predict, the economic stagnation has led to recurrent fiscal crises for the state government, threatening many of the public gains that constitute the Kerala Model in the first place (George 1993; Oommen 1993: 207–16). Declining economic opportunities also threaten to undermine the progressive character of Kerala's unions and its peasant and women's organizations: in times of scarcity, linguistic, ethnic, religious, and caste chauvinism and scapegoating are more appealing—a fact all too well known to far-right politicians across India.[6]

The New Democratic Initiatives:
The Left Democratic Front Ministry of 1987–91

Kerala's left-wing coalition won the statewide assembly elections in March of 1987. With decades of redistribution struggles behind them, many organizers had come to feel that further gains would require new initiatives. Could people be brought into action on the side of the government instead of in opposition? Could the energy of organizing and fighting for benefits be channeled into cooperative action for higher production and greater efficiency? The debates around these issues led to a series of experiments the organizers labeled "The New Democratic Initiatives."[7] They included a mass literacy campaign, a limited cooperative plan in agriculture called "group farming," installation of high-efficiency wood stoves in villagers' kitchens, decentralization of much development planning from the state capital to elected district assemblies, and a creative scheme called "The People's Resource Mapping Programme," in which villagers were taught to make maps of local resources as an impetus to public discussions of resource use, environmental problems, and the concept of sustainability (Franke 1996: 279–82; Franke and Chasin 1994: xiv–xviii; Törnquist 1995). Because the conservative state government elected in 1991 halted or altered these projects, an adequate evaluation of them is difficult.[8] The common theme in all the initiatives is that ordinary people should participate in a far more active manner than just electing one coalition of parties or another.

Further Initiatives: The Left Ministry of 1996

In April of 1996 the Left Democratic Front once again came to power in Kerala. The new ministry almost immediately began a mobilization of the population for what is called "The People's Campaign for the Ninth Plan," referring to India's ninth five-year plan since independence. Instead of making the plans in Delhi or the state capital of Thiruvananthapuram, the government will allot local village assemblies 40 percent of the plan funds to spend on projects developed with direct participation by people and their organizations. The decentralized planning is intended to make the projects more locally relevant, better integrated with the real needs of the people, and more participatory and democratic. More than 3 million people took part in the first phase of the program in August to December 1996. Tens of thousands of volunteers are being trained in appropriate analytical skills and planning to draw up the local projects (Government of Kerala 1996a; 1996b; Thomas Isaac and Harilal 1996). The goals are to create citizen involvement, to overcome cynicism, to unleash local creativity, to apply local knowledge, and to break down the excessive partisanship of development work in Kerala that has led to political party fragmentation and unnecessary hostilities over issues where people often have most things in common. A new Kerala model may be in the making; if local initiative develops as the organizers hope, further campaigns may be carried out to alleviate poverty, promote women's rights, and address other issues.[9]

What does KDB have to do with the new experiments in development? The movements that helped create KDB and that fostered its survival against the odds were central to the creation of the Kerala Model more generally. The New Democratic Initiatives for resolving the crisis of the Kerala Model can benefit from a study of the successful experience of KDB. KDB provides an example of a genuine initiative from below where the democratic consciousness and organized strength of mass organizations were instrumental—with the help of a sympathetic leftist government—in reorganizing production, improving productivity, and raising the living standards of the workers. The New Democratic Initiatives draw their inspiration from the best of the traditions of ordinary people; what better model could there be than KDB? KDB's workers not only own a profitable business with better pay and working conditions; they have also created a successful model of democracy in the arena of production. The right wing in Kerala argues that democratic movements, with their gains in welfare and their protective legislation, are inimical to economic growth. The left, they say, may be good at redistribution, but it has no program to accelerate production. Since accelerating production is the most pressing need in Kerala at the moment, the left should make way for new social forces driven by the market. Is there no democratic, participatory alternative to the right wing critique? The New Democratic Initiatives offer a left-wing answer. And KDB is real-life proof that democratic initiatives can work in the realm of production. The evolution of KDB's democratic initiatives and participatory structures extends over several decades. It begins with the birth and development of Malabar's beedi working class, which we describe and analyze in the next chapter.

CHAPTER TWO

The Making of the Beedi Working Class

Beedis and radicalism have a long history of association in Kerala. In popular satire of the 1950s three essential items defined a rural poor radical: a country towel around the forehead, a Stalin mustache sprouting under the nose, and a smoldering beedi on the lips. In many a village the local shop of the beedi roller was as important a center as the local village library for radical discourse, particularly for the less erudite. In the beedi shop, as someone read the daily newspaper aloud, a beedi roller would listen attentively, his head shaking in rhythm to the angular movement of his arms as he rolled the beedis or cut the wrapper leaves.

In the 1920s, beedi workers were among the most despised members of Kerala's population. They were called by the derisive term *beedi pillaers*, or beedi boys—the use of "boy" connoting a lack of adult personality, just as it did for American blacks in that same period. How the downtrodden, underpaid, and servile beedi workers were able to develop into some of Kerala's most respected agitators of the 1940s and 1950s is the theme of this chapter. Beedi workers participated actively in militant trade unions that laid the basis for a democratic/participatory consciousness among their members, and they were among the main creators of the radical workers' culture of northern Kerala. As we will show in later chapters, this culture has been vital to Kerala Dinesh Beedi's success.

The comparative literature identifies two main factors responsible for KDB's emergence and survival: a strong democratic consciousness

among the workers and a close connection to larger movements for social change. Rothschild and Whitt (1986: 66–68), for example, found
that "non-democratic habits and values" were among the most important constraints on the survival of cooperatives in the United States
and several developed countries. In a comparative study of thirty-one
worker-participation experiments in fifteen different countries, Paul
Bernstein (1976: 493–95; 1980: 91–107) named "a participatory/demo-
cratic consciousness" as one of the six essential features of successful
workplace democratization. Following the well-known psychological
research of Arthur Maslow and others, Bernstein (1980: 93) concluded
that the participatory/democratic consciousness is a set of more precise psychological components including "self-reliance, flexibility, and
activism," along with "a readiness to look for past trends and future
consequences, a sensitivity to the difference between means and ends,
and a strong sense of attachment to one's fellows." The history of
beedi workers in northern Kerala is largely a history of the development of these social-psychological characteristics.

But beedi workers did not create northern Kerala's radical culture
by themselves. Many researchers have noted the importance of a
close involvement in broader social movements by workers in successful cooperatives. Here and in chapter 3 we will show that KDB's
workers connect to these broader movements at every point in their
history.

THE GROWTH OF THE BEEDI INDUSTRY IN KANNUR

Little is known about the origins of the beedi industry around the
turn of the century in Malabar. By the 1920s the adjacent coastal
towns of Kannur and Tellicherry in Malabar and the town of Mangalore farther north in South Kanara had developed into important
beedi manufacturing centers. Muslim entrepreneurs played a large
role in the tobacco processing industry: twenty-eight of the sixty-
seven registered private establishments (42 percent) in the tobacco industry in Madras Province were owned by Muslims in 1921
(Government of India 1921: 30). Muslims made up 32 percent of the
population of Malabar in 1921 (Government of India 1921: 28). They
were also well represented among customers. An author of the 1930
Census of India remarked that "it is among the Muslims that beedi

smoking is most common, a fact borne out by the predominance of tobacco dealers in Malabar and North Arcot districts" (Government of India 1931: 230). The concentration of Muslim traders in and around these towns may have contributed to the establishment of the beedi industry there.

The industry became firmly established in North Malabar after the First World War when Muslim merchants utilized their trade connections to start exporting beedis to Ceylon (Sri Lanka) and later, to Burma (now Myanmar) (Rutherford 1933: 86 and 167; Kannan 1984: 44). The local demand for beedis also rapidly expanded. North Malabar became the main market for the industry when, in the 1930s, exports sharply declined because of trade restrictions imposed by the importing countries. The 1931 census had noted a "general growth in the smoking habit" in Madras Province. There was also a tendency to shift from cigarettes to beedis following the nationalist call for a "boycott of imported cigarettes" (Government of India 1931: 203). One of the largest beedi firms took *Charka* (the spinning wheel), the symbol of the independence movement, as its logo. The Charka brand gained popularity, taking advantage of the popular appeal of the charka. To promote their products, the beedi companies also organized colorful processions through the countryside to the accompaniment of drums and trumpets (Kannan 1984: 44). The beedi firms that were established in the 1930s in response to the expansion of domestic demand, such as Chatta, Madan, Sadhoo, and Haridas, continued to dominate the beedi industry in Malabar for the next three decades.

Prior to the First World War beedi establishments employed only four to five workers each. But by the mid-1930s some had expanded to one hundred to one hundred fifty workers (Tobacco Workers' Union 1984: 13 and *Mathrubhumi* 25 November 1937). The concentration of the beedi-making process at one workplace did not result from economies of scale: there was little division of labor in the production of beedis in large-scale establishments. Therefore, the rise of large establishments is surprising. The only advantage of beedi production in large establishments appears to have been better product quality through closer supervision. Direct production in large establishments might also have been more suited to the scarcity of skilled beedi rollers.

The employers had to compete with one another for the most

skilled workers and usually had to give a lump-sum advance at the time of recruitment (Tellicherry Beedi Thozhilali Union 1984: 19; Kannan 1984: 44). Desertion was a form of labor protest. When a worker left an establishment to join another, he was often able to secure a higher wage and also a lump-sum advance. Beedi workers who were paid 5 to 6.5 annas for rolling a thousand beedis were relatively better paid than workers in the other traditional occupations (Kannan 1984: 41; Tobacco Workers' Union 1984: 21). (Sixteen annas made one rupee.) Wage rates differed among establishments and even within an establishment itself (Tellicherry Beedi Thozhilali Union 1984: 20; Tobacco Workers' Union 1984: 21; *Mathrubhumi* 30 November 1937).

The workforce was predominantly male. Large numbers of children were employed as assistants to tie the rolled beedis, thereby increasing the pace of beedi rolling. They also had to do other tasks such as bringing food and tea to the adult workers and cleaning up the workplace. The children became apprenticed in the craft of beedi rolling. They had no formal link with the employers but were treated as assistants employed by the adult workers.

The number of beedi workers rapidly expanded after the First World War. According to the 1921 Census (Government of India 1921: 30), fourteen beedi establishments in Malabar employed 373 workers. In 1937 there were around a thousand beedi rollers in Kannur town alone (Kannan 1984: 46).

THE SOCIAL BACKGROUND OF THE BEEDI WORKERS

Beedi workers were mostly drawn from the ranks of a lower caste, the Tiyyas (Kannan 1988: 196). Tiyyas—or Ezhavas, as they were known in southern Kerala—were an intermediate caste below the Brahmins and Nairs, the upper castes. Caste segregation rules prescribed for Tiyyas 32 feet as pollution distance from Brahmins and 16 feet from Nairs. But Tiyyas were superior to the Cherumas, the untouchables, and the Malayans, the unseeables. Others included the Mappilas, the Kerala Muslims who were formally outside the caste system but were accorded a castelike status below the upper castes. All these social strata were engaged in reciprocal relations of customary rights and duties, inferiority and superiority, conflicts and bonds.[1] But the caste equilibrium was undermined by capitalist development, which pushed the Tiyya caste onto a trajectory in contradiction to tradition. The Tiyyas were not alone in this social process. In all castes and communities reform movements emerged to challenge the outmoded customs that did not accord with the new acquisitive society that was emerging. Some in the "reform" movements of the higher castes—such as the Nairs—could be drawn away from radical attacks on caste by the idea of moving their particular caste or subcaste to a higher ritual position while leaving the basic caste structure in place. Because the Tiyyas lay in the lower ranks of the caste hierarchy and because they are a large caste group, they could not raise the banner of caste reform without revolting against the caste hierarchy itself.[2] Therefore, the scope of the Tiyya social reform movement was broader than that among many other communities (Thomas Isaac and Tharakan 1986). The Tiyya social reform movement deeply influenced the nascent working class that was emerging in the towns in Malabar.

The incorporation of Malabar into the world economy under colonialism brought about significant economic changes over time. The agrarian subsistence economy was transformed into a food-import-dependent commercial crop export economy. As a result of changes in relative prices, coconut began to replace rice along the coastal tracts while pepper dominated the foothills in the east that were being colonized for cultivation. Coffee and tea virtually monopolized the hilltops of Wyanad. Rice was pushed into narrow irrigated valleys and areas where tribal people practiced shifting cultivation. Changes in land tenure and the tax system also encouraged commercialization, but the cultivation of commercial crops by the tenants did not undermine traditional agrarian relations. After rent deductions, little surplus was left in the hands of the tenant farmers. That, too, was dependent upon the vagaries of international prices for commercial crops (Menon 1994: 9–40).

The commercialization of agriculture led to the development of agroprocessing industries, the most important being the coconut industries. These included toddy tapping, copra making, oil pressing, and coir processing. The coir industry rapidly became a major nonagricultural occupation along the coast (Sharma 1917; Thomas Isaac 1990). Because the Tiyyas' traditional caste obligations emphasized processing of coconut products, they began to benefit from this boom in coir products.[3] Control over the production and distribution of toddy became a lucrative source of accumulation and wealth of some Tiyya families like the Murkothu family of Tellicherry.

In addition to the coconut industries, handloom factories developed in Malabar in the early decades of the twentieth century. Their growth was facilitated by the Basel Evangelical Mission's introduction of fly shuttle technology, and by new cotton products catering to export markets and to army requirements (Raghaviah 1989). The Basel missionaries' motive in starting the textile handloom mills (and also tile factories) was largely to provide employment for their Christian converts, who were mostly drawn from the lower castes. Many of them were Tiyyas who rose to prominent positions in the Basel Mission and later set up their own factories. The new technology attracted enterprising Tiyyas and caused weaving factories to mushroom in and around Tellicherry and Kannur (Aaron 1974: 45–48).

Commercialization of agriculture and the growth of industries gave a fillip to the trading activities in the port towns. While trade with the Western countries was largely monopolized by European trading companies, the Mappila (Muslim) merchants dominated the rice imports and the trade with Arab countries. Niches in the lower links of the trading networks created opportunities for Tiyyas to carve out riches. Some of the Tiyyas had also worked their way up the imperial bureaucratic ladder. Since the early days of British colonial rule, which began in Malabar in 1792, the Tiyya community had provided most of the economic and social intermediaries for the European community in North Malabar, and some of the Tiyya families continued to have kinship ties with the Anglo-Indian community. Tiyyas responded warmly to the missionary schools that were opened, and a Western-educated middle class emerged.

Despite their growing wealth, this new Tiyya elite found to their chagrin that the traditional social hierarchy continued to deny them a social status consonant with their wealth and education. Thus were born the powerful social movements that sought, on the one hand, to reform the customs and traditions within the caste and, on the other hand, to struggle against structures of upper caste domination. The ferment in North Malabar drew inspiration from the vibrant Ezhava Social Reform Movement that was sweeping southern Kerala by 1900.

This movement was led by Sree Narayana Guru, an ascetic from the South. Sree Narayana is often described as the beacon light of renaissance in Kerala. In reinterpreting old traditions, he established the ideological basis for a mass movement that reformed the customs, rituals, and ceremonies of the Ezhavas to bring them into conformity with the practices of upper castes. His program may have been conservative in appearance, but it was a radical challenge to the caste hierarchy and its traditions that denied ritual purity to the Ezhavas. Thus it fully accorded with the aspirations of other Ezhavas and lower caste members in general. The success of his program gave the Ezhavas a new sense of pride and self-respect. "The Society for the Protection of Sree Narayana Dharma" (*Sree Narayana Dharma Paripalana Yogam*, or *SNDP Yogam*), under his patronage, developed into the most important and best-known organization of Ezhavas with a Kerala-wide appeal (Velayudhan 1978). Sree Narayana became a source of authority and legitimacy for a wide spectrum of political and religious thinkers ranging from theists to atheists, caste mobility supporters to caste abolitionists, and nationalist conservatives to radicals.

Tellicherry was the most important center of the Ezhava Social Reform Movement in Malabar. It was there that in 1906 "The Society for Awakening of Knowledge" (*Sri Gnanodaya Yogam*) was founded to promote "religion, business, education and social reform" (quoted in Menon 1994: 67). The Jaganath Temple of Tellicherry, consecrated by Sree Narayana Guru in 1906, developed into a Tiyya pilgrimage center that helped stimulate a powerful movement for breaking out of the traditional temple shrine culture of North Malabar that perpetuated caste inequality (Menon 1994: 40–48).

In the charged atmosphere of caste reform in Tellicherry, the first association of beedi rollers was formed in April 1934. It was named "The Sree Narayana Beedi Workers' Association," (*Sree Narayana Beedi Thozhilali Sangham*), or SNBTS. Its president was Sadhu Sivaprasad, a theosophist and great admirer of Sree Narayana Guru. He had been the prime mover behind the Gautama Lodge and Hall of the Theosophical Society at Kannur.[4] In the late 1920s he had started a branch of the Madras Labor Union at Kannur (Kannan Int: 6 June 1993). It was a general union that workers in all industries could join.

The caste parochialism of the union may have been a response to the influence of Sree Narayana movements in Tellicherry and the hope that it might attract Tiyya workers. One of the first resolutions passed by the Sree Narayana Beedi Thozhilali Sangham was a demand that the birth and death anniversary days of the guru be declared public holidays. Its first procession was to the Jaganath Temple (*Mathrubhumi* 12 April 1934). The major grievance of the Sangham was the disrespect with which the beedi workers were regarded:

> Even the beedi workers have not realized the greatness of their profession. . . . In no way can beedi rolling be considered an unimportant profession. But most of gentlemen greet those engaged in beedi rolling as "beedi boys." It is necessary that the workers organize themselves if the above deplorable situation is to be changed. Organization is necessary for finding solutions to various disabilities that beedi rollers are suffering. Everywhere may you see the proverb "Unity is Strength." May every worker recite the prayer "Sangham Saranam." [5] This alone will stand in their stead in the world that is emerging. (Kunjiraman Nair in *Mathrubhumi* 12 August 1934)

DETERIORATING LABOR CONDITIONS

The formation of the SNBTS was also a response to the deterioration of labor conditions during the 1930s with the onset of the depression. The world economic depression played havoc with the commercialized agricultural economy: exports and prices plummeted, and cultivation and investment in agriculture contracted. The rural unemployed drifted to the urban centers in search of work. Some workers walked five to six kilometers to Kannur town daily to work in the beedi factories.

The system of advance payment ceased. New workers were invariably hired at lower rates. As a result, even within the same factory, the wage rates for rolling a thousand beedis ranged from four annas to six annas (Kannan 1984: 44). According to an estimate by the secretary of the SNBTS, a worker with a child assistant had to work ten hours a day to earn ten to twelve annas, a sum that was barely sufficient to meet necessities in 1934 (Tobacco Workers' Union 1984: 21).

Wage rates in Kannur during the 1930s were significantly lower than those prevalent in Mangalore. In 1934, while the wage rate at Kannur for rolling a thousand beedis ranged between four to six annas, in Mangalore it ranged from nine to ten annas. A large number of workers from Kannur migrated to Mangalore, attracted by the higher wages (*Mathrubhumi* 31 May 1934). Some of the Mangalore firms also began to open branches in Kannur to take advantage of the lower wages (Tobacco Workers' Union 1984: 19).[6]

Besides paying low wages, employers deducted many charges. Every day a worker had to roll a bundle of free beedis for the employer. The practice was known as *ennakettu*.[7] It was supposed to be a payment to the owner for lighting the kerosene lamps so that work could continue late into the night. But the deductions were made even when there was no production at night. Moreover, in establishments where the task of grinding and mixing the tobacco was entrusted to a separate category of workers, the wages of those workers were deducted from the wages of the beedi rollers.

The work space did not expand with increases in the workforce, a situation that resulted in overcrowded work sheds. An official report later gave a graphic description of the situation where

> hundreds of workers are generally massed together in old ramshackle houses with rickety stair cases, unwashed and sometimes unplastered walls. . . . The workers everywhere squat on the floor on tattered mats surrounded by trays containing tobacco, and cut or uncut wrapper leaves; the latter soaked in water emits a peculiar odor while the tobacco exhales its characteristic smell. The mixture of these strong odors pervades the whole workshop. Men, children, heaps of waste, remnants of wrapper leaves, leaf and tin trays stuffed with tobacco or newly made beedis, dirty and torn mats here and there, aluminum, glass and brass tumblers as well as other bottles with dregs of tea and several other odds and ends strewn all over, present a queer picture of jumble and disarray. . . . On the whole working conditions are extremely unsatisfactory from the standpoint of per capita floor space, sanitation, ventilation and lighting. Spending the better part of life in such miserable environments, workers in general and children in particular present a haggard appearance with yellowish eyes and haggard cheeks. . . . (Government of Madras 1947: 41)

It was widely believed that working in beedi factories increased the possibility of contracting tuberculosis, and this possibility was one of the stigmas attached to the occupation.

The employers held that the laborers alone were to blame for their plight. They argued that their employees were not required to work until late at night but did so of their own free will, that it was the workers who exploited child assistants by overworking and underpaying them, and that there was no evidence to prove conclusively any relation between tuberculosis and work in beedi factories (Kunhikannan M. M. in *Mathrubhumi* 26 May 1934). The employers' position was rejected by the SNBTS:

> It is the duty of the employers to the human laborers to provide them with sufficient wages for subsistence and to limit the working time so as to allow a normal person to maintain his health! It is because the employers do not give a return in proportion to their labor expended at the workplace that the workers are forced to sweat like bullocks for 13–14 hours a day. (Krishnan P. K. in *Mathrubhumi* 31 May 1934)

It was not workers' greed but the severity of the poverty that was driving children to the factories, the union argued—and the employers were only too willing to admit them to the factories.

FROM CASTE TO CLASS

The earliest form of industrial protest, as already noted, consisted of workers individually or collectively abandoning their employers. But this became ineffective in a labor surplus situation. There were also instances of individual workers engaging in *satyagraha* (nonviolent "truth struggles," such as fasting at the entrance to a work site) to express their grievances (Kunhikannan 1984: 95).[8] The first recorded strike in the beedi industry occurred within a month of the formation of the SNBTS. Workers in the Charka Beedi Company spontaneously went on strike, protesting against wage reductions and demanding wage increases (*Mathrubhumi* 30 May 1934; Tellicherry Beedi Thozhilali Union 1984: 20). The employers brought in strikebreakers from Muslim centers in South Malabar such as Ponnani, Malappuram, and Kondoti. The union leadership was unprepared to hold the strike, much less to face the imported strikebreakers. The strike soon fizzled out.

The failure of the 1934 strike raised a disturbing issue for the union activists: could the workers' struggle succeed if the workers were divided by caste and religion? Muslim workers, who made up the second largest group in the workforce, had kept away from the SNBTS. Muslim strikebreakers from outside had broken the strike. There had already been Tiyya-Muslim conflicts connected to the temple procession in Tellicherry. The competition that the Tiyya elite was offering to the traditional Muslim traders in the urban areas partly underlay the disturbances (Menon 1994: 71–74). The course of the strike further signaled the danger of communalism.[9]

Some of the employers consciously attempted to exacerbate the situation by segregating Muslim and Hindu workers at the workplaces. According to P. Madhavan, representative to the Madras Assembly in 1937, the abolition of such practices was one of the demands of the workers who had joined the general strike that we shall discuss in the next section (*Mathrubhumi* 1 January 1938).

Despite the caste connotation of its name, the SNBTS was not a mere caste organization. Much to the annoyance of the Tiyya elite, the first appeal for support that SNBTS made to the public contained a searing exposé of beedi working conditions and employer indifference. Not only were the charges made by the union immediately denied by the employers, but members of the Tiyya elite also criticized the union, advising it to strive to discourage alcoholism and use of tobacco among the workers and to improve their moral standards if it was serious about realizing the ideals of Sree Narayana (*Mathrubhumi* 26 May 1934). The Tiyya elite's interpretation of Sri Narayana's ideals did not accord with the aspirations of the workers who were suffering from the deterioration of their working conditions. The need to overcome differences in caste and religion so that all the workers could be united became an important theme of the speeches at union meetings (Kottiath Krishnan, *Mathrubhumi*, 2 June 1934). Within a month, Sardar Chandroth Kunjiraman, prominent nationalist and socialist and a Nair by caste, was unanimously elected vice president of the SNBTS (*Mathrubhumi* 28 June 1934).

The attempts of Sardar Chandroth to start branches of the SNBTS in other beedi centers drew a negative response from the workers in Kannur. Potheri Madhavan, a leading nationalist and later president of a major beedi union, noted that they did not consider it "proper to name the organization of workers from all castes and religions by the Guru of a particular community" (*Mathrubhumi* 16 August 1934). SNBTS was renamed the *All Kerala Beedi Thozhilali Sangham*. As Sardar Chandroth argued in an appeal to the beedi workers in Kerala: "All workers whatever be their caste or religion are basically workers. All workers have the same work, same wages and same working time" (Chandroth Kunjiraman Nair in *Mathrubhumi* 12 August 1934).

BEEDI WORKERS IN THE NATIONAL INDEPENDENCE MOVEMENT

The activist, democratic consciousness of beedi workers developed through several stages, each with its own historical context. First came their exposure to police brutality and political manipulations in the national movement for independence from British colonial rule. This movement in Malabar rapidly veered leftward as caste improvement associations gave way to class awareness, and the national independence movement came to be associated with socialism and then communism. Throughout these stages, beedi workers constantly faced their bosses' arrogance and intransigence as the workers built their ever more radical unions. The constant element in all these stages was the experience of mass mobilization and participation.

The Kannur Beedi Thozhilali Union (KBTU) was formed in August 1934 at a meeting convened at the Gautama Lodge. Its background was more secular than that of the SNBTS. The prime movers behind its formation were workers from Kannur who had been working in Mangalore, where they had come into contact with socialist ideas. Mangalore was the home of two prominent socialists: Kamala Devi Chathopadhyaya and S. V. Ghate. Potheri Madhavan, the leading nationalist in the town, was elected president of the union. He continued to hold that post until he was elected to the provincial assembly in 1937, in a campaign in which the workers played a major role.

The year 1934 was significant for another important development in the national movement in Malabar: the socialists gained a majority in the state committee of the Indian National Congress. E. M. S. Namboodiripad was elected one of the secretaries of the Kerala Pradesh Congress Committee (Kerala Regional Congress Committee, or KPCC). The socialist ascendancy in the congress reflected a change that was occurring within the national independence movement.

Malabar had been drawn into the national independence movement during the nationalist upsurge after the First World War. The Home Rule Movement of Mrs. Annie Besant for dominion status for

India attracted the educated middle class. But by the end of the war the political center of gravity decisively shifted toward the Gandhian agitational program of noncooperation and satyagraha. Gandhi's attempt to link noncooperation with the British to agitations for the restoration of the Turkish Caliphate received a warm reception from the Muslim community in Malabar. Since the mid-nineteenth century, Muslims had risen in revolt several times "against the lord and the state" only to be put down by the armed might of the British (Pannikar 1989). This militant tradition of the Muslim peasantry reasserted itself again once the agitations started. In the face of police repression and the incapacity of the leadership in the congress to resolutely lead the struggle, the Muslim unrest took on communal overtones. The "Mappila Rebellion of 1921" was brutally crushed by the British. It resulted in a communal (caste and religious) divide that was a major setback for the nationalist movement in Malabar.[10]

The political lull in Malabar was broken only by the Civil Disobedience Agitation launched by the national leadership in 1930. But because of the fears lingering from the experience of 1921, this disturbance was confined to the northern *taluks* (subdistricts). Payyanur, a town north of Kannur, was the major center of a salt satyagraha. The new nationalist upsurge brought a new generation of young men like E. M. S. Namboodiripad, P. Krishna Pillai, A. K. Gopalan, and K. Damodaran to the forefront.

The main nationalist activities after the withdrawal of the civil disobedience movement were three: promotion of *khadi* (homespun cloth), uplifting of depressed castes, and temperance. These and other "constructive programs" of Gandhi, along with the electoral politics of the more conservative sections of the congress leaders, could not satisfy the new generation of nationalists produced by the Civil Disobedience Agitation in Malabar. They were even more piqued by Gandhi's persistent refusal to convert the agitations by the lower castes for right of entry into temples into mass movements against caste itself. Their growing disenchantment with the Gandhian program caused them to turn to the ideals of socialism and socialist revolution that were seeping into the highly literate region. Some of them had come into contact with radical agitators while in jail. When the Congress Socialist Party (CSP) was formed in 1934 at the national level, Malabar soon became one of its strongholds (Balaraman 1973; Namboodiripad 1984). In 1935 the socialists won a majority in the organizational elections. Outmaneuvered by the rightists, the left soon had to relinquish office, but it continued to enjoy decisive influence in the lower-level party offices and among the Indian National Congress village committees.

A distinctive feature of the CSP in Malabar was the emphasis it placed on building class and mass organizations within the broad framework of the nationalist movement. Congress Socialists in other parts of the country were more engaged in ideological propaganda. The greatest achievement of the CSP in Malabar was the network of peasant unions it organized. The agrarian movement in Malabar during the 1920s had been dominated by the "upper" tenant farmers, who had the most secure leases and the best financial arrangements with the landlords. After limited tenancy reforms secured their interests, the movement waned. The Congress Socialists' mobilization efforts focused on the lower tenants and agricultural laborers. Peasant unions and agitations sprang up in every corner of rural North Malabar.[11]

The economic depression had pauperized the commercial cultivators. The financial crunch also motivated the wealthier farmers to increase their revenues by denying the poorer peasants their customary rights such as access to common property resources for fodder, fuel, and manure, and enhancing the feudal rent exactions (Menon 1994: 119–59). The rent rates were oppressive and there was no security of tenure. New tenancy reforms to protect the interests of poorer tenants became the central campaign issue of the new peasant movement. This movement, however, was concerned not merely with economic questions but also with social and cultural issues, such as temple entry, that had once been raised by the caste-based social reform movements. The social reform movements were submerged in the peasant and nationalist movements.

Similarly, under the guidance of CSP cadres, trade unions sprang up in all industrial centers, and the beedi trade unions always received special attention. Most prominent CSP leaders, such as A. K. Gopalan, P. Krishna Pillai, K. Damodaran, K. P. Gopalan, and C. H. Kanaran, were at one time or another officers of the beedi unions. It is not difficult to understand the connection: the beedi workers constituted one of the most politically conscious sectors of workers in Malabar. C. Kannan recalls the active participation of beedi workers in picketing foreign cloth shops and liquor shops and in taking part in meetings and campaigns of the 1930 Civil Disobedience agitation (Kannan Int: 6 June 1993). The beedi workers were quick to respond to political developments. For example, the Tellicherry beedi union was the first to protest against the bombing of Gandhi's car in 1934. Only two days later a citizens' public meeting was organized for the same purpose (Kumaran 1978: 83). It was the Kannur beedi union that gave a reception to M. P. Narayanan Nair when he was released after thirteen years in prison for his participation in the Mappila Rebellion of 1921 (*Mathrubhumi* 20 October 1934).

Beedi workers provided a fertile recruiting ground for the CSP. There is hardly a union of any group of workers in Kannur whose officers or organizers at one time or another have not included beedi workers. The union offices were the centers of political activity in the towns. The beedi union was in charge of most of the court cases of hundreds of peasant prisoners who were jailed in Kannur. A number of beedi cadres even went to Travancore in southern Kerala to help the Alleppey coir workers in their month-long strike of 1938 (Tobacco Workers' Union 1984: 25–26; Thomas Isaac 1985).

GROWING INDUSTRIAL TENSIONS

Even though the organizational and political activities of the beedi unions steadily expanded, the industrial scene remained quiet up to the end of 1936. In December the Tellicherry union, after "much quiet deliberation," called for an indefinite strike at Sattar Beedi Factory against wage reductions (*Mathrubhumi* 1 January 1937). The strike dragged on for more than a month but was finally called off on the recommendation of P. Krishna Pillai. The union executive committee concluded that only an industry-wide general strike could settle the issue of wage reductions (*Mathrubhumi* 30 January 1937). A major organizational activity of the union during the new year was to raise a volunteer corps of workers for the inevitable showdown.

After prolonged discussions, the Third Annual Conference of the Kannur Union in August 1937 drew up a charter of demands for all beedi workers, of which the following were the most significant:

1. Standardization of the wage rate at ten annas for rolling one thousand beedis
2. Provision by the employers of tools like scissors

3. Appointment of separate workers for mixing and powdering the tobacco and for dyeing the threads
4. Ending of deductions from wages for such things as *en-nakettu* (lighting fees)
5. Abolition of child labor
6. Establishment of workday from 8:00 A.M. to 6:00 P.M.
7. Public holiday on Sunday
8. Payment of all wages every Saturday
9. Provision of individual ventilated work spaces and mats for seating
10. Implementation of the Factories Act in the beedi industry and its extension to all establishments employing more than ten workers (Tobacco Workers' Union 1984: 2; *Mathrubhumi* 25 August 1937)

The announcement that the government was extending provisions of the Factories Act to beedi establishments employing more than twenty workers had appeared in the press two months earlier (*Mathrubhumi* 27 June 1937). This added to the industrial tensions and led to a confrontation in November 1937 when the factories inspector from Coimbatore visited Kannur to inspect the beedi establishments. The employers indulged in widespread falsification of records. In many factories a majority of the workers were refused work during the day of the inspector's visit so as to keep the workforce below twenty. The trade union leaders exposed this foul play, and protest meetings were organized (*Mathrubhumi* 25 August 1937). In Tellicherry the beedi workers were asked to work in their houses until the inspection was over. Instead, during the visits of the inspectors, they held demonstrations at the company work sites, holding up the raw materials they had been ordered to work with at home (*Mathrubhumi* 4 December 1937).

The visits of the factories inspector convinced the employers that their forced compliance with the Factories Act was imminent. They were aware that as a result, trade union pressures were bound to increase. Within one week of the visit of the factories inspector the large beedi firms started to open new, smaller establishments—called branches—in rural areas closer to the beedi workers' homes. The rollers were asked to work in these new branches, which almost always employed fewer than twenty workers, thus placing them outside the regulations of the Factories Act. The employers also started to victimize union activists. In both Tellicherry and Kannur the beedi employers and rollers were moving toward a major confrontation.

The Union General Body at Kannur called for a general strike from 6 December 1937 to press for their charter of demands and to end the breakup of the larger factories intended to escape the provisions of the Factories Act. The strike was meticulously planned. A. K. Gopalan, one of the senior CSP leaders, was the president of the strike committee. Under his leadership a volunteer camp was set up that in the evening became a lively center for public political education. Peasants in neighboring villages came to the town daily in solidarity processions, carrying grain and vegetables for the striking workers. Every day the volunteer picketers marched to the factory gates singing the strike anthem, "We starving thousands laboring in the town" (Tobacco Workers' Union 1984: 22–23).

The employers were adamant, refusing to concede any demand even at the conference convened by government officials (*Mathrubhumi* 11 December 1937). Only some of the smaller employers who were not threatened by the Factories Act were willing to reach settlements by granting small wage increases (*Mathrubhumi* 21 December 1937 and 24 December 1937). The employers threatened to move their factories from Kannur. Finally, through the mediation of the local member of the legislative assembly, P. Madhavan, a compromise was worked out: a one-anna wage raise was conceded, but employers were unwilling to give assurance of a uniform wage. Beedi rollers were exempted from the tasks of grinding tobacco and dyeing the threads, and wage deductions for lighting the shed were eliminated, but the employers were not willing to consider any of the other demands. They refused to give any assurance that they would not break up the units. The strike had to be withdrawn after thirty-eight days with only some marginal gains (*Mathrubhumi* 1 January 1938).

In New Durbar Factory at Tellicherry workers had walked out even before the general strike in Kannur had started. The provocation was that the company had reduced the rolling wages from 8 annas to 7 and then 6.5 annas (*Mathrubhumi* 25 November 1937). After two workers who protested were dismissed, ninety of the one hundred workers joined the walkout. The strike at New Durbar became a rallying point for workers in and around Tellicherry. When it become known that Krishna Pai, the owner of New Durbar Factories, was trying to continue production at his residence, his house gates were picketed (*Mathrubhumi* 14 December 1937).

Peasant solidarity marches during industrial strikes, later popular in Malabar, started during the New Durbar Strike. This is how A. K. Gopalan (quoted in Tellicherry Beedi Thozhilali Union 1984: 43; *Mathrubhumi* 3 December 1937) recalled the incident:

> It was at that time that in the suburban areas like Pinarayi and Erinjoli peasant unions were being organized. At a meeting in Erinjoli I appealed to the peasants to help the striking workers. The next day there was to be a meeting at Tellicherry Beach. Peasants from Pinarayi, Erinjoli and other villages flowed to the meeting place in processions. They carried jack fruits, mangoes, bananas and so on on their heads. . . . They were heaped together at the meeting place. When I had finished speaking an old man stood up and cried out: "As long as we live the factory boys need not be afraid. We will feed them."

The popular backing that the strike enjoyed forced the New Durbar owner to reach a compromise partly restoring the pay that had been cut. But before long he once again began to victimize the workers, reducing the amount of work. A temporary truce worked out by the government subcollector did not last long, and in 1938 the workers went on a forty-one-day strike. In the process the company lost its market and had to be closed down soon after reopening (Tellicherry Beedi Thozhilali Union 1984: 21). The workers had to seek employment elsewhere.

Thus the first round of major industrial confrontations ended disastrously for the workers in economic terms, but the strike proved to be an effective school of political education for the beedi workers. They experienced comradeship in a common struggle and saw the power of peasant solidarity. They also learned for themselves the true colors of the police and state machinery. There had been great expectations that provincial Indian National Congress governments that had come to power would take a sympathetic attitude to the struggle, but those hopes were betrayed. The anti-working-class bias of the rightists within the congress was fully exposed in a dramatic manner at Tellicherry. It became clear to everyone that C. L. Prabhu, a prominent local congress rightist once held in the highest esteem in the town, who offered to mediate in the dispute, was the major obstacle in reaching a settlement. Finally, workers had to picket his house (Tellicherry Beedi Thozhilali Union 1984: 36). In contrast, every leftist congress leader in North Malabar was in the thick of the day-to-day struggle at the side of the workers, a struggle that proved to be a decisive turning point in the radicalization of the beedi workers.

THE CULTURE OF SELF-STUDY

The high level of political awareness of the average beedi worker resulted not only from the hard-won experience of the 1930s strikes, but also from a tradition of study that was built up over time. Organizing reading rooms and night schools was an important part of trade union activities in Kerala in the 1930s. One of the first actions taken by the SNBTS after its formation was to open a reading room for the workers. Before long a night school was also established. In Kannur, Hindi, English, and Tamil classes were conducted. Within four months of the formation of the union, a library with a full-time librarian was opened.

Study was a part of the work routine. The seated posture and the quiet, repetitive process of beedi rolling that could be done mechanically allowed freedom for discussion or listening to others reading. One of the union demands of the New Durbar Beedi Company strike of 1937 was that "while the workers are idle without work, they should be permitted to read newspapers or books, without breaking the discipline of the factory or creating difficulties for other workers" (*Mathrubhumi* 30 November 1937). It became customary for one of the workers to take a turn at reading while the others listened. Each worker contributed a bundle of beedis to the wages of the reader. Literacy became a social requirement, and the experience of reading to fellow workers raised everyone's knowledge. The result was a wider democratic consciousness that KDB would later utilize to its benefit.

Here is a description of the schedule for a working day at Great Durbar Beedi Company during the 1940s:

Morning, newspaper reading. In the afternoon, reading of political texts and discussion. Twice a week there used to be training in public speaking. No one was left out of this duty. Therefore comrades who were illiterate were forced to join the night school to study. Every worker used to contribute from his meager wages to buy books. Some work centers were like mini libraries. . . . (Nanu 1946: 71)

Socialists considered political activity to include establishing village libraries and selling literature. Under their initiative reading centers and libraries sprang up in so many localities that in 1937 a Malabar Reading Room Conference was organized. The beedi workers were very much a part of this vibrant new culture.

The cultural troupes of the beedi workers created some of the best amateur theater in Malabar. From 1937 on, the Kannur Union had a central troupe whose performance was an essential item of any major political conference. The story of this grassroots cultural movement remains to be documented (Sreedharan 1984: 37–43). Scripted and directed by the worker-artists themselves, these new plays and songs brought to center stage the ordinary workers and peasants and their daily struggles.

FROM CONGRESS SOCIALISM TO COMMUNISM

The spread of trade unions and peasant unions and the militant groundswell created momentum for a further shift of the Indian independence movement in Malabar. Living in an export-oriented region in the grip of deep economic crisis due to the depression, CSP cadres had developed an admiration for the Soviet Union, which seemed to have escaped the worldwide economic malaise. This ideological position began to distinguish Kerala socialists from the national leadership of the Congress Socialist Party, many of whom were virulently anticommunist. With the formation of a Communist Party secret cell in 1937 by E. M. S. Namboodiripad, N. C. Shekhar, K. Damodaran, and P. Krishna Pillai, the availability and systematic dissemination of Marxist literature increased. The left congress organizers had published *Prabhatham [Dawn]* since 1934. After a lapse, it resumed regular publication in 1938 and was supplemented by pamphlets and other literature. Systematic study classes and schools were organized. In the six-week training camp for raising a sixty-five-member Communist volunteer corps of workers at Kannur at the initiative of the beedi workers' union, the topics included Marxist philosophy, political economy, the history of revolutions, and socialism in the Soviet Union. As a participant put it, "Each topic and each word of it was new. Before the camp, most of the participants had only vague notions of revolution and socialism. The camp was a turning point in the ideological education of the participants" (Tobacco Workers' Union 1984: 25).

The leftists who had gained the leadership of the KPCC (Kerala Pradesh Congress Committee) in 1935 and had been thrown out by the rightists within a year once again captured the leadership in 1938 in alliance with progressive Muslims. E. M. S. Namboodiripad was once again the secretary of the KPCC, but now he was a Communist. An important new activity initiated by the leftist KPCC was the raising of a disciplined and politically conscious volunteer organization for the nationalist movement. Initially thirty volunteer officers were given nearly two months' training. This was followed by taluk (subdistrict) and village training programs to produce at least ten volunteers for each of the five hundred village committees of the congress. These village committees had been organized after the 1935 provincial elections at the initiative of the leftists. Though the target was not reached, an army of three thousand volunteers and around the same number of volunteer officers was formed (Namboodiripad 1990: 272). These disciplined volunteer cadres formed the cutting edge of the increasingly radicalized peasant movement that was sweeping North Malabar at the end of the 1930s.

With the onset of World War II, the leftist KPCC set out to mobilize the masses against Indian participation in the war efforts while the national leadership, even though opposed to the war, continued to maneuver indecisively. On 1 September 1940, at the outbreak of the war, beedi workers at Kannur organized an antiwar rally. Beedi workers were at the forefront of picketing army recruitment offices. The leadership of the KPCC were arrested by the government, which only drew a more militant response. The KPCC resolved to observe 15 September 1940 as "Protest Day" (*Mathrubhumi* 10 September 1940 and 15 September 1940). All over North Malabar peasants and workers defied government bans to organize public protest meetings. The most serious confrontations took place at Morazha, where a police subinspector was killed as he led a *lathi* (nightstick) charge to disperse the crowds; at Mattannur, where the police had to retreat after losing their rifles and ammunition; and at Tellicherry Beach, where two protesters were shot dead (*Mathrubhumi* 17 December 1940).

One of the two workers killed at Tellicherry Beach was Chathukutty, a beedi roller at Great Durbar factory. Of the twenty-seven convicted on riot charges, fourteen were beedi workers. Despite the police terror, beedi workers struck the next day and thronged in thousands to the funeral of their fallen comrade (*Mathrubhumi* 18 September 1940). The police retaliated viciously: reserve police surrounded the Great Durbar Beedi Company and arrested nearly one hundred workers, many of whom had to be hospitalized after being tortured. The beedi workers were special targets of attack. "Nail examination before beating" became a common police practice. (The beedi workers normally grow slightly longer nails on the index finger to facilitate closing the tip of the beedi).

The All-India Congress Committee disbanded the KPCC, using the Protest Day as a pretext (*Mathrubhumi* 19 September 1940 and 14 October 1940). Thus the communists formally parted ways with the congress but carried along with them the militant peasant and trade unions and some of the best cadres of the national independence movement. For the beedi unions, too, 1940 was the year of transition from Congress Socialism to Communism.

THE WAR PERIOD

A respite from repression came only in 1942. With the entry of the Soviet Union into the war, the Communist Party reversed its militant opposition to the war efforts. Survival of the first socialist state and defeat of the fascist forces were viewed to be of paramount importance to national liberation. The new line was to oppose the Quit India Struggle launched by the congress and direct all efforts toward arousing antifascist consciousness through campaigns such as "Anti-Jap *Melas*." [12] At the level of peasant and worker mass organizations this implied a new tactical line that came to be known by the phrase "production policy" (Ranadive 1943).

The textile workers of Tiruvannoor who had raised the per capita output of thread from 5,240 pounds to 6,240 pounds a day were hailed as models to be emulated (Sekhar 1943: 3). The workers were asked to form productivity committees. The capitalists who tried to create scarcity and crisis were to be isolated and exposed. On the other hand, the workers were to cooperate with capitalists who were patriotic and sympathetic to the people. Explaining this approach, an All Kerala Trade Union Congress pamphlet concluded: "Class struggle today means increasing production. It means creating the unity to end the war and save the country" (Sekhar 1943: 2). The production of beedis and productivity of the workers could not have been of any critical importance to the war efforts. However, the production policy for the beedi industry meant relative industrial peace during the years 1942–44 despite a rapid escalation of prices.

Data on wage rates collected by the Court of Enquiry into Labor Conditions in Tobacco Industries suggest that the wage rates increased only marginally, if at all, during 1942–44. The wage differential between Mangalore and the Kannur-Tellicherry belt tended to widen. The Kannur wage rate was 27 percent lower than the Mangalore rates in 1939. By 1943 the differential had increased to 50 percent. By 1946 the trend was reversed but the differences persisted.[13]

The lower wages caused beedi firms in Mangalore such as Ganesh Beedi (1942) and Great Durbar Beedi (1943) to open branches at Kannur. PVS Beedi had opened a branch in 1938. As a result, industrial employment expanded, and average employment in the branches increased. The Madras government had exempted the beedi industry from the provisions of the Factories Act in 1941. While previously the employers had been careful to keep employment in the branch establishments below twenty, in the new situation larger numbers were accepted.

The trade unions distinguished themselves with their unstinted efforts to give relief to the famine- and pestilence-threatened population. With the disruption of grain imports from Burma and Southeast Asia, an acute food scarcity had arisen in Malabar. Near-famine conditions prevailed. The peasant organizations launched a program to expand food cultivation in the wastelands. Food committees were set up for the prevention of hoarding and black marketing and for the introduction of informal rationing of available grains. The volunteer organizations of the unions were at the forefront of relief activities for those stricken with cholera and smallpox that spread into large parts of Malabar in epidemic proportions. The Kannur union opened a special relief center in the town. Medical relief squads were sent to villages in the foothills. The fearless and selfless service rendered by the worker volunteer squads won general admiration.

The intense involvement of the unions in relief work was not solely the result of wartime political exigency. The union had adopted the "constructive work" tradition from the nationalist movement. The best-known example of it was the 1939 construction of the Eengayil-Peetika-Kannachira Palam Road, a long-standing unmet demand of villagers near Tellicherry town. Every day a squad of thirty workers set out from the union office with baskets and shovels to do free road construction. A special song was prepared for this daily march. This event received widespread publicity at the time (Kumaran 1984: 82). Beedi workers were cementing their ties to other Kerala movements for self-improvement and social justice.

THE GENERAL STRIKE OF 1946

After the failure of the strike of 1937–38, the beedi unions did not resort to any major strikes for nearly a decade. But the wartime inflation and erosion of real wages made a struggle for wage increases unavoidable. The major weakness of the strikes of 1937–38 had been the lack of coordination among the various industrial centers, which allowed employers to divert production to locations where there was no strike. In August 1946 union leaders planned a general strike covering all the industrial centers in South Kanara and South Malabar as well as Kannur and Tellicherry in North Malabar. The demands varied from center to center, but the major common demands were a wage increase of four annas (15–20 percent) for rolling one thousand beedis, a dearness allowance—cost of living increase—and three months' wages as a bonus from the wartime superprofits made by the beedi owners.

The government was determined to put down the "Communist conspiracy." The rival congress trade unions joined the strike for varied periods in some centers but largely played the role of strikebreakers. The confrontation led to violence.

Those who picketed the factories were arrested, and unusually stern sentences were handed down: one to two months' imprisonment. In Kannur alone 120 union workers were so sentenced. Strikebreakers physically confronted the strikers. *Goondas* (thugs) attacked the strikers.[14] The Ganesh Beedi Factory in Kannur town, along with a stock of more than a million beedis, was burned down by the strikers (*Mathrubhumi* 24 November 1946). Many working-class neighborhoods were subjected to generalized repression by special police (Punchayil Nanu 1984: 69–71). But the workers refused to back down, and the strike continued successfully for fifty-seven days with no end in sight. Finally, the government referred the dispute to adjudication, and the strike was withdrawn (*Mathrubhumi* 28 November 1946 and 1 December 1946).

The adjudication was held in Mangalore. It lasted six months before awarding a wage raise of one anna, a dearness allowance of one anna for every one rupee of wages earned, and one month's wages as a bonus. The award was not implemented, however, until 1952. The reason for the delay was that the unions meanwhile had fallen victim to the general repression against the communists and their sympathizers that occurred during 1948–50. The Communist Party of India, encouraged by the militant upsurge of mass struggles at the dawn of independence, had made an unsuccessful effort to capture state power, and as a result, the party and many of its mass organizations were banned. The beedi trade union cadres found themselves in the vortex of the turmoil. Some of them even joined the armed peasant resistance groups. Chinta Poduval of the Payyanur union was one of seven who fell to police bullets on the slopes of Munayan Kunnu (Munayan Hill) in 1948 (Shenoi 1986: 20; Narayanan 1986: 24). In North Malabar beedi workers became a special target of police repression: beedi work centers were raided, and more than three hundred members of KBTU were arrested and tortured (Tobacco Workers Union 1984: 27). The union office was raided and torched. After these events, the day-to-day functioning of the unions ceased until 1951.

By the time the unions reemerged into the open, the whole industrial scene had changed. In place of the direct production of beedis in large establishments owned by the companies, an indirect system of production in small establishments owned by middlemen or contractors had come into being. Alarmed by the militancy of the strike of 1946, employers had also felt threatened by the impending labor legislation. Following the exclusion of the beedi industry from the provisions of the Factories Act in 1941, the government had set up a Court of Enquiry to study labor conditions in the tobacco-related industries. The court was to submit proposals for new legislation. Under pressure from trade union agitation, its report, published in 1947, recommended bringing the beedi industry under the New Factories Act, strictly regulating child labor, and enforcing the Payment of Wages Act, the Maternity Benefit Act, and the Workmen's Compensation Act in the beedi industry (Government of Madras 1947). The government accepted the recommendations. The owners then set up smaller establishments so that they would not be bound by these acts.

The first major firm to initiate indirect beedi production was Sadhoo Beedi in 1950. Mangalore Ganesh Beedi, the other large beedi firm, followed suit later in the same year (Tobacco Workers' Union 1984: 27). While Sadhoo Beedi engaged middlemen under the "trade system," Ganesh Beedi used middlemen under "commission systems".[15] Once these two largest beedi firms changed over to indirect production under middlemen, the smaller firms also switched.

INDUSTRIAL EXPANSION AFTER INDEPENDENCE

The changeover to indirect production was accompanied by a phenomenal expansion of beedi production in North Malabar, which now came to constitute the district of Kannur. According to the census, the number of workers employed in the beedi industry in Kannur district increased from 4,061 in 1951 to 18,501 in 1961 and further to 40,378 in 1971. Industrial employment in the district thus increased by almost ten times in twenty years. Kannur's share in the beedi workforce of the state of Kerala rose from 14 percent to 45 percent between 1951 and 1971.[16]

The industry in Kannur was able to take advantage of the expanding beedi markets because of its organized nature and lower wages. In the Travancore (southern Kerala) and Cochin (central Kerala) regions, beedis were produced by independent petty producers catering to neighborhood clienteles. Seventy-two percent of the beedi establishments in Travancore-Cochin in 1961 were single-worker establishments, and another 26 percent employed fewer than five workers. In contrast, establishments employing more than five workers constituted more than 50 percent of the beedi producers in Kannur district. More than half the beedi establishments employing more than twenty workers were situated in Kannur district (Government of India 1961). The size distribution may not reveal the extent of concentration in Kannur, where indirect production was becoming the norm. The giant Mangalore-based Ganesh Beedi employed more than ten thousand workers, but by the mid-1960s many of them were contracted to middlemen.

The large firms enjoyed significant economies in raw material purchase. Because of their control over raw materials, they could also regulate the quality of their products. By strictly adhering to certain quality specifications, they were able to develop brand loyalties and expand their markets. In the early 1970s, it was estimated that nearly half the beedis consumed in Kerala were marketed under brand names (Ravi 1979: 35).

An added advantage of the Kannur-based firms was their lower wage cost. Minimum wages for beedi rolling were fixed for Travancore-Cochin in 1952 but were introduced in Malabar only in 1966, following the recommendation of the Minimum Wages Committee Report of 1964. The actual wage rates in Kannur even in the mid-1960s were about 16 percent lower than in southern districts of Kerala.[17]

Because of the lower wages in Kannur, Mangalore firms continued to move there until the middle of the 1960s. During this period four of the top five beedi companies—Ganesh Beedi, Great Durbar Beedi, PVS Beedi, and Bharat Beedi—were from Mangalore. Only Sadhoo Beedi originated in Kannur. Almost all of this expansion took place in small-scale production units owned by middlemen. Most of the large units were broken up, and direct production by the companies drastically declined. Those units registered directly under the companies specialized in preparation of raw materials for distribution to the contractors and for packaging and labeling. The share of employment in the larger registered private beedi establishments declined from 50 percent of the total employment in the industry in Kannur district in 1951 to a negligible figure by 1971. In contrast, the share of the unregistered small-scale establishments in industrial employment increased from 24 to 78 percent during the same period. Legally these small-scale establishments were owned by the middlemen, and the workers in them were not officially employees of the big beedi companies. The household sector employed 22 percent of beedi workers by 1971, down slightly from 26 percent in 1951 (Raghavan 1986: 56).

The unions had lost the battle against decentralization. Now they faced an uphill task: to mobilize the scattered workers to prevent further decentralization into household units, or "outwork," as it was popularly known, and to regain at least some of the hard-won rights of the past.

More than ever workers' unity seemed important. The Communists tried a new approach. Instead of reviving their old unions whose registration had been withdrawn, leaders on the left appealed for a common union of beedi workers regardless of political affiliation. The experiment did not last more than a year. Instead, the trade unions splintered along party lines. The socialists left to form their separate union affiliated to the HMS (*Hind Mazdoor Sabha,* or Indian Workers' Assembly) in 1952.[18] The Communist-led Tellicherry Beedi Thozhilali Union (TBTU) then revived its old registration. In Kannur, Communists renamed the reorganized union the Tobacco Workers' Union (TWU). After the end of the war, the Indian National Congress had organized its own trade unions at Tellicherry and Kannur to counter the influence that the Communists wielded among the beedi workers. The Swatantra Beedi Thozhilali Union (Independent Beedi Workers' Union) in Kannur and the Beedi Thozhilali Congress (Beedi Workers' Congress) in Tellicherry were established. Both were later affiliated with INTUC (Indian National Trade Union Congress), the Congress Party's national union federation.[19] A beedi trade union of Muslim workers owing allegiance to the Muslim League also arose. The pioneering unions in Tellicherry, Kannur, and Payyanur continued firmly within the fold of the Communist-led All-India Trade Union Congress (AITUC). But the employers were only too willing to negotiate with the newly formed rival unions, and trade union rivalry at times led to clashes between the workers. The Communist-led unions continued to be the predominant organizations.

The structure of the unions had to be significantly altered to suit the situation created by industry decentralization. In earlier times the primary units of the unions were the factory committees, but now the major factories had ceased to exist. Union organizers responded by creating village or regional division committees to become the primary units of the unions.

Three major trends in the trade union struggles of the 1950s and early 1960s can be noted (Tobacco Workers' Union 1984: 26–28; Tellicherry Beedi Thozhilali Union 1984: 23–25; Narayanan 1986: 23–25). First, strikes and agitations for wage and other economic benefits started up again. The major issue taken up by the unions after the reorganization was the implementation of the adjudication award of 1947. Since mobilization for a general strike was not organizationally possible, a satyagraha was announced at the May Day rally of 1952. The satyagraha was utilized to mobilize all workers, including those in other industries, into mass solidarity rallies. The employers were forced to agree to implement the award. With the formation of the first left ministry in Kerala in 1957, the TWU secretary C. Kannan was one of those elected to the Kerala State Legislative Assembly. The extension of the minimum wages act from Travancore-Cochin to Malabar, though challenged by the employers in courts, gave rise to a spate of strikes for wage increases. Industry-wide strikes were organized in 1960, 1962, and 1964 for wage increases. The 1964 Minimum Wages Committee for the first time recommended payment of a dearness allowance to beedi workers. The wages in Malabar began to climb; the wage disparity with other regions narrowed.

The second trend was a resistance movement against workforce dispersal. As wages rose, the pressure for decentralization of the industry also mounted. Workers resisted attempts to reduce the workforce and shift the production to middlemen. Some of the middlemen started to put out work to home-based rollers.

> Even then the industry was decentralized into small groups of workers. Due to the effective and vigilant union interventions it was not possible for the employers to manipulate things as they wanted. It was then they adopted the tactic of the outwork system. Their motive was to scatter the workers. Initially some of the workers fell into the trap. But active propaganda and education by the union successfully countered the tactic of the employers. (Tellicherry Beedi Thozhilali Union 1984: 25)

Even though the unions were successful in preventing the spread of the domestic putting-out system, everyone felt that the tendency could not be prevented through sporadic resistance. It was clear that a lasting solution lay in comprehensive protective legislation that would make it impossible to deny legal benefits even to workers employed indirectly. The campaign for such legislation, which became the most important theme of trade union agitation and propaganda, was the third trend in the post-independence trade union movement.

In 1954 the Tobacco Workers' Union president C. Kannan led a *jatha* (procession) that marched more than four hundred kilometers from Kannur to Madras, touring the major beedi centers en route and demanding immediate legislative action. A memorandum was submitted to the chief minister at Madras after a mass rally. Partly in response to the agitation, the Beedi and Cigar Industrial Premises Regulation Act was passed by the Madras Legislative Assembly in 1956. But the act created a mini-crisis in the industry as many of the companies closed their factories and shifted to neighboring states free of labor regulations. The Madras government beat a hasty retreat in 1958 by formally repealing the act.

Given the footloose nature of the beedi industry, national legislation was seen as the only solution. A. K. Gopalan was the opposition leader in the national parliament. He had a lifelong association with beedi workers. In 1956 he introduced the Beedi and Cigar Labor Bill in Parliament, but it went nowhere. The provisions of the proposed national legislation were major themes at the All-Kerala Conference of Beedi and Cigar Unions convened in 1957 at Chalakudy. Incorporating the suggestions made at this conference, A. K. Gopalan made another unsuccessful push for comprehensive legislation for the beedi industry.

Gopalan's efforts eventually led the Indian national government to pass the Beedi and Cigar Workers' Conditions of Employment Act in 1966. It was weaker in many ways than Gopalan's original bill. It recognized the contract and domestic outwork systems but only attempted to regularize the employer-employee relations in those sectors. The most important weakness of the act was that although it sought to improve working conditions in beedi establishments and provide workers with a provident fund, gratuity, maternity benefits, and medical allowance, it was left to the individual states to draw up their own schedule for implementation of these provisions. This was a strange aspect of the legislation since it ran counter to the basic rationale for having a nationwide act in the first place (Gopalan 1962: 305–8). Despite its limitations, beedi workers and their employers realized that a long-cherished dream of the beedi rollers had come true, at least on paper.

THE COUNTEROFFENSIVE OF THE EMPLOYERS
AND THE UNION CRISIS

In the 1967 Kerala state elections the left parties again came to power. Beedi workers had been a mainstay of the left voting block in all elections since the 1930s. The left government formed in the first general elections of 1957 had been dismissed by the central government following a "liberation struggle" launched by vested interests.[20] The 1967 left government was committed to the implementation of the central government legislation for the beedi-cigar industry. No state government had so far implemented the law passed in 1966. In 1968 Kerala did so.

The employers moved to the courts and got a stay order delaying the state government's notification. The unions joined the legal battle in the courts while mobilizing the workers for action. The employers declared that the Communist menace had created an industrial climate that was not conducive to normal functioning. The most prominent of the beedi firms, with headquarters in Mangalore, declared their intention to close down operations in Kerala. On 15 October 1968, Mangalore Ganesh Beedi closed down all its units in Kerala. Overnight twelve thousand workers lost their livelihoods. The company made it clear that the factories would not reopen unless the unions voluntarily renounced their demand for the implementation of the Beedi and Cigar Workers' Conditions of Employment Act and accepted the domestic outwork system as a legal form of industrial organization.

Beedi workers and union activists were shocked. The workers had decades of activism behind them. They had taught themselves to read, to study world events, to lead discussions, and to speak at meetings. They had learned to dream of a better future but to plan for it strategically and to analyze their own strengths and weaknesses before taking action. They had learned to organize, to sacrifice, to plan. They had developed strong attachments to their fellow beedi workers, to their nearby peasant comrades, and to the overall movements that were generating the Kerala Model, a set of ties like those Rothschild and Whitt (1986) found essential to building cooperatives worldwide. They had developed a democratic, activist consciousness within their unions, a consciousness surely as strong as any in Bernstein's (1976) comparative study that we cited at the beginning of this chapter. But were their unions to suffer their greatest blow just as their long-drawn-out struggle for comprehensive labor legislation seemed to be on the verge of success? The memories of the past were not encouraging. The 1937 general strike had not stopped the emergence of the branch system of production to evade the Factories Act. The gains of the 1946 general strike were undermined by further branching out of beedi rolling through middlemen. True, the workers had a leftist government that was sympathetic to their plight. But how could a state government stop the owners from moving out? Was the industry now to be decentralized into household units or to be removed to a safer area, totally eliminating union strength and the gains of the past? What was to be done?

CHAPTER THREE

Solidarity versus Retrenchment:
The Birth of KDB

Sree Narayana Beedi Thozhilali Sangham leaders should collect a good amount of capital and independently organize production. The profit from it should be equally distributed among the workers.

So advised Kottiyath Krishnan at the inauguration of the union's reading room in 1934 (*Mathrubhumi* 2 June 1934). His suggestion marked the beginning of a long and checkered struggle for a beedi workers' cooperative. The first recorded strike at the Charka Beedi Company had just ended in a fiasco, leaving many unemployed. Possibly persuaded by Krishnan's advice, the workers who left the company collected shares and established "Thozhilali Beedi Factory" (Workers' Beedi Factory) (Tellicherry Beedi Thozhilali Union 1984: 20). A union press release shortly afterward expressed satisfaction that the Thozhilali Beedi brand was being purchased by the liberal public. But this cooperative, organized "independently of the union, as an enterprise of the workers themselves" (*Mathrubhumi* 28 June 1934) did not survive for long. Nothing is recorded or remembered of how the end came. Suggestions for a workers' cooperative reemerged in the wake of the 1937–38 strikes. V. R. Nayanar, of *Bharat Seva Sangam* (Society for Service to India), issued a public statement in exasperation after a futile attempt to get the employers to grant concessions: "People who are sympathetic to workers should try to organize a cooperative beedi firm in order to help the workers. Only then can the exploitation of the workers stop . . . and [the workers] receive a decent wage rate" (*Mathrubhumi* 19 December 1937).

The idea received support from radical quarters. P. Krishna Pillai—to whom had fallen the unpleasant task of conveying to the militant workers the need to withdraw the strike without winning their demands—became an ardent supporter of beedi cooperatives. These two episodes illustrate utopian and survival elements in the formation of cooperatives, which we discuss below.

If in 1934 beedi workers were expressing a democratic, activist, cooperative impulse, as we saw in chapter 2, many years of experience lay before them in which these qualities were invested in a series of mostly unsuccessful strikes and agitations. The growth of a democratic consciousness alone could not produce a viable workers' cooperative.

THE HISTORY OF THE COOPERATIVE MOVEMENT
IN EUROPE AND NORTH AMERICA

The comparative literature indicates that cooperatives tend to arise when one of two general historical factors is present: a capitalist economic contraction or a broad-based wave of social and political movements. In early-nineteenth-century Europe, cooperative firms and communities were central to the efforts of utopian reformers to realize their ideal of a nonexploitative, egalitarian society. The utopians expected that their rational and just models of cooperation would attract and be emulated by others, leading to a gradual transformation of society. Robert Owen's New Lanark cotton mill and other practical experiments with cooperative communities were major landmarks of this utopian tradition. Owen's influence is evident among the Rochdale pioneers, who were among the most famous of the nineteenth-century cooperative experimenters. The Rochdale pioneers opened a cooperative store in 1844 to start building a common fund with which to finance a complete cooperative community (Fletcher 1976: 173–75). By the middle of the nineteenth century the Christian Socialists had emerged as the most vocal advocates of cooperatives. Drawing inspiration from their reading of the New Testament, they saw cooperatives as part of a social order that God had entrusted to them. Later in the nineteenth century, Marxism and anarchism also proved to be sources of inspiration for cooperative experiments. We shall consider these ideas and their relationship to cooperatives in more detail in chapter 7.

Apart from the cooperatives that were set up by utopian reformers, a large number of workers' enterprises made their appearance as self-defense mechanisms of the workers during periods of economic retrenchment. Such cooperative enterprises—more a practical response to the threat of unemployment than a reflection of utopian ideas—are documented from the late eighteenth century, even before the appearance of Owen. The history of the cooperatives in Europe and North America reveals broad phases of cooperative upswing mostly coinciding with industrial recessions.[1] Most of these self-defense cooperatives were short-lived because of financial, technological, marketing, and managerial problems inherent in the circumstances of their origin. Only in France and Italy did industrial cooperatives come to be a significant long-term presence.

Idealism, movements, and economic or political crises sometimes combined to bring on a wave of self-management experiments. Workers' cooperatives were organized during the Paris Commune of 1870–71 and in every socialist revolutionary upsurge of the twentieth century. As old structures of authority were toppled, ordinary people tried to take over and manage the production and distribution of goods and services and even their neighborhoods. Most of these experiments, too, were unsuccessful in the long run. The reasons remain subject to intense debate.[2]

Interest in cooperatives resurfaced in Europe and North America during the 1970s. The upsurge of radical movements in the 1960s combined with a long wave of industrial recession starting from the early seventies that forced even some conservative trade unions to take an active interest in workers' cooperatives. Rank-and-file workers faced with unemployment were willing to experiment with self-management to keep their jobs. In many cases governments were also willing to assist such experiments to hold down unemployment (Coates 1976). The New Left movements and ideologies that came to prominence during the seventies also experimented with various participatory organizational forms for carrying out production and providing services. Though largely unacknowledged, many of these microexperiments drew inspiration from earlier utopian and anarchist socialist traditions (Rothschild and Whitt 1986: 14–18).

What if this kind of broad movement for social change combines with a long process of democratic worker activism? What if that movement has put a government in power that is sympathetic to the workers? And what if this combination of forces in turn is confronted with a sudden, dramatic crisis of capitalist retrenchment? As we saw in chapter 2, beedi workers in Kerala had fought for four decades for better wages and working conditions. Then, on 15 October 1968, they found themselves laid off, victims of that most singular and dramatic capitalist weapon, the employer's willingness to fire them all before giving in to certain worker demands. A conjunction of social and historical forces in Kerala was developing that would force beedi workers to set up a cooperative. It was a conjunction of forces that would test the qualities we outlined in chapter 2 and—beyond that—would call forth the individual courage, determination, and creativity of hundreds of individual workers and their political allies.

The Cooperatives of 1958

Though KDB's ancestry can be traced as far back as the 1930s, it was at the end of the 1950s that a major breakthrough occurred when the government of the newly formed state of Kerala sponsored beedi cooperatives. The history of these early cooperatives is worth analyzing as a background to the formation of KDB, which came a decade later. In 1945 P. Krishna Pillai came forward with a novel scheme to popularize the idea of a cooperative. The 1946 general election was around the corner. He suggested that the beedi workers' unions should draw up a program for the new government for the beedi industry and should place it before the candidates seeking the votes of beedi workers. An important component of the program was the government's encouragement of cooperatives through liberal financial aid. The follow-up to Krishna Pillai's suggestion is best described in the words of Azhikodan Raghavan, a beedi worker himself in the

1940s and later one of the foremost leaders of the Communist Party in Kerala.

> At that time many did not have clarity regarding the practical aspects of organizing the beedi and cigar industry on a cooperative basis. Doubts were expressed. There were also serious differences of opinion. The beedi and cigar worker union executive committee and general bodies were called to draw up a program to be placed before the candidates. Reorganization of the beedi and cigar industry on a cooperative basis was given a special emphasis in the program. The Communist candidate in Chirakkal Taluk was comrade K. P. Gopalan and Manikoth Kumaran the Congress candidate. The program was submitted to both the candidates. K. P. Gopalan accepted it and raised our issues in his campaign. (Azhikodan Raghavan 1955: 439)

K. P. Gopalan, who was also the president of the Kannur union for a brief period, received an opportunity to redeem his election pledge to the beedi workers a decade later. The first election to the legislative assembly of the newly formed state of Kerala in 1957 saw the Communists rise to power. K. P. Gopalan was chosen as the industries minister. The formation of the Communist ministry raised the expectations of laborers throughout Kerala. The beedi workers began to draw up comprehensive plans for the reorganization of the industry. The trend toward fragmentation of production units in the beedi industry—described in chapter 2—lent a sense of urgency to the task.

As noted in the previous chapter, with the dispersal of production and the entry of middlemen during the late 1940s, the relation between the real employer and the employees in the beedi industry ceased to have any legal dimension. An All-Kerala Conference of Beedi and Cigar Unions was convened in 1957 in Chalakudy in central Kerala to formulate a counterstrategy for labor. The conference drew up a two-pronged counteroffensive. First was the demand for comprehensive industrial legislation to protect the workers in the context of decentralized production. Second was the demand for introduction of workers' cooperatives in the industry. It was believed that the existence of a cooperative would increase the bargaining power of the workers.

The demands of the Chalakudy conference had a quick, sympathetic response from the industries ministry. A Tripartite Committee for the Beedi and Cigar Industry, with the representatives of the government, employers, and employees was appointed on 17 June 1957.

The committee finalized its report in a record time of six months. It recommended new legislation to "enable the bulk of the new employers also to carry on in the industry without unbearable financial problems," but with provisions regulating "the hours of work, granting workers weekly holidays, annual leave with wages, health facilities and sanitary conditions" (Government of Kerala 1958: 15). It proposed licensing work premises, restricting new workers in the industry, and extending the Minimum Wages Act to Malabar. The committee realized that the new legislation would cause "some of the present employers [to] close down the establishments and leave the industry. . . . To meet such a contingency in case it arises the committee proposed to organize the industry on a cooperative basis" (Government of Kerala 1958: 16). A model scheme for beedi cooperatives was drawn up.

Accordingly, the industries department took initiatives to set up fourteen beedi cooperatives in the major centers of the industry.[3] Five years later the Minimum Wages Committee reported that the cooperatives were found to be financially unstable and unable to provide the workers with benefits due to them under the protective legislation (Subramaniam 1965: 33).

Detailed information on these cooperatives is slight, but the Kannur Beedi Workers' Industrial Cooperative, said to be one of the more successful cooperatives, provides a good example of the kinds of difficulties they faced.[4] It had started production sometime during the middle of 1958 with a membership of four hundred. The cost of a membership share was Rs 10, of which only Rs 5 had to be paid at the time of joining. The government gave a loan of around Rs 12,500. The director board included prominent trade union cadres. For the first two weeks only four workers were employed. Over time, the number of workers increased to fifty. The beedis were marketed under the brand name "Society Beedi," with the packet having a symbol of two hands held together in a handshake.

By 1961 the cooperative was in serious financial difficulties. An attempt was made to revitalize it with some new officers. A Communist Party sympathizer from Trichur arranged for the raw materials on credit. The cooperative survived, but its financial condition did not improve. Another revitalization attempt involved an outlay of

Rs 50,000. This was drawn up when the second left ministry came to power in 1967. The government was very sympathetic to the proposal, and the loan was approved. But the union decided to forgo the loan because by then the Kerala Dinesh Beedi Cooperative was about to be formed. An attempt was made to convert the society into a branch of the Dinesh Beedi Cooperative, but it failed for legal and political reasons. The cooperative continued to function for a few more months but finally liquidated itself and donated its movable assets to the Kannur Town Primary Society of the Kerala Dinesh Beedi Cooperative.

The Tellicherry cooperative, also formed in 1958, had disbanded even earlier, in 1962. Most of the other cooperatives also failed. Why did this happen? The experiences of the Kannur and Tellicherry cooperatives suggest five reasons.

First, the cooperatives lacked professionalism in marketing. K. C. Kunhiraman, a worker-director, remembers their marketing strategy:

> Squads of five to six workers would go out on Sundays to market our beedis at different places. We would go out in the morning and work till late evening. Even on working days squads of two workers would go to all important areas. These workers would be given wages. The *modus operandi* was that each worker would contribute two beedi bundles to workers in the marketing squads. Different workers would volunteer for the marketing squad on different days. (Kunhiraman Int: 9 June 1993)

According to T. C. Kumaran, the president of the cooperative in 1961, the methods had hardly changed after almost ten years. The marketing strategy was based entirely on the enthusiasm of the worker members; no marketing network of agents was built up to sustain it on a commercial basis.

The second reason for the failure of the cooperatives was the inability to maintain quality. The blend of tobacco is the most vital component for determining the taste of the beedi. At the Kannur cooperative a cheap variety of tobacco was used as the base, with disastrous consequences:

> A lot of complaints came from the market and beedi stocks started to accumulate. We workers of the cooperative tried various things to improve the quality of the beedi. . . . We tried various blends. We found

that the tobacco exempted from excise did not light properly or give smoke. This tobacco was largely composed of finely powdered tobacco stem pieces. . . . These powdered tobacco stems expanded when the beedi was lit and it blocked up the smoke channel of the beedi. . . . We workers decided that this tobacco should not be used in our beedis and told the secretary and the president. . . . They did not initially appreciate our viewpoint . . . but finally agreed. . . . But by that time our reputation in the beedi market had been affected. The demand had gone down. . . . A lot of debtors did not pay us back. (Kumaran Int: 10 June 1993)

Beedis produced by the Tellicherry Beedi Workers' Cooperative were also of poor quality because of the tobacco blend used.

A third cause of the cooperatives' demise was that the scale of operation was not sufficient to take advantage of economies of scale in the purchase of raw materials or in marketing the beedis. Only limited advertisements could be undertaken, and often raw materials had to be purchased from the local market at high prices. The cooperatives thus found it difficult to compete with the large private beedi companies.

Moreover, working capital was insufficient. A mistake like a wrong blend would lead to an accumulation of stock. Even a brief period was enough to push the cooperative into a permanent financial crunch. Political forces compounded the financial problems. By the time the cooperatives were set up, the right-wing "liberation struggle" against the Communist government had reached a fever pitch, and the cooperatives were viewed as Communist outfits. The new experiment had started in a very hostile environment. Panniyan Bharathan, the secretary of the Kannur union in the period, recalls that the hostility of the anticommunist front government that came to power after the left ministry was dismissed in 1959 also significantly contributed to the failure of the cooperatives. The government refused all requests by the cooperatives for additional financing (Bharathan Int: 9 June 1993).

Finally, the extent of the commitment of the unions to cooperatives at that time is open to question. Union resolutions had demanded workers' cooperatives, and the cooperatives were led by the unions. But remarks made in the interviews leave one with the impression that the 1958 cooperatives may have been viewed as a scheme of the industries department. They were not the major focus of union activity. This comes out all the more sharply when we contrast the 1958 cooperatives with the formation of the Kerala Dinesh Beedi Cooperative in 1969.

A Political Challenge

The Kerala Dinesh Beedi Cooperative arose from one of the gravest crises the beedi workers in northern Kerala ever faced. This crisis produced a major political challenge to the unions and the left political parties. As we recounted in the previous chapter, in September 1968, the major beedi companies threatened to close their shops in Kerala. The private beedi employers claimed that they were forced to close down their factories because "normal functioning of the factories had become impossible in the situation created by the workers *gheraoing* [surrounding and holding] and physically attacking the employers and management personnel" (*Mathrubhumi* 26 September 1968). They further alleged that constant labor unrest was the direct outcome of the labor policies of the 1967 left government, which prohibited police from interfering in labor disputes unless an exceptional breakdown of law and order occurred. Such a breakdown was the stated reason for dismissal of the first Communist ministry in 1959. It became the common refrain of the right wing on every advance of the left movement. Thus, the allegation made in a context in which nearly twelve thousand workers could be rendered jobless touched a very sensitive spot.

The unions stoutly denied the allegation. They pointed out that there was not a single strike going on, and no industrial violence had occurred in the beedi industry for the sixteen months since the strike in June 1967 (*Mathrubhumi* 16 October 1968). The unions argued that the real reason for the closings was the threat that the Kerala left government would implement the Beedi and Cigar Workers' Conditions of Employment Act. Nonetheless, the employers' claim of a deteriorating law and order situation was taken up by the opposition political parties.[5]

The state government invited the beedi owners to Trivandrum, the state capital, for talks. An all-party delegation went to Mangalore for discussions. It was suggested that the implementation of the Beedi and Cigar Workers' Conditions of Employment Act could be phased in over a period of time. But the talks made it clear that the owners were in no mood for a settlement. The state government was informed that the owners were too busy with the Dasra Festival in Mysore to visit Trivandrum for talks. On 15 October Mangalore beedi firms stopped all their activities within Kerala (*Mathrubhumi* 16 October 1968). Twelve thousand workers were instantly unemployed.

What could be done? The beedi unions in Kannur district formed a Joint Action Council. The left trade unions held that agitations would have to be carried out simultaneously on three fronts: (1) against the central government to demand uniform implementation of the Beedi and Cigar Workers' Conditions of Employment Act in all the states, (2) against the state government to demand immediate relief and intervention, and (3) against the employers to demand reopening of the factories. Even as preparations for combined agitations by all the unions were going on, conflicts developed between the left trade unions—All-India Trade Union Congress (AITUC) and Indian Workers' Assembly (HMS)—on the one hand and right trade unions—Indian National Trade Union Congress (INTUC) and Independent Workers' Union (STU)—on the other.[6] The right trade unions wanted to aim the campaign at the state government. They refused to support any agitation against the center. The debate became acrimonious, and the Joint Action Council broke up at its second meeting (*Mathrubhumi* 21 October 1968). The left trade unions announced a program to picket central and state government offices from 22 October onward. A few days later the other trade unions came up with their own agitations.

At A. K. Gopalan's initiative, the beedi owners agreed to start negotiations (*Mathrubhumi* 29 October 1968), but they refused to come to Kerala. The hill town of Mercara, in the Karnataka border district of Coorg, was chosen as the venue. The first round of talks raised hopes of a settlement, but at the second round of discussions in the middle of November the owners' positions visibly hardened (*Mathrubhumi* 3, 13, and 16 November 1968). They realized that neither the trade unions nor the Kerala government could pursue them across the borders.

Ganesh Beedi Company's legal adviser spoke through the owners' chief negotiator at the talks:

There have not been any conciliation talks. Conciliation talks are held when there is a labor dispute. There is no labor dispute between the workers and management of Ganesh and Bharat Beedis because the employee-employer relationship has ceased to exist. . . . The rightness or wrongness of closure of factories was not a subject of discussion in the last round of talks. The discussion was about the possibility of providing new work for the unemployed workers. (*Mathrubhumi* 18 November 1968)

He put forward two conditions for management's agreeing to provide employment to the locked-out beedi workers. The first was to the state government. There was no question of reopening the factories or accepting any of the past labor liabilities. The state government was to agree to the denial of service benefits to the beedi workers (*Mathrubhumi* 17 November 1968). The second condition was to the trade unions. They were to formally accept the domestic putting-out system, which the owners insisted was the most suitable organization for the beedi industry (*Mathrubhumi* 18 November 1968).

The employers' demands were a virtual declaration of war against the left government and the beedi unions. The government of Kerala was being told to formally agree that the employers could break the law, and the trade unions were being told to virtually disband themselves. The right trade unions—who had rejoined the Joint Action Council on the eve of the second round of talks—broke ranks once again. They expressed willingness to experiment with the beedi companies' demands. They argued that it was better to reach a collective agreement with the employers regarding the terms and conditions of the domestic putting-out system than to leave the system entirely unregulated (*Mathrubhumi* 18 November 1968.[7]) After a fleeting hesitation, the left trade unions rejected management's proposals. The Rubicon was crossed; there could be no going back now. The unions would have to disrupt the attempts to introduce the domestic putting-out system, demanding that the displaced workers be rehired with past gains intact.

The Struggle Turns Violent

The socioeconomic crisis in the district worsened as the impasse continued into its second month with no end in sight. The unemployed workers were running out of resources. After the relief ration granted by the government ended (*Mathrubhumi* 9 November 1968 and 16 December 1968), relief was taken up by a Struggle Solidarity Committee, but it was not enough (*Mathrubhumi* 7 November 1968). So helpless were the workers that many agreed to roll beedis under any conditions if they could earn some income. Management declared its willingness to provide them work to do at home. In effect, the owners would impose the domestic putting-out system through the sheer misery of its alternative: no work at all. At the other end of the spectrum, a small minority of the workers were drifting from desperation toward extremism. In Tellicherry on the night of 22 November, three hundred people, many of them beedi workers, attempted to storm the police station (*Mathrubhumi* 23 November 1968).

December saw the opening of two new fronts for agitation. The head offices of Ganesh Beedi Company in Mangalore in the nearby state of Karnataka were picketed. The Karnataka state government declared the agitation illegal, citing the threat to peace in the town. Batches of workers broke the ban daily, and were arrested and convicted. More than three hundred workers were jailed.

Simultaneously the trade unions had to confront yet another threat back in Kerala. To undermine the strike, Maha Laxmi Traders, Guru Kripa, and Deepak tobacco depots were being opened, often on the premises of the closed Ganesh Company itself to distribute raw materials to any workers who were willing to roll beedis for the domestic putting-out system. The right trade unions began cooperating with management (*Mathrubhumi* 17 December 1968), but the left unions picketed the depots, facing severe and unexpected police brutality (Sahadevan Int: 9 June 1993).

Given the promanagement stand of the right trade unions and the depth of the workers' desperation, the struggle to stop the spread of the putting-out system was being lost. The workers resorted to the only weapon they had left: beedi tobacco depots were set on fire (*Mathrubhumi* 11 and 22 December 1968).

Far-right vigilantes now entered the scene: RSS squads appeared in Kannur. The RSS—*Rashtriya Swayam Sevak Sangh*—forms the militant core of the fascist Hindu communal movement in India. Though their popular support in Kerala has always been very limited, they have a strong network of cells in the state. In the rest of India they mostly attack Muslims. In Kerala, however, they act primarily as a violent anticommunist force. *Jan Sangh,* then the political wing of the RSS, had already appealed to the beedi workers not to be communist pawns

(*Mathrubhumi* 18 November 1968). The unions alleged that RSS squads were guarding the new depots against attacks from the workers (Vasu Int: 7 June 1993; Sahadevan Int: 9 June 1993). Occasional confrontations soon developed into a war of attrition. Knives and bombs were freely used. This street war subsided only a decade later, having claimed more than fifty lives. After its formation, Kerala Dinesh Beedi Cooperative proved to be a favorite target of RSS attacks. All six beedi workers who were killed in RSS attacks were employees of the Kerala Dinesh Beedi Workers' Cooperative (Pandakal 1984: 55–56).

FORMATION OF THE KERALA DINESH BEEDI
WORKERS' COOPERATIVE

Retrenchment and the wave of social movements in Kerala in the 1960s now intersected to produce a new beedi cooperative. Acceptance of the domestic putting-out system would mean the loss of all that the unions had struggled for. How could the jobs be kept without losing everything else? Suggestions for a workers' cooperative were again in the air. The Kerala State Industries Minister had hinted at it (*Mathrubhumi* 26 October 1968). The trade unions had also raised it in their memorandum submitted to the government (*Mathrubhumi* 9 November 1968). But it took another six weeks before a concrete policy could be announced by the state government. One reason for the delay was that hopes of a compromise continued until the failure of the second round of talks at Mercara. The other reason was that an involved debate was going on behind the scenes: was the best approach a government-owned beedi corporation or a worker-owned beedi cooperative?

The labor minister favored a government corporation. The industries minister threw his weight behind worker ownership. The fissures in the Left United Front government that were to be the cause of its downfall later in the year had already made their appearance. It was reported that the CPM (Communist Party Marxist), the dominant partner in the coalition, was more sympathetic to the government ownership proposal of the labor minister, with whose splinter party it had more cordial relations.

Opinions in trade union circles were also divided (Kannan Int: 6

June 1993; Bharathan Int: 9 June 1993). Some voiced strong support for a government corporation, for two main reasons. First, the trade unions needed speedy reemployment of the laid-off workers to continue their struggle against the spread of the domestic putting-out system. The formation of a complicated worker-owned cooperative could be a time-consuming affair, and a delay would defeat its very purpose. Second, the failure of the 1958 cooperative was still a vivid memory. The unions had failed then to keep a fifty-member worker cooperative afloat. Now it was being proposed that the trade unions virtually take over the responsibility for guaranteeing employment and wages for twelve thousand workers. How could they hope to succeed?

Even among the proponents of the worker-owned cooperative there were differing views on the form it should take: should it be a federation of small-scale dependent primary cooperatives or one large unitary cooperative with small-scale work branches? The debates could not go on endlessly. Finally, the state cabinet, on 18 December 1968, put an end to speculation by announcing a cooperative with twelve primaries and one apex central society. The state government committed itself to the speedy implementation of the program. In an extraordinary decision, the industries minister and other concerned officials were ordered to proceed to Kannur and camp there until the cooperative was properly organized (*Mathrubhumi* 19 December 1968).

The cooperative finally started production on 15 February 1969. The first few weeks proved to be a period of hectic activity. The government had created one of the largest beedi industrial firms in the country with a cabinet directive—an event that had no precedent. Beedi firms start small and then expand as their brand wins consumer loyalty and demand increases. But here was a firm that was going to push millions of beedis onto the market from day one. What were the planners and organizers thinking? Two months of hectic activities ensued. The Industries Minister, a veteran trade union leader of the coir workers of Alleppey, with the Industries Secretary, the Director of Industries, and their assistants, moved from Thiruvananthapuram and set up camp in Kannur (*Mathrubhumi* 19 December 1968); Kannan Int: 6 June 1993). The first days were spent in marathon discussions with the trade union and political party leaders to finalize the cooperative scheme. While the trade union leaders set about to convene the general-body meetings of the unemployed workers in various locations to explain the scheme and recruit members, a team of specialists in industrial cooperatives drafted the bylaws and cut short the normal procedures to have the central society and the twenty primary cooperatives registered in record time (*Mathrubhumi* 24 December 1968). There were meetings and consultations every day. A number of important production decisions had to be taken: What was to be the blend and brand of the new beedi? Where would beedi leaves and tobacco be purchased as per the requirement of the blend? Where would they find godowns [warehouses], headquarters for the primary societies and the central society and buildings for more than twenty work centers? Who would print the labels, draw up a marketing scheme, organize the advertisement campaign? The list of tasks that had to be completed before production could start seemed endless (Gopalakrishnan Int: 10 June 1993). The industries minister had set the tone of action in his speech at the first meeting on his arrival in Kannur. No financial, legal, or procedural barriers were to delay the project. Necessary governmental orders were drafted and notified from Kannur itself (Panikkar 1974: 4–7). Finally, at a ceremony on 15 February 1969 the minister for industry, T. V. Thomas, inaugurated the working of the Kerala Dinesh Beedi Cooperative by handing a day's supply of tobacco and *tendu* leaves to a beedi worker—President of the Hosdurg primary society (Ramunni 1974).

Along with grassroots pressure and participation, an important feature of the formation of the Kerala Dinesh Beedi Workers' Cooperative was the role played by the Kerala state government. Initially, the cooperative was almost entirely financed by the government. The workers, who had been unemployed for four months, were unable to come up with Rs 20 to purchase a share in the cooperative. Therefore, the government extended Rs 19 as a share capital loan so that each worker had to pay only Rs 1 to buy his or her share. The government also contributed Rs 1.35 million as share capital of the central society and sanctioned a working capital fund of Rs .71 million. An arrangement for Rs 1 million overdraft facilities with Kannur District Cooperative Bank on government guarantee was also made available. Because of the substantial government investment in the cooperative, the bylaws required that both the chairman of the board of directors and the secretary of the central society would be government officers. Even the primary society director boards were initially appointed by the government.

Such a high level of government involvement and control would appear to be contrary to the idea of a worker-owned cooperative. It could give rise to a privileged, order-giving bureaucracy that would stifle shop floor participation and initiative. Promotion of small-scale industrial cooperatives and cottage industries had been an important part of the development strategy of the government of India since independence. Therefore, government involvement in the formation of the beedi cooperative was not exceptional, but the *level* of involvement was. The evolution of Kerala Dinesh Beedi shows that state sponsorship does not have to make a cooperative into an appendage of a government bureaucracy. Grassroots strength and government commitment can combine to create conditions for the rise of workplace democracy.

TOWARD A NEW CULTURE OF DEVELOPMENT ACTION

Surveying the daunting tasks ahead in setting up KDB, P. V. Kutty, a trade union representative at the organizing conference, had warned that the entire scheme would fall through if those who "head the apex [central] society are not honest and efficient" (*Mathrubhumi* 23 December 1968). Kerala Dinesh Beedi has been fortunate in having the services of officials of proven integrity whose commitment to the cooperative has been exemplary.

G. K. Panikkar, the Joint Director of Industries in charge of Northern Kerala, was persuaded to be the first chairman of the board of directors of the new central society. Panikkar had begun his civil service career as a block development officer, distinguishing himself in the early 1960s by organizing one of the largest land development cooperatives (Panikkar Int: 18 January 1993). He continued to hold the position of chairman of the cooperative concurrently with his official posts in the industries department, and, even after retirement, was nominated to stay on as chairman. His identification with KDB was so total that he became popularly known as "Beedi Panikkar."

N. P. Gopalakrishnan, the cooperative organizer from the industries department, was made the secretary of the central society. He carried out his duties with a skill and dedication that have won widespread admiration.

Panikkar hesitated to take charge of KDB at first. On the fifth anniversary of the cooperative he confessed: "What I was worried about was that as workers and their leaders belonged to different political camps, trouble would be from that side. But I must say that aspect has not bothered me very much at any time during the past five years . . ." (Panikkar 1974). The dedication of the trade union leaders and their intimate knowledge of the industry drew admiration from the administrators. The respect was mutual. The blend of popular mobilization and the best features of bureaucracy produced a cooperative leadership as smooth as a fine beedi.

Besides the chairman, the board of directors of the central society consisted of a nominee of the finance department of the government and five workers' representatives from all the major political formations in the district: P. V. Kutty, Communist Party of India—Marxist (CPM); C. C. Balan, Communist Party of India (CPI); P. T. Pavithran, Congress; M. C. Kannan, Socialist; and K. P. Cheriya Abdul Khader, Muslim League. The zeal for participation and democracy is revealed by the fact that even members of the Indian National Congress and the Muslim League, groups that had supported the domestic putting-out system and had ridiculed the idea of a cooperative, were placed on the board. There were practical reasons for this arrangement as well. The all-party nature of the board ensured that there was no major political opposition to the cooperative. Similarly, the primary society director boards included all the parties.

Initially, government appointment rather than elections was a practical and political necessity. The Congress Party, the Muslim League, and the Socialists were unlikely to receive any seats on elected boards. This would leave them an outside, alienated minority. K. P. Sahadevan (Int: 9 June 1993), the Tobacco Trade Group secretary, explained: "We were stepping into a new venture—into a new experience—and we wanted the cooperation of all. We were eager to create a broad front to carry on."

Analyzing the first five years of expansion of the cooperative, AITUC leader C. C. Balan (1974) judged the political style to be the most important factor in KDB's success:

It is well known that the workers who have been brought together in the field of this cooperative belong to different political parties. Precisely for this reason, a feeling among many was that the workers would soon start quarreling among themselves. But not only did it not happen, but further, we were also able to function keeping the interests of workers above everything else. The structure and style of functioning of the Central Executive of the society was such as to compel and encourage the above trend. There may have been some exceptional instances, but on the whole our experience is one of unity among various political factions in action for common goals.

Central society secretary N. P. Gopalakrishnan concurred: "There was a strong team spirit. Everybody wanted the cooperative to succeed irrespective of political differences. . . . The team spirit, which prevented political interference and corruption, was the most important factor which led to the success of the cooperative" (Int: 10 June 1993).

This team spirit survived through the 1970s, which was otherwise a decade of sharp rivalry between the two communist parties, with the CPI heading a coalition government that included conservative parties while the CPM led the opposition. In a sense, KDB could be described as a forerunner of what the left today calls the "politics of development action." Political fragmentation in Kerala has made the unity of the people difficult for even mutually beneficial development activities. Most mass organizations have evolved into front organizations of one or another political party. These political alignments have become such a divisive force that cooperation at the grassroots is often impossible. The patriarch of communists in Kerala, E. M. S. Namboodiripad (1909–1998), was in the forefront of a campaign to self-critically analyze the sectarian traditions that have crept into Kerala's political life. Namboodiripad (1992) emphasized the need for a new political culture that would make it possible for political parties, whether in power or in opposition, to work together on the basis of issues, particularly in the area of economic development. The creation of such a culture became an important item of the left agenda in the 1980s. The 1990–91 total-literacy campaign in Kerala was a dramatic exhibition of the potential of a new political culture of development (Tharakan 1990).

Elections to KDB's director board were to take place at the end of three years, but the system of appointments continued until 1986. The CPM insisted on the elections, arguing that the cooperatives had stabilized well enough to accommodate more democratic procedures of selecting the director boards. There was widespread apprehension that the elections would generate bitterness and factional feuds within the cooperatives, but the feuds did not materialize. The lack of conflict was due partly to institutional mechanisms such as the Pension and Welfare Committee that represented all the trade unions and partly to the traditions of accommodation and mutual consultation that had been built up over the years prior to 1986.

FROM GANESH TO DINESH

An advertisement was placed in the newspapers calling for designs for a KDB emblem. A village art teacher won the prize with a portrayal of dawn breaking over the coconut trees from behind distant hills (*Mathrubhumi* 5 January 1969). Dinesh—the morning sun—became the brand name of the beedi produced by KDB. The wrapper was pink, like the wrappers made by the Ganesh Beedi Company.

Creating a new tobacco blend for the Dinesh beedi was a drawn-out and tedious process. The trade union leaders had learned a bitter lesson from the 1958 cooperative. Widespread opinions were solicited regarding the blend. P. V. Kutty and C. C. Balan, both members of the central society director board, proved to be master blenders (Balan Int: 9 June 1993), creating a blend that was similar to that of Ganesh but less harsh. There was no doubt that for the new cooperative to establish itself, it would have to capture a substantial part of the market catered to by the popular Ganesh beedis.

The logo, the name, and the blend were not without opposition. Ganesh Beedi complained of trademark violations; Ganesh and Dinesh sounded similar, and both wrappers were pink. Ganesh spokespersons charged that even the trunks of the coconut trees in the Dinesh logo looked like the trunk of Ganesh—the elephant god who appears on Ganesh Beedis' packages. At first Ganesh Beedi had thought KDB would collapse into bankruptcy, and had decided that lying low would be wiser after being so long in the limelight of antagonistic public attention.

However, KDB not only survived but began to eat into Ganesh's market. After nearly twenty months, Ganesh Beedi filed a trademark infringement case in Mysore District Court (Panikkar 1988: 7–14). A court injunction was issued prohibiting the production and marketing of Dinesh beedis. Stopping production at KDB would have been calamitous. G. K. Panikkar, at his own personal risk, decided to ignore the order. He rushed to Mysore. The court refused to vacate the stay order and postponed further deliberations for two weeks. This unusual delaying action meant that Ganesh would win the battle even if it lost the case: two weeks without production would destroy KDB's infant market network. KDB went on producing beedis.

Eventually, the judge at the high court in Bangalore was moved by the story of the fledging cooperative and its unequal struggle with Ganesh, the beedi giant. He vacated the stay to stop the production. The court case dragged on for three more years. The initial court verdict was in favor of KDB; it was appealed by Ganesh. To avoid endless litigation, an out-of-court settlement was reached by which KDB agreed to make minor changes in the trademark.

Considerable apprehension was created by the litigation, particularly the stay order of the Mysore court, but it proved to be a blessing in disguise. Panikkar recalls, "The court helped us because it won us popular support. People like martyrs and they [Ganesh] were once again trying to destroy us" (Panikkar Int: 8 June 1993).

THE POLITICS OF CONSUMER CHOICE

The widespread political sympathy that the cooperative enjoyed among the working population facilitated rapid penetration into the beedi market by breaking the barriers of brand loyalty. Tens of thousands of consumers suddenly switched over from the traditional brands to Dinesh beedis. This was largely a conscious political act of solidarity with the workers' cooperative. There is no other way to account for the ability of the cooperative to sell millions of beedis each day after only a few months in operation. The secretary of the cooperative recalled that "in the case of our Dinesh beedi, there was no time to undertake any market surveys. We had to give jobs immediately to the workers who had been unemployed for months" (Ramunni 1974). Though there were ups and downs, Dinesh beedis received a sympathetic response everywhere: people bought them and smoked them.

The product of the cooperative came to symbolize the unequal battle being waged between the beedi barons and the starving workers. Struggle solidarity committees, with representatives of mass organizations and prominent citizens, had long been in existence in Kannur district. Beedi workers took their product to political conferences and meetings, where the leaders would often appeal for a switch to Dinesh beedis. P. Vijayan, a beedi worker and current district president of the Centre for Indian Trade Unions, CITU, recalls numerous such instances (Vijayan Int: 7 June 1993). Some government employee organizations sent circulars urging their members to change over to Dinesh. Tobacco Workers' Union president C. Kannan recalled that even beedi workers of private firms conducted large publicity campaigns for KDB beedis: "Actually, they were cutting into their own job security. When the cooperative grew in size and captured more of the market, many of the smaller beedi firms closed down. Some of the private sector workers who campaigned for Dinesh Beedi lost their jobs" (Kannan Int: 6 June 1993).

Worker volunteers formed marketing squads. They met distributors and shopkeepers and persuaded them to sell Dinesh beedis. Two central squads toured outlying areas in decorated vans fitted with microphones. Punchayil Nanu, a member of the squad that toured plantation areas, remembers their activity: "We would wait till workers came out after work and talk to them for five to ten minutes. We would explain the circumstances in which our cooperative was formed and appeal for class solidarity. We used to say that this product should be seen as the symbol of struggle of the working class against capitalist exploitation" (Nanu Int: 7 June 1993). Pookkadan Chandran (Int: 6 January 1993), a member of the other central squad, had similar narratives in the rice belt of Kuttanad in Central Kerala.

The popular campaign was supplemented with innovative advertising campaigns and creation of a network of sales agents. Advertisements were taken in the press calling for agents. They were interviewed and selected. We give a detailed discussion of this marketing network when we analyze the activities of the central society in chapter 4. Here we note that even the commercial marketing agents in their promotional activities emphasized "the fact that the ownership of Dinesh beedi unit belonged to the workers. Therefore the campaign to patronize Dinesh Beedi, in addition to its quality, had a worker-oriented undertone" (Ramankutty 1974: 73–74).

From 1969 to 1992, KDB increased its sales from 1 million to 588 million rupees. Even though the sales have continued to increase every year, there has been some slowing of the rate of expansion. On the whole, the picture that emerges is one of phenomenal expansion. KDB is now reportedly the fourth largest beedi firm in India. Its rival—Mangalore Ganesh Beedi Company—is the largest (Rama-krishnan 1990: 11).

As KDB's market expanded, the workforce increased. Initially, only three thousand of the twelve thousand displaced workers could be hired at the cooperative. The market was still too small. By 1974, when the cooperative celebrated its fifth anniversary, KDB could justly claim to have fulfilled its objective of rehiring all the displaced workers. By 1985, total employment had increased to around thirty thousand. Since then, market expansion has slowed, leading to a slowdown in the growth of the workforce. Employment peaked in 1991 at just over thirty-five thousand. In 1995 the actively employed workforce numbered just under thirty-two thousand (see table 3.1).

Until the early 1970s, recruitment was almost entirely from the displaced workforce from Ganesh Beedi and the other Mangalore-based companies that had closed down in 1969. Once the task of rehabilitation was completed, formal recruitment procedures had to be adopted to select new workers. Demand for employment at KDB far outpaces its ability to offer jobs. Membership in the cooperative has become a coveted goal for beedi workers.

The expansion of KDB's workforce has been accompanied by changes in its composition. At the time of the formation of the cooperative, the workers were almost entirely male, except for the primary societies in the Kasargod area. But a majority of the new workers have been women, who today constitute over 50 percent of the workforce. The shift to female beedi workers at KDB parallels the shift taking place in the gender makeup of beedi workers in Kerala generally. Between the 1961 and 1981 Indian censuses, the number of male beedi workers in Kerala increased only from sixty-nine thousand to

Table 3.1. Growth of KDB

| Year | In the Primary Cooperatives | | Concerning the Central Cooperative | | Concerning the Workers | | | | | |
| | Membership | Employment | Sales (thousands of rupees) | Net Profit (thousands of rupees) | Per Capita Annual Earnings, in Rupees | | | | Nonwage Per Capita Real Earnings in (1971) Rupees | Benefits As a Percent of Total Earnings[a] |
					Wages	Benefits	Bonus	Total		
1969	13,000	3,000	1,100	50						
1970	n.a.	5,000	5,200	30						
1971	n.a.	7,000	10,800	98						
1972	n.a.	8,000	14,100	-11						
1973	n.a.	10,000	16,900	-18						
1974	n.a.	12,000	24,500	92						
1975	n.a.	14,000	38,800	-38	1550	57	64	1671	1006	7
1976	n.a.	16,500	49,200	34	1363	90	72	1525	947	11
1977	n.a.	18,000	64,900	-27	1677	201	133	2011	1281	17
1978	n.a.	18,000	76,100	80	1766	271	183	2220	1354	20
1979	n.a.	19,246	80,300	66	1678	311	192	2181	1246	23
1980	n.a.	19,036	93,100	88	1896	388	236	2520	1254	25
1981	n.a.	22,330	125,400	93	2131	497	291	2919	1275	27
1982	n.a.	22,065	141,500	114	2483	607	362	3452	1426	28
1983	n.a.	28,569	171,900	27	2407	563	350	3320	1253	28
1984	n.a.	27,148	201,500	101	2718	685	394	3797	1266	28
1985	n.a.	30,590	234,200	315	3239	791	493	4523	1454	28
1986	47,768	32,633	287,300	708	3463	852	582	4897	1436	29
1987	46,623	30,658	342,000	3,388	4061	1008	799	5868	1573	31
1988	48,510	33,518	361,700	3,151	4245	1053	859	6158	1532	31
1989	49,077	32,670	280,800	2,611	3315	857	943	5115	1224	35
1990	50,727	33,771	456,600	3,892	5081	1267	1051	7400	1697	31
1991	50,051	35,035	531,800	3,217	5366	1399	1102	7866	1576	32
1992	49,120	33,372	587,800[b]	3,642	6652	1747	1399	9799	1775	32
1993	48,604	32,632	638,000	2,706	7043	2013	1519	10575	1742[c]	33
1994	45,775	33,095	714,500	4,821	8537	2340	1949	12826	1890	33
1995	45,224	31,817	736,098	4,111	9331	2578	2148	14057	—[d]	34

Source: Kerala Dinesh Beedi Workers' Central Cooperative Society, Annual Reports.

[a] Benefits plus Bonus divided by Total Earnings.

[b] This figure (for 1992) differs from the similar figure in table 6.1 because table 3.1 includes the value of sales after the central society markup has been added. The figure in table 6.1 includes only the profits of the primary societies.

[c] The constant rupees figure for 1993 is based on nine months' data only.

[d] Cost-of-living data are not yet available for computing the 1995 constant rupees wages and benefits.

seventy-eight thousand. During the same twenty-year period, the number of female workers rose from one thousand to forty-one thousand (Government of India 1961, 1981a). The same trend has probably continued into the 1980s.[8] The main reason for this shift is the relative decline in beedi wages compared with the wages of construction workers and agricultural laborers. Younger rural male workers in the beedi production belt have tended to go into other vocations. Ironically, the rapid entry of female workers into the beedi industry was stimulated in part by the spread of the domestic putting-out system, initially in the villages on the Kerala-Karnataka border and then into the interior villages in Kasargod, which were outside the traditional beedi production centers. This is the process we described in chapter 2.

With no militant trade unions in the new areas of Kasargod, little could be done to disrupt the spread of the putting-out system, and once the domestic industry had come, it could not be disrupted unless alternative employment could be guaranteed to the domestic workers. The expansion of KDB might have been the answer, but today the number of domestic workers in Kasargod is estimated to be at least 20 to 25 percent higher than the number of workers in the cooperative. To absorb them, KDB would have to penetrate markets outside Kerala. Almost the entire output of the domestic industry in Kasargod is taken by Mangalore-based firms for sale outside the state. For reasons that we shall discuss in the next section, the cooperative is finding it difficult to rapidly expand its market even within Kerala. The low wages in the states outside Kerala create cheap beedis that limit KDB's sales in new Kerala markets and outside Kerala.

Because of this low wage competition, the trade unions have been forced to accept the domestic putting-out system as a reality. The system has been steadily creeping into traditional areas in Kannur district. Union efforts have been directed toward organizing the home workers to ensure them statutory minimum wages and other benefits. A protracted campaign has been going on since the late 1980s in which KDB's success in generating profits even after paying more than the statutory wages and benefits has been a powerful inspiration.

As indicated in table 3.1, except for four years during its first decade, KDB has registered profits. The accumulated central society profits came to Rs 33.3 million in 1995. In addition, the primary societies had accumulated considerable profits of their own. The accumulated profits and other funds generated by the cooperative make it completely self-reliant in providing its working capital. Apart from trade credit, KDB does not borrow from any financial or other institutions. It has been able to build up considerable fixed assets. The current value of KDB's land and buildings is estimated at above Rs 100 million. The financial strength of the cooperative was dramatically displayed in 1988 when it came to the rescue of the state government, which was in financial distress. With the state treasury so low it could not pay its bills, KDB came through with a short-term loan of Rs 30 million.

KDB—THE STANDARD BEARER OF IMPROVEMENT
IN LABOR CONDITIONS

The measure of success of KDB is not merely its rapid business expansion but the fact that this expansion has been achieved while improving the workers' standard of living. Because traditional industries such as beedi production are based on handicraft skill, there is little scope for increasing the competitiveness of firms other than through reducing wages, increasing workloads, or worsening working conditions. Periods of sharp market rivalry therefore prove to be periods of increasing misery for the workers. The Kerala Dinesh Beedi experience is a dramatic contrast to this scenario.

Table 3.1 shows the trends in wages, bonuses and other benefits enjoyed by KDB workers since the mid-1970s. The wages are periodically raised according to rises in the cost of living in compliance with decisions of the state Minimum Wages Committee appointed by the government. As a result, wages for rolling one thousand beedis have risen from Rs 3.36 (Rs 2.30 basic wage and Rs 1.06 dearness allowance) in 1969–70 to Rs 39 (Rs 30 for basic wage and Rs 9 for dearness allowance) in 1994 and Rs 50.10 in 1995. The average annual earnings of a KDB worker have risen from Rs 1,550 in 1975 to Rs 6,652 in 1992 and to Rs 9,331 in 1995. Table 3.1 shows that the general trend of wages and benefits in 1971 constant rupees—adjusted to correct for inflation—has also been upward, from Rs 1,006 in 1975 to Rs 1,890 in

1994. This is a gain of 88 percent, truly impressive for any group of Indian workers in the factory or nonfactory sectors.

The most important new wage benefit is the annual bonus declared as a percentage of wages. In 1972–73 the first bonus of 2.25 percent was declared by the cooperative. The rate slowly crept upward to 16.5 percent in 1992–93 and rose to 17 percent in 1995. KDB workers enjoy a number of other new wage benefits (see table 1.1). May Day of 1970 was KDB's first paid holiday. Today KDB workers are entitled to eighty-one paid leave days—fifty-two Sundays, fourteen other holidays, and fifteen casual leave days, one for every twenty days worked. Maternity benefits received little attention until the 1980s, partly because the number of women workers was very small. Even today full statutory maternity benefits are not paid. Three months' leave and a payment of Rs 400 per month, or the average of the immediate past three months' wages, whichever is higher, is granted as maternity benefit.

A truly innovative welfare scheme voluntarily implemented by the cooperative is the Welfare Cum Pension Scheme of 1986. It was instituted by integrating two existing welfare schemes. The Death Benefit Scheme, started in 1977, guaranteed a death benefit of Rs 5,000 to the family of every worker who had paid Rs 1 per month. At the end of 1995, 1,159 families had received such payments. The Employees' Retirement Benefit Scheme, started in 1982, guaranteed a lump sum of Rs 3,000 and other statutory benefits on retirement, on payment of another Rs 1 per month. In 1994, the lump-sum retirement benefit was raised to Rs 4,000. Every worker who has completed fifteen years of service and reached the age of fifty-five is guaranteed a monthly pension of Rs 150 until his or her death. The worker's contribution is fixed at Rs 4 a month, while KDB contributes annually Rs 0.4 million to the fund, subject to a review from time to time. The death benefit continues as in the past. The Rs 4,000 retirement benefit is still available to any worker with fewer than fifteen years' service at retirement. As of September 1995, 774 lifetime monthly pensions were being paid out. The pension trust funds were financially sound.

While wages have kept pace with the requirements of the Minimum Wages Committee, benefits have risen more rapidly. As a result, the share of benefits that was 7 percent of a worker's total earnings in 1975 had risen by 1992 to around 32 percent and to 34 percent by 1995 (see table 3.1.). In 1995, workers also received a festival allowance of Rs 500, given to Hindus and Muslims at appropriate times at the major annual festivals.

Improving the Workplace

Workers' gains go beyond wages and pensions. One of KDB's most ambitious undertakings is its program to construct new work sheds—the buildings in which beedi rolling, labeling, and packaging take place. Since the mid-1980s, primary societies have constructed about 14 new buildings per year under a plan controlled by the central society. Of the 326 work sites in 1992, 139, or 43 percent, had been reconstructed. New buildings also mean purchase of land so that the primary societies no longer have to pay rent. Constructing their own buildings, in the long run, constitutes an investment in higher future profits and bonuses for KDB workers.

In the short run, the new buildings offer significant improvements in work surroundings and working conditions. The old sites are improvised out of old buildings, usually large houses, shops, or storage spaces. They are often dirty, uncomfortable, poorly ventilated, and poorly lighted. Washing and latrine facilities may be absent. The new buildings have a minimum of about 1.5 square meters of floor space per worker. They also feature backrests and reasonably comfortable benches for rollers to sit on. Workers may opt to sit on the floor against the backrests. Each new building has at least two toilets, two urinals, and some water faucets where workers can wash up at the end of the day. Airy window openings and fluorescent lighting are also installed. If the local water supply is not sufficient, KDB builds its own well. The most recent work sheds are now also featuring an area set aside for workers to eat lunch at a distance from the tobacco fumes. In addition to the work areas and amenities such as latrines, the work sheds also house a small office for the staff and a storage area for raw materials.

In 1992–93, new work sheds were costing about Rs .6 million to construct. Through intensive efforts by Chairman Panikkar, some recent work sheds received grants of Rs 75,000 each from the central government's Beedi Workers' Welfare Fund. The fund, which was created by an act of Parliament in 1976, is currently collected from beedi firms by a tax on beedis manufactured. The welfare schemes under the fund include medical aid to beedi workers, scholarships for their children, group insurance, and a housing program. As part of the housing program a provision has been made to give financial assistance of Rs 75,000 each for beedi workers' cooperatives to build work sheds. The grants have proved to be difficult to get and administer. Finally, in March 1994, after substantial lobbying and personal effort, Chairman Panikkar convinced the labor department to release Rs 3.9 million toward the construction of thirty-three new work sheds. Central government subsidies account for only 13 percent of the construction costs; the rest must be borne by KDB. In 1994, 50 work sheds were built; by the end of 1995, 172 work sheds—53 percent of the total number of work sheds—had been upgraded. The 15 sheds under construction in 1995 represented 10 percent of the remaining sheds to be upgraded.

Absence of Child Labor

One of the most striking features of KDB's workforce is the absence of children. All cooperative members must be eighteen or over, and no one is allowed to employ a child assistant. In the private sector, rollers often employ child assistants. Some of the tasks associated with beedi rolling—tying thread around the beedi and pushing in the ends of the wrapper leaf—are technically well suited to children because of their small fingers. Children as young as eight or ten may work all day in some private-sector beedi centers and in privately contracted home production even in Kerala. The numbers are not known but may be large in some parts of India. S. Giriappa (1987: 41–47) found in a sample in suburban Mangalore (just north of Kerala's northern boundary) that 4 percent of all children were working as beedi assistants, while in a nearby rural beedi-making area 15 percent of the children were so employed. They worked almost as many hours per day and days per year as adults. In addition to assisting rollers, some children worked as labelers in the factories without adequate ventilation or other facilities (Giriappa 1987: 90).

Child laborers get very low wages, paid by the rollers themselves. The children are not on the payroll and do not receive any wages or benefits from the firm where they assist the rollers: management and owners look the other way, avoiding Indian national laws protecting children against such labor. Abolition of child labor has been a demand of the trade unions in Kannur since the 1937 strike. Some workers initially resented the demand as harmful to their ability to earn higher wages and refused to join the strike. Union leaders convinced many with the argument that restricting the children's entry would curtail the supply of labor and eventually drive up wages (Kannan Int: 6 June 1993).

Children were not allowed in the 1958 cooperative, and KDB today considers the abolition of child assistants one of its major achievements. Kerala society as a whole benefits from the children's being able to go to school, where they can learn skills more useful to society than beedi rolling and where they can also better their individual lives through acquiring knowledge.

The absence of child helpers creates hidden costs for KDB, however. Rollers paying almost nothing to child assistants can increase their output substantially more than those who must push the ends and tie the threads themselves. In private shops or in households where the workday may go late into the evening, a roller and child assistant can produce as many as three thousand beedis per day. This gives private-sector firms a competitive edge in pricing their beedis below those of KDB. It is difficult to estimate how much of this difference in pricing results from reliance on child labor, but the use of child workers no doubt contributes to the price differences we will discuss in chapter 4.

Abolition of child labor also costs KDB in loss of comparative worker skill. As the child becomes effective at quickly tying and end-pushing, he or she may be given additional tasks, including eventually the chance to start rolling beedis. After two or three years' experience, child workers have enough skills to become effective apprentices or even to go into beedi work directly—eventually hiring younger children as their assistants. Long child apprenticeship makes for highly efficient cutting of the wrapper leaves. This is done at first with a small tin pattern or template around which the worker cuts the leaf. Because children's hands are smaller and more flexible, they can learn more quickly how to cut the leaves without the tin piece. Holding the leaves flexibly in the hand allows cutting of more wrappers per leaf—a major factor in productivity, as we shall see in chapter 6. The private firms thus get very skilled workers—albeit previously much exploited ones—who produce a larger output and better quality than do the newer KDB workers, who often train for only two to three months (Vasu Int: 7 June 1993).

The victory over child labor at KDB is part of the more general Kerala phenomenon of low child labor. Because of Kerala's nearly 100 percent school enrollment, children are learning, not working in low-paid jobs. This is in sharp contrast with most of the rest of India. The 1981 census reported only 80 million of India's 159 million six- to eleven-year-olds attending school. Various government studies in the 1980s indicated from 14 to 44 million working children under the age of fourteen (Kanbargi 1991: 17; Weiner 1991: 8).[9] In 1986, the *Lok Sabha*—India's national parliament—passed the Child Labor Prohibition and Regulation Act. This act specifically bars children under fourteen from any work in specified dangerous occupations, including cement, soap, and explosive manufacturing, road and building construction, and beedi making (Kanbargi 1991: 16–17). Enforcement has not been highly successful.

Helping Private-Sector Workers

Unfortunately, KDB has no mechanism for abolishing child labor outside its own work centers. Otherwise, the impact of KDB's programs on labor conditions in the private sector has been substantial. As can be seen in table 3.1, KDB employed 22,330 workers in 1981. The Indian census for that year reports a total of 119,000 beedi workers in Kerala. This means that KDB accounted for 19 percent of all beedi employment in the state. KDB's influence in Kerala is thus significant. Private beedi establishments in the organized sector that survive in Kannur give their workers wages and benefits comparable to those provided by KDB, the pacesetter for wages and benefits. Even the domestic workers of the Kerala-based beedi firms in and around Kannur get many of the statutory benefits. The Mangalore-based firms that operate the putting-out system, mainly in Kasargod district, continue to flout the law, however. Evidently a protracted struggle will be necessary to improve the lot of the domestic rollers. Directly or indirectly KDB will play a role in that struggle.

THE COOPERATIVE THAT SUCCEEDED

How did worker solidarity overcome the bosses' determined retrenchment campaign? At the beginning of this chapter, we noted that one or more of three elements are usually present in the formation of workers' cooperatives: an idealistic vision, a capitalist crisis, or state intervention. In KDB's case, all three elements converged to produce a powerful conjuncture, but each element was intense in its own right. As we saw in chapter 2, KDB was forged in part by workers and leaders with long-standing socialist visions, a high level of democratic consciousness, a willingness to engage in self-sacrifice, and a sense of community and solidarity with other workers and sympathetic professionals and intellectuals built up over four decades of organizing experience and struggles. Their vision was nearly shattered by a capitalist crisis of the most extreme type: the sudden and arrogant lockout by the beedi barons forced the idealists to take the plunge and try to realize their vision. They hesitated but then went forward. Their earlier struggles gave them a crucial strategically placed short-term ally in the left state government of 1967–69. Their long struggles also gave them essential longer-term allies in their fellow radicalized workers, peasants, and left sympathizers, who bought and smoked Kerala Dinesh beedis as acts of political solidarity. To these dramatic historical and political conjunctures, KDB's workers added particular elements of their own: their highly developed beedi rolling skills and the special talents of a few expert workers who fashioned a beedi with the quality to sustain their politically initiated markets.

After twenty-five years, KDB can justly be called "the cooperative that succeeded." Though not all the dreams of the workers and the union activists have been realized, the Kannur Tobacco Workers' Union leader C. Kannan (Int: 6 June 1993) spoke for most when he summed up KDB's first quarter century:

> The Dinesh Beedi Workers' Cooperative is an instrument of the workers in their struggle for better wages and living conditions. For the first time in India, beedi workers are guaranteed what is legally due to them. Whatever the other limitations of this experiment, to that extent, at least it has succeeded.

Kannan's unpretentious evaluation is typical of the humble and constantly self-critical style of Kerala's worker-leaders. Kerala's beedi workers had done more than guarantee basic wages and benefits: they had created a democratically run, worker-owned cooperative against the determined machinations of some of India's most powerful capitalists. They had shown that vision, sacrifice, struggle, and mobilization could overcome the built-in powers of the rich. Their success, however, was only a beginning. Now they would have to build a business structure that could stay afloat in a hostile, competitive, capitalist industry.

CHAPTER FOUR

From Mobilization to Efficiency: The Role of the Central Society

Strikes and marches, meetings and resolutions, fighting the police, enduring hunger, the anxiety and euphoria of a prolonged struggle, and the mutual solidarity of the oppressed—all these may contribute to the democratic consciousness, but such combined emotions and events cannot run a business indefinitely. The dramatic struggles that gave birth to KDB continue to influence its development, but to succeed, the cooperative also had to create structures of efficiency that would allow it to compete in a hostile capitalist market economy. How can a cooperative, dedicated to paying its workers decent wages with good benefits, stay afloat in a sea of competitors who pay much less and give almost nothing in benefits? How could KDB come to set the standards for pay and benefits in the private sector rather than be drowned by it? First, KDB had to solve the problem that holds back the development of most workers' cooperatives in the first place: lack of capital.

The comparative literature makes it clear that problems of initial funding are a major reason so few workers' cooperatives are set up worldwide (Fanning and McCarthy 1983: 136–39). The workers' savings are too meager for any substantial investment, and it is unlikely that the workers would have collateral or enough credit access to raise capital from the market (Bonin et al. 1993: 1316). Most workers' enterprises are thus undercapitalized or too small to be economically viable. Furthermore, the social, legal and economic environment of a capitalist economy is hostile to nonconformist forms of production.[1]

Workers' cooperatives have to incur extra costs in obtaining appropriate information, identifying solidaristic worker members, and overcoming legal, institutional, and attitudinal barriers (Fanning and McCarthy 1983: 126–36).

As a result, few cooperatives are founded, even fewer are successful, and those that survive are mostly small and account for only a minute portion of economic output. The Italian network of workers' cooperatives, the largest of its kind in the developed countries, had only around five thousand units in 1981 (Thornley 1983). These cooperatives employed 2.5 percent of the nonagricultural labor force in that year (Bonin et al. 1993: 1291). Outside Italy, only about 1 percent of workers are in the cooperative sector in Western Europe (Bonin et al. 1993: 1291).[2] The French workers' cooperatives in 1981 numbered only around six hundred (Batstone 1983), and there were only three hundred in Britain (Cornforth 1983: 163).[3] The U.S. record is perhaps the worst: fewer than six hundred could be traced to an entire century since 1835 (Aldrich and Stern 1983).

As we saw in chapter 3, KDB overcame the traditional capital shortage and institutional barriers because of government intervention to extend sufficient short-term credit, to make available efficient and effective administrators, and to provide a legal and institutional framework to establish the cooperative. Another important element of KDB's success is its structure. In particular the central society (also known as the central cooperative)—a cooperative that unites the smaller production cooperatives—provides the smaller units with a shelter organization that offers economies of scale, adequate finances, and shelter from the market's fiercest competitors. The lack of a shelter organization has been the downfall of many cooperative experiments (Scurrah 1984). The failure of the beedi cooperatives in the 1950s may be traced in part to this factor. The effectiveness of KDB's central cooperative as a shelter organization, an important theme in the present chapter, gives the central cooperative an effective control over the surplus generated. Coordinating the tradeoff between distributing the surplus as extra wages via bonuses (see chapter 3) and investing for the future has been critical to KDB's success. A long academic tradition has argued that long-run efficiency of workers' cooperatives is impossible because of the accumulation dilemma.

The Yugoslav cooperative theorist Jaroslav Vanek has stated this argument in its strongest terms. In Vanek's model, the objective of a cooperative firm is maximization of earnings per worker. Adjustment of the workforce or of capital intensity to worker-earnings maximization can result in the eventual degeneration or self-extinction of the firm. Degeneration can occur when, in the attempt to maximize earnings per worker, the workforce is reduced and the number of nonmember workers is increased. The efforts to maximize current earnings can lead to underinvestment and capital consumption. Therefore, Vanek is against self-financing of cooperative investment. Jensen and Meckling argue that a pure rental model of the cooperative firm would be inefficient because the time horizon of investment would be limited by the duration of employment of the worker members, causing a reduction in investment to suboptimal levels. The common-property nature of the accumulated assets would act as an impediment to optimization of investment and employment. The problem of nontransferability of the residual claim would cause inefficient monitoring and portfolio adjustment. Problems may also crop up because the preferences of the members are not identical (Jensen and Meckling 1979: 480–89).

How KDB's central cooperative has resolved the tension between distribution and investment is one of the important analytical issues we take up in this chapter. We will also examine how the central society benefits KDB's smaller units but also generates tensions and disputes within and between KDB's two levels. The dynamics of the interaction between the central society and the primary societies are among the most important features of KDB.

THE STRUCTURE OF KDB

The Kerala Dinesh Beedi Workers' Cooperative is organized into three kinds of units at two structural levels. At the top, the Kerala Dinesh Beedi Workers' Central Cooperative Society, with its headquarters in Kannur, manages the overall affairs of the cooperative. Under the central cooperative are the twenty-two primary cooperatives. The primary cooperatives in turn branch out into work centers. Figure 4.1 shows how raw materials pass through the cooperative structure to become finished beedis. First, the central cooperative purchases wrapper leaves, tobacco, thread, and packaging materials. These are sold to the primary cooperatives. The central cooperative also advances the necessary finances for wages and other production costs. The primary cooperatives in turn ship out the raw materials to the work centers where the beedis are rolled. The rolled beedis are purchased by the central cooperative and marketed to consumers through a network of distributors and sales agents.

In its role as shelter organization, the central cooperative fulfills four main functions:

1. purchasing raw materials in bulk and supplying them to the primary cooperatives,
2. raising funds to meet the financial needs of the primary cooperatives and managing the overall finances of KDB,
3. marketing the beedis produced by the primary cooperatives, and
4. coordinating and supervising the primary cooperatives.[4]

These four functions of the central cooperative create a delicate balance of power between the central and primary cooperatives, a situation that has led to contention in KDB's history. As we noted in the previous chapter, two models were actively considered when KDB was set up: a centralized cooperative with branches and a federation of smaller production cooperatives with a central coordinating body. KDB is a blend of the two. The idea of a highly centralized cooperative was given up, and dispersed, independent primary cooperatives were chosen as the basic units of production. But the central cooperative formed by these primary cooperatives became more than a shared marketing agency: government decrees gave it overall supervisory and financial control over the primary cooperatives. The cooperative structure adopted was thus more unitary than federal in character.

The balance of power between the central and primary cooperatives has also evolved over time. Conflicts have developed between the two layers of KDB, but the basic relationship has remained one of mutual support. One reason that the conflicts between the central society and the primary cooperatives have not undermined the structure has been the remarkable success of the central cooperative in raw material purchase, beedi marketing, and financial management. Our discussion in this chapter first revolves around these three vital roles

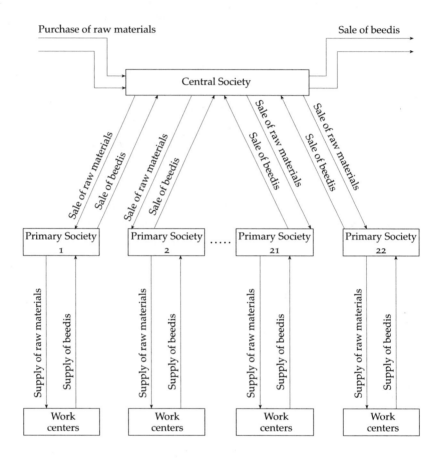

Figure 4.1. Organization of production at Kerala Dinesh Beedi Workers' Central Cooperative Society

of the central cooperative. At the end of the chapter we take up issues relating to the fourth role: coordination and supervision of the primary cooperatives.

KDB's central cooperative is managed by three representative groups: a twenty-two-member general body, a seven-member director board, and a pension and welfare committee. Figure 4.2 illustrates how the main components of KDB relate to one another.

The Elected General Body

The general body is composed exclusively of the twenty-two representatives directly elected by the worker members of each of the twenty-two primary cooperatives (described in detail in chapter 5). Usually the president represents the primary cooperative, but any member of the local director board or any other worker can fulfill that task. The general body normally meets once annually. The democratic character of the central cooperative is partly ensured by the fact that the general body retains the "ultimate authority in all matters relating to the administration of the society" (KDBWCCS 1969: 7). The general body of the central cooperative has the powers to elect or remove the directors, to approve or reject the annual budget, and to enact or amend the bylaws.

The authorized share capital of the central cooperative is Rs 5 million, subscribed by its members, the primary cooperatives, and the Kerala state government. The maximum primary society contribution is Rs 100,000. At the formation of the central cooperative in 1969, the shares owned by the member societies were at the minimum requirement of one share of Rs 1,000. The Kerala state government contributed the rest, nearly 93 percent of the original subscribed share capital. This high level of government participation not only in share capital but also in other KDB funds was partly responsible for the government's insistence that the bylaws of the central cooperative give the government the right to appoint the chairman and the secretary.[5] In 1994 the total subscribed share capital of the central cooperative was Rs 3.5 million, of which the contribution of the member

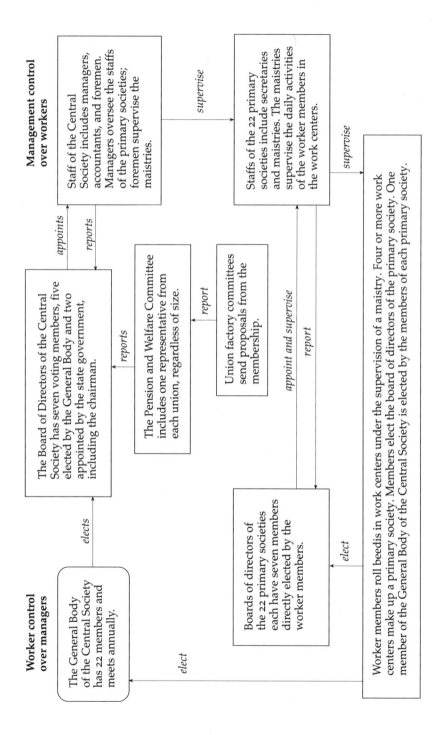

Worker control over managers

Management control over workers

Staff of the Central Society includes managers, accountants, and foremen. Managers oversee the staffs of the primary societies; foremen supervise the maistries.

supervise

Staffs of the 22 primary societies include secretaries and maistries. The maistries supervise the daily activities of the worker members in the work centers.

supervise

appoints

reports

The Board of Directors of the Central Society has seven voting members, five elected by the General Body and two appointed by the state government, including the chairman.

reports

The Pension and Welfare Committee includes one representative from each union, regardless of size.

report

Union factory committees send proposals from the membership.

appoint and supervise

report

elects

The General Body of the Central Society has 22 members and meets annually.

Boards of directors of the 22 primary societies each have seven members directly elected by the worker members.

elect

elect

Worker members roll beedis in work centers under the supervision of a maistry. Four or more work centers make up a primary society. Members elect the board of directors of the primary society. One member of the General Body of the Central Society is elected by the members of each primary society.

cooperatives accounted for 44 percent. Government ownership thus declined from 93 percent to 56 percent.

The Board of Directors

Despite government ownership of more than 50 percent of KDB's shares, the cooperative is run primarily by its workers. The government appoints only two members of the board of directors of the central cooperative. One of these two is the chairman; the other is usually a district industries officer. The five representatives of the primary cooperatives to the director board were also appointed by the government until 1986. Since 1986, five director board members have been elected from among the twenty-two representatives in the general body. All of the five current board members were previously full-time beedi workers for many years and are also current elected officers of the primary cooperatives.

The Chairman

According to article 15 of the bylaws, the board of directors is the competent "authority to frame regulations for the conduct of business" and also to take key business decisions (article 17). But the chairman has "overall control in the affairs of the society" and is "responsible for the executive administration of the Central Society." He or she is the ex officio treasurer and also has the powers to

(1) "inspect the affiliated societies and to ascertain by enquiry by deputizing one or more of the members or any persons authorized by them to see whether the affiliated societies are working on proper lines and to point out to them the defects in their working," and to
(2) "call for any information, statement or return concerning the working of affiliated societies. The societies concerned shall give all facilities for inspection and furnish the information, statement or return called for" (KDBWCCS 1969: 6).

These powers of the chairman are greater than those of the head of a typical Indian cooperative. They could easily lead to serious confrontation with the elected director board, but no confrontation at this level has occurred in the history of KDB. This is testimony to the sincerity and integrity of KDB's chairman and the accommodating and flexible style of the worker directors.

Activities of the Director Board

   The directors of the central cooperative are deeply involved in the functioning of KDB. In addition to their contributions to overall policy deliberations, KDB's worker-directors provide competent field leadership in purchasing and marketing operations, maintenance of the Dinesh tobacco blend, coordination of the primary societies, and liaison with the trade union leaders. N. Pavithran, one of the current directors, detailed his typical monthly schedule at the central cooperative:

Director board meetings	4 days
Pension and welfare committee meeting	1
Tobacco testing	3
Identifying counterfeit beedis and court appearances to testify	10
Visiting primary societies regarding purchases of land and construction of buildings	3
Total (minimum)	21

If we count thirty days in the month, Pavithran seems to have about nine days' vacation—four of them Sundays—but he generally comes to the central cooperative every working day and finds miscellaneous tasks waiting. The other directors may not be involved to quite this extent in the day-to-day operations of the central cooperative, but their essential duties would require around ten days in a month (Pavithran Int: 21 June 1994). Three of the present (five) directors are also presidents of their primary cooperatives with responsibilities there as well.

   Though the bylaws require only one board meeting a month, it has become customary for the director board to meet every Wednesday and sometimes more than once a week. A typical director board meeting starts with a review of the stock and sales of beedis in the past week and moves on to the report on counterfeit beedis (discussed later in this chapter). Next, the reports of the quality-control squads and inspection teams are considered in detail. Then the board reviews the arrival and supplies of wrapper leaves and tobacco, and the reports on the leaf cutting output of the primary cooperatives are discussed. Other major issues include purchase of land and building construction or any other extraordinary expenditures. The board does not confine itself to broad policy issues but takes an active role in all major decisions affecting the cooperative. The tradition of activism and involvement has come to characterize the board much more than the written bylaws imply.

The One-Union-One-Representative Pension and Welfare Committee

Another representative body at the central cooperative is the pension and welfare committee. Its role has increased in scope since the elected director boards assumed office in 1986. The minor unions today do not have representation on the central cooperative director board. The pension and welfare committee has one representative from each of the nine unions with any presence at all at any work center of KDB, irrespective of their strength. It has therefore become an important consultative body. It meets once a month, and all decisions are made by consensus. The chairman of the central society and some other central society representatives sit on this committee. Along with the proposals for improvements in benefits such as those described in chapter 3, the pension and welfare committee has taken up difficult issues such as the decision to reduce working days for all members equally in times of accumulating stocks of unsold beedis.

The Secretary

After the chairman, the secretary is the highest-ranking nonelected management figure in the central cooperative. According to the bylaws, the secretary must be a government officer appointed by the director of industries of the state government. The secretary manages the day-to-day operations of KDB with the help of the office staff. His or her powers are delegated by the chairman and the board of directors. Though the secretary has no voting rights, he or she is an active participant in director board discussions.

A special feature of the beedi industry in Kannur is that none of the necessary raw materials are produced within the state of Kerala. The tendu leaf for wrappers has to be brought from the forests of Central India, while the tobacco comes from the Nippani tracts in Karnataka or even farther north from Gujarat, or east and north from the Virginia tobacco belt of Guntur in Andhra Pradesh.[6] Purchasing tendu leaf turns out to be a long drawn-out affair extending over four to five months. The logistics of the transportation alone are astounding. In 1992–93, the central society purchased sixty-five thousand bags of leaves worth over Rs 127 million. An initial lot is transported in full trainloads. The rest is staggered over the year in individual boxcars to minimize warehousing costs. In times of boxcar shortage—which are frequent—the tendu leaf supply line has to be kept open by using trucks. Tobacco is usually transported in trucks. A truck loaded with tobacco arrives almost daily at KDB headquarters. Tobacco purchases for 1992–93 totaled 1.4 million kilograms valued at Rs 25 million.

A major advantage of KDB's primary cooperatives over the 1958 beedi cooperatives is this large-scale purchase of raw materials directly from the sources. In the early years, raw materials had to be purchased from nearby markets at Calicut and Mangalore. As soon as KDB could generate enough resources, it began searching for direct sources of wrapper leaves and tobacco. Three advantages derive from direct source purchasing: (1) KDB is able to eliminate middleman profits and thus get raw materials at lower rates, (2) it is able to maintain more consistent product quality, and (3) significant economies are achieved in the handling charges.

The central cooperative takes great pains not to buy the wrapper leaves from private traders because the tendu wrapper leaf business in India is famous for its corruption. When Madhya Pradesh Marketing Federation—one early source of wrapper leaves—privatized its marketing, the central cooperative switched its purchases of wrapper leaves to the Orissa Forest Development Corporation owned by the Orissa state government. As a gesture to another government-sponsored firm—and because KDB is its largest customer—the Orissa Forest Development Corporation allows KDB to bypass the trader auctions; its purchases are settled through separate negotiations. The chairman usually negotiates the price of shipments at the average of the auction prices. At times, through aggressive bargaining, KDB has been able to get special rebates. In 1992–93, the rebate came to Rs 46 million (KDBWCCS 1994: 5). The landed price (including delivery) that KDB incurs on tendu leaves at Kannur is usually almost 35 percent lower than the local market price (Gopalakrishnan Int: 22 June 1994).

Private traders resent KDB's privilege in selecting leaves right at the godowns (warehouses). The traders who buy at the auction have to purchase the tendu leaves in lots; they cannot pick and choose. KDB sends in two or three squads of experienced foremen and workers, at times accompanied by a director board member, to carefully inspect and select the leaves. The selected bags are marked and numbered for verification on delivery. The purchase of wrapper leaves highlights the importance of the large-scale federation that can make bulk purchases. It also indicates the fragile dependence of the central cooperative on the continued existence of and sympathy from a government-owned firm—the Orissa Forest Development Corporation. Conditions could alter if the present "reform" program in India for privatization as a part of the structural adjustment program spreads to the collection and marketing of tendu leaves.

Unlike the tendu leaf business, the beedi tobacco trade is dominated by private traders (Doshi 1991). Therefore, KDB must take special care to avoid corruption. Price quotations and tobacco samples are invited by the central cooperative secretary. The samples received are numbered and passed on to a taste selection committee, composed of foremen and experienced workers. The tasters roll and smoke different tobaccos from the samples supplied and make their recommendations. Their reports are then placed before the director board. Before the purchase decision, some of the directors personally do random checks on the recommended and rejected samples (Radha Madhavan Int: 22 June 1994). The sources of the samples are not revealed, even to the directors; only the secretary has that information. So far this system has worked so well that there has not been a single corruption charge in tobacco purchase at KDB (Bharathan Int: 9 June 1993).

After arrival in Kannur, samples of the tobacco purchased are removed from their sacks and randomly tested for quality. Now the tobacco must be ground and blended. The various types of tobacco in appropriate proportions are trucked daily to a blending center. The work environment at the center is an unhealthy one. Workers jump, kick, and thrash about in the various stacks to produce the blend, which is then sifted in the next room. The blending area is enclosed, but even from ten meters outside, one can begin to smell the strong tobacco wafting out through cracks in the building. The workers inside must be exposed to incredible amounts of nicotine and other possibly carcinogenic materials: they wear no safety clothing. Management has provided protective masks but does not insist that the workers wear them. Mechanization of blending has been suggested but has not received much consideration from KDB.

The thread for tying the beedis is bought at local markets, and the central cooperative dyes the thread to the desired color. Finally, the cooperative purchases labels from Sivakasi in Tamil Nadu, one of the leading printing centers in India. As a precaution against printing of counterfeit labels, KDB has stuck with a couple of major presses in Sivakasi from the very beginning. The rates are decided through negotiations.

The central society sells the raw materials to the primary cooperatives after adding 3 percent to cover overhead costs, and it pays transport costs to the primary cooperatives' headquarters. The primary cooperatives bear the cost of further transport of the raw materials from their headquarters to the sometimes scattered work centers.

The raw materials inventory fluctuates depending on a variety of complex factors, such as the speed with which leaves are loaded onto the trains in Orissa and the availability of boxcars. During the period 1970–75 the inventory dropped from thirty-three days' worth of beedi sales to fourteen because of the cooperative's improved management. From 1975 to 1985 it ranged from twelve to twenty days' worth of sales. In the late 1980s, average stocks rose, partly as a result of the bulk purchases. In 1988 they began to rise as a result of a stagnation in beedi sales, reaching a forty-six-day supply in 1992, the highest figure in KDB's history. In 1995 the inventory of raw materials had dropped again to thirty days of beedi sales.

The central cooperative was able to reduce stocks of unsold beedis from a high of forty days' worth in 1970 to three days' worth in 1975. From there it has remained consistently below four days. In 1995, the figure was 3.4 days.

Successful Marketing Strategies

The central cooperative purchases the beedis produced by the primary cooperatives (figure 4.1) and markets them under the common brand name "Dinesh." The brand name's goodwill among consumers is one of KDB's greatest assets. The name is owned by the central cooperative, and its exclusive right to market beedis under that name is an important deterrent to any tendencies among the primary cooperatives to break away and market beedis on their own.

Marketing beedis is a highly competitive business. In chapter 3 we discussed how widespread political sympathy and the excellent quality of its product enabled KDB to break loyalty to other brands and quickly create a market for itself. In addition to the worker sympathy and enthusiasm generated by its initial sales campaigns, four other elements in KDB's marketing strategy have proved effective.

The first is the creation of a reliable distribution network throughout Kerala. As noted in the last chapter, soon after KDB's formation, public announcements invited agents to apply to distribute the new Dinesh beedis. The large response was partly due to the cooperative's high profile in the press. Agents were selected after careful screening and personal interviews; those not found up to the mark were rejected. Beedis were never given to agents on credit; KDB always insisted on cash because in a fast-moving market capital could not be locked up. An important feature of the agency network is that the central cooperative deals directly with every agent. KDB rejected the private-sector sales structure, in which main agents have their own subagents (Gopalakrishnan Int: 10 June 1993).

KDB decided not to amass a fleet of vehicles because this often leads to their misuse. Instead, agents were given a vehicle allowance, depending on the quantity of beedis sold, to maintain their own sales vehicles. The only condition was that the name "Dinesh Beedi" should be prominently displayed on the vehicles to advertise the product. Of KDB's eighty or so agents within Kerala, nearly sixty have utilized the vehicles scheme.

A second marketing strategy is product differentiation. KDB caters to different consumer tastes in different regions. Medium Beedis were KDB's original product, and even today they constitute more than 50 percent of output. Medium Beedis are sold mainly in Kerala's northern districts and, as we have already noted, are similar in size and taste to the Mangalore Ganesh Beedis that were already popular in northern Kerala. Special Beedis were introduced in the early 1970s, after KDB had stabilized itself, in an effort to capture the market in southern Kerala, where smokers prefer larger beedis with a different taste. Small Beedis were introduced for the highland regions, especially central Travancore (southern Kerala). The Rajadhani Special caters to the export market, mainly to migrant Keralites in the Middle East, and to the metropolitan areas. The market share of Rajadhani and Small Beedis remains very limited.

The imaginative use of official and nonofficial media to cover KDB achievements is a third KDB marketing tool. The government-owned radio, the directorate of audiovisual publicity, and the leading newspapers generate thousands of rupees' worth of free advertising by reporting important and even mundane events occurring at KDB. For example, twelve leading newspapers published editorials about KDB's achievements on the day the cooperative celebrated its twentieth anniversary.

Finally, KDB launches special intensive short-term sales drives when beedi stocks pile up. The most dramatic of these was the matchbox campaign. In July of 1969—at the height of its first monsoon sales lull—the fledgling cooperative faced unsold stocks worth Rs 2 million. With brilliant insight, Chairman G. K. Panikkar came up with the idea of offering a free box of matches with every packet of beedis. Although the matches cost a quarter million rupees, the overstock sold, and KDB actually increased its outreach by this promotional novelty (Raghavan 1995: 271; Panikkar 1974). When stocks accumulated in 1991–92, a gift coupon scheme was launched. Coupons worth Rs 5 to Rs 50 were distributed randomly in beedi packets for consumers to reclaim and cash in. The scheme was tried first in Madras city (in nearby Tamil Nadu state) and then for Special Beedis throughout Kerala. In 1994 KDB again successfully promoted gift coupons in its beedi packets. Central society officers ·credit the scheme with temporarily increasing beedi sales enough to clear out the stock backlog and keep beedi workers from having to take too many unwanted leave days.

Factors Contributing to Decline in Sales

As we noted in the last chapter, KDB's beedi sales have tended to stagnate in recent years (see table 3.1). The number of beedis sold declined in several recent years, though each time sales picked up immediately thereafter. In 1987–88 and 1991–92 the accumulation of unsold beedis necessitated a temporary slowdown in production in the primary cooperatives. KDB's advertising and marketing strategies may thus be less effective than what is required to meet the needs of the workers for regular employment. In 1995, the central society responded to the combined factors creating declining demand with an intensified advertising program. Additional prize coupons were developed, including a grand prize of an automobile, several televisions, radios, and other smaller prizes. (One difficulty with the plan is that inserting the coupons in the packages is tedious work that slows down the labeling and packing. It thus costs KDB more than is apparent to the consumer.) KDB has also repainted and increased the number of its color posters across Kerala, organized an automobile rally from Kannur to Calicut, and given out KDB caps to spectators at the popular annual boat races in Alleppey and Kottayam.

Most of the problem in beedi sales probably comes from uncontrollable forces outside KDB. The most important factor responsible for the stagnation in demand seems to be counterfeit Dinesh beedis. A spate of companies have attempted to imitate the brand name of KDB with closely parallel names—Kerala Swadesh Beedi and Kerala Desh Beedi—or its package and label. Other companies market true counterfeit beedis in packets made to look identical to those of Dinesh Beedi and carrying the brand name "Dinesh Beedi" on the wrapper. Counterfeit beedis are mostly rolled in Tamil Nadu or in pockets in Kerala where wages are very low. They are of lower quality, since the producers use cheap tobacco and leaves, but a consumer cannot tell whether the beedi is genuine until he buys and smokes it. The recent increase in consumer complaints of the deteriorating quality of Dinesh Beedis results from these spurious beedis.

The total quantity of counterfeit KDB beedis in the market is anybody's guess. KDB central society director N. Pavithran, who is in charge of the special central cooperative squad constituted to pursue counterfeit beedis, places their share in KDB's market at between 30 and 40 percent. This estimate is supported by a team of professional investigators engaged by KDB (Pavithran Int: 21 June 1994). The detection squad of the central cooperative has been successful in bringing some of the culprits to justice. In tracking down counterfeit beedi producers, central society board members and investigators have sometimes received physical threats from criminal elements. Despite their courage and persistence, KDB investigators face numerous legal loopholes that make it very difficult to win convictions in court. A more effective deterrent seems to be the negative public image given to the culprits. They often turn out to be established and well-known traders, whose cases attract local newspaper attention. KDB makes a point of giving wide publicity to every case of spurious beedis it uncovers. In 1995, KDB was finally able to win a case based on a police raid in which duplicate labels and beedis were discovered. The court gave a penalty of Rs 3,000 and a two-year prison sentence. On the whole, however, the cooperative is losing the battle against counterfeit beedis.

Another marketing handicap for KDB is the higher price of its beedis. Cost-push factors have been responsible for increases in the price of beedis from Rs .25 (25 paise) for a bundle of twenty-five beedis in 1969 to Rs 2.50 for a bundle of twenty beedis in 1994.

Private-sector beedi firms are able to make significant savings because of lower wage costs and through partial evasion of excise duties. The 1994 prices of KDB's main competitors, Sadhoo and Ganesh Beedi, are around 20 percent lower. The organized-sector beedi brands constitute the upper end of the market. The lower end is catered to by smaller beedi companies or beedis manufactured in Tamil Nadu at much cheaper labor costs and sold for Rs 1.75 a packet or even lower. Camouflaging its periodic price increases has been a delicate exercise for KDB's management. The other major beedi manufacturers usually wait for KDB to raise prices first and then follow suit. At times fear of backlash to the price increase has prompted KDB to reduce the number of beedis in a bundle rather than raise the price.

Private manufacturers also pay higher commissions to their sales representatives, particularly the retailers, who therefore have an incentive to push brands other than Dinesh Beedi. Table 4.1 shows the price and commission differentials between KDB's Medium brand and the most immediate direct competitors.

The manner of collecting the excise duty on beedis has been another serious disadvantage to KDB. Until 1976 the central govern-

Table 4.1. Prices and Sales Commissions for Selected Beedi Brands in Kannur, June 1994

Brand Name	Producer Price Per Packet (Rs)	Wholesale (Agents') Price Per Packet (Rs)	Retail Price Per Packet (Rs)	Agents' Commission As Percentage of Price	
				Wholesale	Retail
Dinesh Medium	45.00	45.50	50	1.1	9.0
Sadhoo	35.00	36.30	40	2.8	9.3
Ganesh	36.25	37.10	42	2.3	11.7
China	39.25	40.00	44	1.9	9.1
C. C. Beedi	35.90	36.75	42	2.3	12.5
Vimal	31.50	33.00	38	4.7	13.2
Surya	31.50	33.00	38	4.7	13.2
Sadhoo Super	33.40	34.40	38	2.9	9.5

Source: Information supplied by KDB.
Notes: The agents' wholesale commission percentages result from dividing the difference between the wholesale price and the producer price by the wholesale price. The agents' retail commission percentages are derived by dividing the difference between the retail price and the wholesale price by the retail price.

ment collected excise duty from the tobacco growers, but from that year on the point of taxation was shifted to beedi manufacturers, with exemptions given to petty producers. The change in the law was intended to protect small producers, but these independent producers are largely extinct today, and the market is controlled by large manufacturers. KDB dutifully pays its entire excise duty of Rs 5.30 for each one thousand beedis. The total excise tax remitted in 1993–94 came to Rs 37.9 million. But even some manufacturers larger than KDB do not pay excise duty for their entire production, and the smaller manufacturers totally avoid it. The new tax system has also added an incentive to the producers of counterfeit beedis: they sell at KDB prices but don't pay KDB taxes. Shifting the excise duty back to the point of sale of tobacco has been one of KDB's major demands, and it is supported by the trade unions (KDBWCCS 1975). So far their efforts have not borne fruit.

Although counterfeit beedis and an unfriendly tax structure are the major impediments to KDB's increasing its share of the market, the central society may also be contributing to the problem with its policies. KDB's higher prices reflect its honest tax payments and its higher wages and better benefits. Its lower agent commissions, however—as shown in table 4.1—suggest that it might be missing an opportunity to increase its sales.

The data in table 4.2 raise doubts as to whether KDB is allocating sufficient resources to marketing its beedis. Marketing costs as a per-

**Table 4.2. Marketing Costs of the Central Cooperative
As a Percentage of Total Sales, 1970 to 1995**

Year	Total Sales (in Rs Thousands)	Marketing Costs As Percentages of Sales			
		Van Allowance	Sales Commission	Advertising	Total Percentage
1970	1,100	0.0	29.7	21.8	51.4
1971	5,200	1.5	11.8	3.9	17.2
1972	10,800	0.6	6.8	2.0	9.5
1973	14,100	0.3	6.0	1.7	8.0
1974	16,900	0.7	6.4	1.5	8.6
1975	24,500	0.8	6.1	0.8	7.6
1976	38,800	0.6	4.8	0.8	6.1
1977	49,200	0.6	4.9	0.6	6.0
1978	64,900	0.5	3.7	0.5	4.6
1979	76,100	0.4	3.1	0.4	3.9
1980	80,300	0.4	3.0	0.0	3.4
1981	93,100	0.4	3.3	0.4	4.1
1982	125,400	0.3	2.7	0.3	3.2
1983	141,500	0.3	2.8	0.3	3.4
1984	171,900	0.3	2.5	0.3	3.1
1985	201,500	0.0	2.4	0.0	2.4
1986	234,200	0.2	2.6	0.2	3.0
1987	287,300	n.a.	n.a.	n.a.	n.a.
1988	342,000	0.2	2.2	0.2	2.5
1989	361,700	0.1	1.7	0.2	2.0
1990	280,800	0.2	3.4	0.3	3.9
1991	456,600	0.1	2.4	0.2	2.7
1992	531,800	0.1	2.2	0.2	2.5
1993	638,000	0.1	2.0	0.2	2.3
1994	714,500	0.1	2.1	0.2	2.3
1995	736,098	0.1	2.1	0.2[a]	2.3[a]

Source: Computed from KDB reports and records.
[a] See explanation in the text.

centage of sales have steadily come down from 9.5 percent in 1972 to only 2.5 percent in 1992. The sharpest decline has been in advertising, from around 2 percent in 1972 to a meager 0.2 percent in 1992. The share of commissions paid to the agents and retailers has also declined overall but stabilized at just above 2 percent in the 1990s.

In 1995, government tax policy began favoring producers of "small cigarettes," as they are known in Kerala. These small cigarettes do not exceed 60 mm in length and are therefore similar in size to beedis.[7] This came on top of a change in consumer behavior following the boom in remittances from the Middle East since the mid-1970s (Sunny 1988; Thomas Isaac 1993). Though no hard statistics are available, it is widely believed in Kerala that the market is beginning to shift from beedis to cigarettes. Fearing that the small cigarettes had begun to eat into its markets, KDB launched a special promotion campaign in 1995 in which it spent over one million rupees on extra advertising. This campaign, however, still left KDB with only .3 percent of sales spent on advertising, far below the 1.5 percent or more it spent in its first five years (see table 4.2).

The decline in advertising has been exacerbated by the recent segmentation of Kerala's news media. Over the last decade, major newspapers have started separate editions or have created separate pages for local district news. News about KDB often fails to be reported outside Kannur or North Malabar. Unlike KDB's tenth anniversary, which received statewide coverage in all the major papers, the silver jubilee celebrations were covered only in the northern editions. Low spending on advertisements and a more localized media may have combined to produce the more severe market stagnation for Dinesh beedis in Kerala's southern districts.

Finally, a trend may be developing away from smoking altogether as the Indian public becomes more aware of the health risks associated with tobacco. Already, Indian national television has begun airing antismoking messages, and schools are encouraged to teach children about the dangers of tobacco. (We shall consider KDB's initial moves towards diversification out of beedi production in the afterword.)

FINANCIAL MANAGEMENT

The Thrift Fund

The most remarkable feature of KDB's present financial position is that the cooperative does not resort to any borrowing from external sources, despite the impeccable credit rating that it enjoys. The thrift fund collected from the workers is the major source of internal financing for KDB. This fund is a creative device by which KDB partly solves the problem of investment and the need for accumulation to which we referred at the beginning of this chapter. As explained in chapter 3, because the first twelve thousand charter members could not even afford the twenty rupees to purchase a single share, nineteen rupees per member was advanced as a loan by the government. This loan was repaid in a few years by a 5 percent deduction from the workers' wages. This deduction has continued; it applies to all cooperative members and goes into a credit pool called a "thrift fund." Workers can take interest-free loans up to 50 percent of their deposit or six hundred rupees, whichever is lower. Up to 20 percent of the fund is out on loan at any time. On 31 March 1993, the fund totaled Rs 74 million, of which Rs 10 million (14 percent) was out on loan. The loan is repaid automatically over ten months through a second wage deduction (Panikkar Int: 11 October 1993). On leaving the cooperative, the worker is entitled to the amount contributed to the fund without interest. The thrift fund not only benefits workers in time of need, but the 80 percent not out on loans constitutes 25 percent of the working capital pool for the central cooperative. During 1995 the fund totaled Rs 99 million, of which Rs 10.2 million (10.3 percent) was out on loan. KDB's thrift fund provides a major mechanism by which the possible demands of the workers for immediate distribution of surplus as wages or bonuses can be channeled into investment, thus avoiding the trap of the Vanek model noted at the beginning of this chapter.

The Debate over Price Enhancements

KDB's other major source of internal finance is its accumulated surplus. The substantial surplus generated each year is utilized for bonuses, working expenses, and the creation of fixed assets. As with the thrift fund, central society management of the accumulated surplus through the elected director board of experienced and forward-looking worker-managers provides a restraint on possible demands for excess distribution. KDB also pays the government an annual dividend for its share capital investment. The division of KDB's surplus among the central society, the primary societies, and the workers has resolved the accumulation-distribution dilemma in a way not apparently thought of by the critics of cooperatives to whom we referred at the beginning of this chapter. KDB's solution is not without its own attendant problems, however. The central cooperative has earned profits continuously since 1978 (see table 3.1). The declared profit has to be allocated to various funds as required by the bylaws. The largest allocation is to the reserve fund, "which may be utilized with the sanction of the registrar to meet unforeseen losses" (KDBWCCS 1969). By convention the central cooperative keeps its formal profit to a minimum by transferring a substantial proportion of the surplus back to the primary cooperatives in the form of purchase price enhancements or rebates.

These rebates are necessary because at the time the central cooperative purchases the beedis from the primary cooperatives, it fixes an ad hoc price that does not fully cover the wage costs, let alone the overhead. Temporary accommodation is provided to the primary cooperatives in the form of advances to meet their deficits. At the end of the year the central cooperative calculates the total surplus, declaring a portion of it as its own net profit, and then transfers the rest to the primary cooperatives as price rebates. These rebates constitute a uniform percentage of the total value of beedis purchased from each primary cooperative.

In 1993–94, the central cooperative declared a surplus of Rs 40.2 million. The director board declared a price enhancement of 5.3 percent of the purchase value of beedis. This totaled Rs 35.3 million. Before the price enhancement only five primary cooperatives had recorded profits, and the primary cooperatives as a whole recorded a net loss of Rs 4.1 million. With the rebates, all the primary cooperatives registered profits totaling Rs 31.2 million.

Though the price enhancement of Rs 35.3 million is formally transferred to the primary cooperatives, in reality the central cooperative continues to be the custodian of the funds. This is facilitated through a practice of the central cooperative whereby it maintains a running account called the "suspense account (members)." The costs of raw materials supplied and the advances given for wages and other expenditures are debited to this account; the value of beedis purchased by the central cooperative is entered as a credit. At the end of March 1993, the amount due to the members in the suspense account was Rs 139.5 million. These funds—formally owed to the primary cooperatives but kept in the custody of the central cooperative—are utilized for working capital or are deposited in banks as income-earning assets.

In 1984–85, KDB's auditors questioned this practice. The central cooperative responded:

> We do not find any injustice in pooling the resources of the primaries in the Central Society, since whatever profits are derived in business are plowed back to them at the close of each year. All the more, the

outstanding dues are derived in the primaries for payment of thrift, gratuity etc. which are of long-standing nature and for which there is no immediate necessity for discharging the funds. Whenever the society requires amounts for payment of such liabilities we give the funds without any delay. . . . This policy was adopted by us from the very beginning on mutual discussion and bilateral understanding between the central [cooperative] and the primaries. (KDBWCCS 1988)

Today the wisdom of the central cooperative's being the custodian of surplus funds is generally accepted in principle. However, the officers of many primary cooperatives have expressed resentment against this effective denial of financial autonomy. Any financial expenditure above Rs 1,000 requires prior permission of the central cooperative. Such a provision reportedly makes speedy responses to emergencies, such as repairing buildings in the monsoon, difficult. A proposal has to be sent to the central cooperative for its approval, which is granted at times only after an inspection by a central team (Haridasan Int: 1 April 1993; Govindan Int: 7 April 1993). "It [financial control] is good in many ways. But it also creates problems. . . . It helps to prevent misuse of funds," says K. Raveendran, the president of the Chala primary cooperative. "But we are not able to tackle certain issues promptly" (Raveendran Int: 2 April 1993).

The central cooperative's arbitrary manner of determining the purchase price has also been a cause of resentment. The main complaint is that a primary cooperative does not know whether it has registered a profit or a loss until the price enhancement is declared by the central cooperative. Therefore, some primary society officers have demanded that the purchase price reflect the market price of beedis minus a fixed deduction for the overhead charges of the central cooperative (Haridasan Int: 1 April 1993). The annual general body meeting of the central cooperative passed a resolution in 1989 supporting this demand. The general body suggested that the central cooperative deduct only 3 percent of the sale value of the beedis and credit the rest to the primary cooperatives. It was argued that such a procedure would allow the primary cooperatives to monitor their financial position more accurately throughout the working year (KDBWCCS 1989 *Ann. reports:* 72).

As a consequence of the general body resolution, the traditional procedure was modified. Higher purchase prices were given to the primary cooperatives. The ratio of price enhancement to direct prices has come down. In the 1980s, it averaged around 20 percent, but for the financial year 1993–94, it was only 5.3 percent. The funds of the primaries continue to be held by the central cooperative, as before. "Our philosophy of financial management is not to allow funds to accumulate at the lower levels of management," explained G. K. Panikkar (Int: 11 October 1993).

REGULATION OF OUTPUT OF THE PRIMARY COOPERATIVES

Another vital role played by the central cooperative is the coordination of primary cooperative production with market demand. Here again, the central society acts as both a shelter organization and a resolver of the problem of accumulation and distribution. If every primary acted as an independent production unit, marketing could become a serious problem. Accumulation of stocks would lock up large amounts of working capital and endanger the continued functioning of the cooperatives. If the beedi stocks are not properly stored, especially during the damp monsoon season, they can deteriorate rapidly in quality. Fears of overstocking and loss of quality were two of the reasons behind the initial proposal for one large centralized cooperative with regional branches in place of a more decentralized organizational structure.

The central cooperative tries to regulate the output of the primary cooperatives in three ways: (1) controlling the recruitment of new workers, (2) imposing restrictions on the production of existing workers in times of occasional market glut, and (3) determining product composition.

Control over recruitment has proved to be the most important instrument for regulating the output of the primary cooperatives. According to its bylaws, each of the primary cooperatives has the right to give membership to any beedi worker residing within its defined area of operation. But an entirely different tradition of recruitment has been built up over time. As we saw in the last chapter, when KDB started functioning, all the primaries voluntarily restricted production to three thousand workers—that is, only one-fourth of the total membership. Over time more and more workers were absorbed into the workforce in batches, each batch being added by decision of the central cooperative made on the basis of its judgment of market conditions. Later, when workers other than those originally retrenched by the Mangalore firms were allowed membership, the central cooperative continued to determine the overall expansion of the workforce and also the quota of new workers for each of the primary cooperatives.

As we noted in chapter 3, the demand for work in KDB is much larger than the number of new openings. Primary cooperative officers are sensitive to local pressures for employment at KDB. The urge to recruit more workers on their own occasionally takes the form of criticism of unutilized work space capacity in the new buildings (Bediaduka Int: 25 March 1993) and leads to demands that the primary cooperatives be allowed to replace retired workers without asking permission from the central society (Govindan Int: 7 April 1993). Some primary cooperatives have exceeded their new worker allocations. In 1993 the central cooperative had to threaten to stop wage advances to recalcitrant members. A special general body meeting was convened to discuss the problem and to ensure that such instances would not occur in the future (KDBWCCS 1993 *Ann. reports:* 3). There was no support for the erring members in the general body.

The central cooperative also decides which of the four beedi types each primary cooperative should produce. The product mix has to be fine-tuned to changes in demand. In recent years, sales of Special Beedis have declined and more work centers have been reoriented to producing Medium Beedis.

At times the central cooperative has also been forced to impose restrictions on production. A ceiling of seven hundred fifty beedis per day was imposed by the central cooperative on the three thousand workers initially employed. It had to be reimposed with the onset of the first monsoon. The second monsoon proved even more crisis-ridden: layoffs were declared and workers were given only two days' work a week (KDBWCCS 1989: 2, 6). With the stagnation in demand in the late 1980s, restrictions on production once again had to be imposed in the monsoon seasons of 1987–88 and 1991–92. Production was curtailed to reduce stocks. But there were no layoffs: in consultation with the trade unions, workers were asked to make use of their annual paid leave days (KDBWCCS 1988 *Ann. reports:* 8 and 1992 *Ann. reports:* 10).

Although stocks built up to crisis levels during some monsoons,

KDB experienced scarcity of beedis during some busy seasons (KDBWCCS 1989: 8 and 1990: 6). The central cooperative management claimed that the scarcity was due to lax worker discipline, such as unauthorized absences, and to a decline in the per-worker daily output of beedis. The annual output of KDB was estimated to be only 65 percent of its potential. Consequently, efforts to increase the per-worker daily output of beedis have developed into important central cooperative campaigns in recent years.

MONITORING OUTPUT QUALITY

Monitoring the quality of beedis produced by the primary cooperatives is an important task of the central cooperative. Supervising production at the work site is the task of the supervisors—maistries (the shop floor supervisors) and foremen (who supervise the maistries)— in the primary cooperatives (see figure 4.2), but the central cooperative draws up the norms for local supervision. It monitors whether these norms are being maintained by the primary society staff.

The central cooperative has fixed an outturn norm of 5,500 beedis from one kilogram of tobacco for Medium Beedis and 4,750 for Special Beedis. Higher outturn would lower quality, whereas lower outturn could reduce profitability. Similarly, the central cooperative sets a wrapper leaf outturn norm, which has to be periodically revised to reflect variations in leaf quality. A squad of skilled workers and central cooperative foremen sample and cut some tendu leaves into wrappers on arrival at Kannur to set a norm for the number of beedis expected from each kilogram of wrapper leaf.

The chief means of monitoring primary society productivity are the weekly reports sent by the primary cooperative secretaries. The foremen at the primary cooperatives, who are in fact employees of the central cooperative, also submit periodic reports with detailed remarks. The foremen at the central cooperative also undertake random checks of the bundled beedis that arrive from the primary cooperatives. The packaged beedi bundles are also randomly weighed to detect deviations from optimum tobacco use. The central cooperative periodically conveys suggestions for improving quality to the primary cooperatives. No punitive mechanisms are used to ensure that the suggestions are heeded, but negative remarks in the annual reports and the social pressures at the general body meetings tend to prod the laggards.

Market complaints regarding the quality of beedis have been increasing over the years. Every year's annual report since the mid-1980s has detailed these complaints: insufficient tobacco in beedis, damp wrapper leaves, deterioration of tobacco quality due to overexposure to air, improper rolling, and even the presence of foreign particles in the tobacco. The spurt in counterfeit beedis accounts for a large proportion of these complaints, but the central cooperative is convinced that a general laxity in quality maintenance has crept in at the work sites. Negligence of the maistries in their supervisory role is mentioned particularly often (KDBWCCS, *Ann. reports*, 1992: 9).

To counter these trends the central cooperative has initiated several measures. In 1986 it called four zonal conferences of maistries and foremen to discuss quality and output shortcomings (KDBWCCS 1986: 5-6). A special central cooperative squad consisting of the most efficient foremen was constituted to undertake surprise inspections of work centers. In 1991 the special quality control squad was made a permanent agency headed by a chief foreman.

ENSURING UNIFORM LABOR CONDITIONS

KDB's central society further regulates the relationship between accumulation and distribution by its control over the wages and benefits of the workers in the primary societies. Uniformity in wages, salaries, and other benefits across the primary cooperatives was an important concern of the trade unions at the time of KDB's formation. Apart from the ethical desirability of equal benefits to all workers, there were practical reasons for uniformity. Differences in wages and working conditions might sow disunity among the workers and lead to demands for parity with the better-paid workers—a process leading in turn to wage and benefit costs that the productivity levels might not justify. Differences in wages and benefits within the cooperative would also weaken the struggle of the trade unions for the standardization of wages and benefits in the private sector. Therefore, the wages, salaries, and other benefits and the service conditions of all the employees in KDB are negotiated between the central society board of directors and the leadership of the trade unions.

During KDB's early years, the differences in the salaries and service conditions of the salaried employees in the primary cooperatives were a source of controversy. Reviewing KDB's first five years, C. C. Balan, a prominent central cooperative director, described these discrepancies as a major organizational weakness that urgently needed to be remedied. Unlike the wages and working conditions of the production workers, those of the staff were decided on independently by each primary cooperative. Significant differentials had cropped up. Attempts to standardize them became difficult because of opposition from some of the primary cooperatives. "There may be differences of opinion whether the salaries are high or low. But it is not proper that the employees within the same firm working in similar jobs should receive salaries at different rates or under different conditions" (Balan 1974: 53). The problem was overcome after protracted negotiations. Not only have the salaries and service conditions of the staff been standardized, but the ratio of staff to production workers is also supposed to be uniform: one clerical staff member for each two hundred fifty production workers and one maistry for every work center. If the number of workers exceeds one hundred at a particular work center, a helper is provided to the maistry.

Another undertaking to improve working conditions—KDB's most elaborate—is the work shed construction program, which is closely monitored and controlled by the central cooperative. All building plans have to conform to central society norms and must receive the approval of its consulting engineer. The land can be purchased only after a team of central cooperative directors and other officials physically inspects the site and verifies the land price. Even if the primary cooperative has surplus in its suspense account with the central cooperative, it cannot start construction without formal approval by the central cooperative director board. The inevitable delays in such a centralized process have been a major source of irritation to the primary cooperatives because they can prove costly in the land purchases. A site identified by the primary cooperative may be snatched away by other buyers or the price hiked up through competitive bidding (Raghavan Int: 23 March 1993; Raveendran Int: 2 April 1993).

As we reported in chapter 3, on average around fourteen work sheds are being built each year. Neither the financial performance of the primary cooperatives nor their accumulated profits are considered in the allocation of new work sheds. Bediaduka primary, one of the worst performers in profitability, has newly constructed all but a couple of its work centers. The difficulty in renting large buildings in its area of operation and the predominance of women workers, whose need for clean, modern facilities was considered greater than men's, seems to have weighed in favor of Bediaduka primary's securing a higher priority for construction of new work centers. Thus need, rather than the financial strength of the particular primary cooperative, seems to have been the determining factor in the allocation of new work sheds.

The equal treatment of unequal performers sometimes gives rise to resentment among the more efficient primary cooperatives whose members believe that higher efficiency and better management should be more substantially rewarded. The problem has been compounded because some of the primary cooperatives have consistently lagged behind in profitability. In a surprise move in 1980, the general body of the Chala primary decided to pay dividends to its members from its accumulated profits. The central cooperative vehemently objected to the move, saying that a majority of the other primary cooperatives were incurring losses and that it would not be proper for one primary alone to pay dividends. The Chala primary decision was described as a "threat to the unity of the cooperatives" (Govindan Int: 7 April 1993). The dividends were not paid.

The Chala dividends dispute could arouse fears of an overly centralized cooperative structure. Even though total centralization was rejected at the time of KDB's formation, the idea continued to receive strong support. In 1971 a subcommittee of the central society board of directors was constituted to review KDB's structure, following a memorandum from the Tobacco Workers' Union. After much debate, it was decided that no formal change in the structure was required, but in practice the central cooperative came to exercise greater supervisory power over the primary cooperatives. Thus, for instance, in 1978 the general body meeting of the central cooperative, through a special resolution, instructed all the member cooperatives "to strictly abide by the instructions of the central cooperative in the general interest of the Dinesh Beedi movement" (KDBWCCS 1989: 22). This was followed by another resolution the following year instructing the central cooperative that "supply of raw materials should be cut to the societies [primary cooperatives] who acted against the directions [of the central cooperative]" (KDBWCCS 1989: 29). According to some primary society officers, the central cooperative over time has come to exercise so much power that "the relationship between the central cooperative and the primary [cooperatives] is like that of a head office and its branches" (Haridasan Int: 1 April 1993).

So far there has been only one serious challenge to the authority of the central cooperative. Certain irregularities in granting nonwage benefits, payment of advances to workers, and office procedures in the Bediaduka primary were detected by the inspection squad in 1990. The directives of the central cooperative to rectify the mistakes and recover the losses from the officials responsible soon ballooned into a major confrontation. The Bediaduka cooperative president claimed autonomy, citing its bylaws. He even went to the extent of filing a legal case against the central cooperative. The central cooperative stopped the supply of raw materials and advances of finances to the primary and convened a special meeting of the general body to discuss the issue. The Bediaduka primary president's autonomy claim was rejected by all the other members; he failed even to get the support of his political party colleagues at the general body meeting (*Deshabhimani* 2 December 1991).

The desire for some change seems to be gaining ground, however. Some primary cooperative officers express fears that the absence of any serious decision-making powers at the lower levels is adversely affecting morale and involvement. Lack of initiative at the primary level and dependency on the central cooperative for all decisions and policies was a criticism voiced by the members of the director board of the central cooperative at their meeting on 21 June 1994 to discuss our preliminary profit analysis (see chapter 6).[8] The secretary of the Chala primary cooperative seemed to concur when he said "they [primary cooperatives] rely more on the central cooperative, waiting for them to improve the situation. This attitude is more visible since the 1980s" (Govindan Int: 7 April 1993).

EMERGING ISSUES

The energy and commitment that built KDB originally has been channeled into a structure remarkably well suited to surviving in a competitive, capitalist economy. The structure of a powerful central cooperative uniting federated local (primary) cooperatives has allowed KDB to solve the problem of sheltering as well as to maintain an effective balance between the distribution of the surplus and the need for investment for the future. KDB has overcome the negative predictions of theorists such as Vanek by creating a structure that complements its high worker consciousness and activism. Its centralized marketing and financial management allow it to operate as a giant corporation, while the elected local director boards guarantee at least formal workplace democracy. Centralizing the surplus for redistribution as a bonus rather than paying dividends on shares standardizes the workers' incomes. A payment of dividends is a reward for ownership while a bonus is a reward for work. Construction of new work sheds seems to fit the principle of standardization by improving the facilities of those workers most in need of them. Over the years, KDB has also displayed a considerable ability to innovate when new policies were needed and to respond effectively to external and internal challenges. Despite tensions in the organizational hierarchy, the basic relationship of the primary cooperatives to the central society has remained one of mutual support. C. C. Balan summed up their experience of the first five years:

> Each society [primary cooperative] is independent in the eyes of the law. Assets and liabilities of each are its own. But we have not been functioning as per the clauses of the written law. Though the primary and the central cooperatives have been functioning as two units of the same firm, the style of work has been fashioned so as to strengthen each other. . . . Both the central cooperative and the primaries perform different roles, but functions of both are equally important. If one works so as to undermine the other, the entire movement will suffer. (Balan 1974: 56)

No one in KDB would question this statement. But an issue that emerges from our survey of the evidence is the need for a greater degree of autonomy in the primary cooperatives so that their work does not degenerate into the routine mechanical activity of carrying out central society dictums. Can the creative potential of lower levels of management be developed without destabilizing the overall organization that has evolved and that has proved to be such a success? Do the shelter functions of the central cooperative require the present level of central cooperative control over the daily activities of the primary societies?

A related issue is the absence of material incentives to the better-performing primary cooperatives. How completely egalitarian do the workers and lower management want to be? In our survey of primary cooperative directors, fifty-four refused to comment on the subject and thirty-two were opposed to any change. But fifty-seven directors favored experimenting with measures such as linking the annual bonus to primary society profitability after guaranteeing a certain minimum to all. The introduction of material incentives might pose a threat to the political resolution of the wages-versus-investment problem, which KDB has so far achieved.

The third problem that is likely to worsen in the future is the recent decline in the demand for beedis. As a result, the expansion of the cooperative has slowed. The related problem of counterfeit beedis seems to be eluding solution. KDB will also have to face the growing opposition to the use of tobacco. Many public institutions have already prohibited smoking on the premises, and legislation to discourage smoking is being currently discussed in the Indian national parliament. Should KDB start taking measures to diversify production and slowly move away from tobacco? We shall take up these emerging issues in the next several chapters.

CHAPTER FIVE

The Dynamics of Shop Floor Democracy: Empowerment versus Supervision in the Beedi Primary Cooperatives

How democratic can a workplace be? Can the necessary discipline and work routine be maintained if bosses have no real authority? Can a business operate effectively when managers who need to make quick decisions have to wonder if their workers will question or disobey them, or vote them out of office? These and similar questions have dogged the worldwide cooperative movement since its inception in the nineteenth century. One aspect of the debate concerns the general phenomenon of inequality. Cross-cultural research seems to show that, once instituted, inequality tends to perpetuate and to reinforce itself (Fried 1967; Kerbo 1996: 10–11; Lenski 1966).[1] If inequality is self-perpetuating, isn't it utopian to think workers could become their bosses' equals?

More specifically with reference to workers' cooperatives, two theoretical approaches have influenced the literature. Economists speak of the "degeneration hypothesis." Imagine an economy with all worker-owned cooperatives. The entire surplus within a cooperative is distributed or accumulated within each unit, so the incomes of the members of cooperatives with higher capital-to-labor ratios or more favorable market conditions rise faster than the incomes of the less fortunate ones (Estrin 1981). Members of successful cooperative firms—motivated by their self-interest—might expand by hiring new workers at lower wages rather than expanding cooperative membership. The cooperatives degenerate into virtual traditional capitalist firms (Bonin et al. 1993: 1312). Even within single cooperatives, the degeneration hypothesis is supported by substantial data. Empirical studies on agricultural cooperatives have noted that they "very often fall into the hands of the rich, being the most interested and powerful, and thereby entirely negate any redistributive ideals" (Worsley 1971: 21; cf. Nash and Hopkins 1976: 12–15). The emergence of cooperative sugar mills in western India represented a movement of capitalist elements among the peasantry into industrial capitalism (Baviskar 1971; Chiteleen 1982). Some scholars coined the term "cooperative capitalism" to describe the phenomenon (Breman 1978). Even in radical Kerala, in the 1950s, coir (coconut fiber) cooperatives degenerated into virtual cartels of merchants or agencies for marketing and financing of larger producers (Thomas Isaac 1990).

The sociological version of the degeneration hypothesis goes back at least to Max Weber ([1910] 1958: 253–64), who wrote about the "routinization of charisma." Unlike Karl Marx, who saw in workers the possibility of transforming society through collective action, Weber saw society bureaucratizing radical movements by the forces of "discipline." Sociologist Robert Michels ([1915] 1962) formulated this process into "the iron law of oligarchy" to denote the transforming power of structures over people no matter how idealistic and committed they are.[2] As Chasin and Chasin (1974: 65) summarize his law for cooperatives, "Workers who become leaders are transformed into petty bourgeoisie by their way of life."

Cooperatives like KDB face the problem of how to institutionalize the charismatic, revolutionary, participatory forces that were essential to their creation. The iron law also operates at the psychological level. The participants in radical movements eventually develop a stake in preserving the organizations they created for the struggle, regardless of the ability of those organizations to achieve the original goals. This "goal transformation" is accompanied by an emphasis on "organizational maintenance" and "oligarchization" (Zald and Ash 1966: 327). The ideals of the movement eventually become subordinated to the needs of the organization and are no longer what holds the organization together. The cooperative becomes similar to a capitalist firm.

Can cooperatives circumvent the iron law of oligarchy and prevent degeneration (Egan 1990)? KDB offers mixed and complex evidence on these issues. In this chapter, we shall consider the dynamics of management-worker interactions at the shop floor—in this case the 326 beedi rolling sheds of KDB's twenty-two primary societies. We

Workers insert finished beedis into drying racks. The beedis are baked dry in charcoal ovens to prevent mold from collecting on them. Photo by Richard W. Franke.

Mixing the KDB blend at the central society warehouse in Kannur. The unprotected workers absorb tobacco dust and fumes. Photo by T. Rajesh.

shall see that tensions and disputes occur but that the worker-owners and their elected management seem to be hammering out a mix of empowerment and supervision that suggests workers can be optimistic over the pessimistic voices of the degenerationists.

ROLLING BEEDIS

The workday at KDB begins at 7:00 A.M. Workers have a flexible schedule: they can arrive between 7:00 and 9:00 and can leave between 4:00 P.M. and 6:00 P.M. Work centers do not remain open at night. The work center maistry gives out the appropriate day's supply of materials to each worker on arrival and keeps a record of all the transactions. For the first two hours or so, workers cut the tendu wrapper leaves, as we described in chapter 1. When they have finished their supply of the leaves or have cut as many as they intend to roll into beedis, they switch to rolling. This usually takes up the remaining six hours of the workday. Experienced workers now on the director boards state that an average worker can roll a thousand beedis in six to six and a half hours. Two hours is sufficient to prepare a thousand wrapper leaves (Central Society Director Board Int: 21 June 1994).

The rolled beedis are stacked in drying trays and delivered at day's end or the following morning to the primary society headquarters, where they are re-checked for quality, baked dry in a charcoal oven, labeled, and packed. Workers take lunch and tea breaks. Some primary societies have strict policies to regulate break times, while others are rather lax.

THE WAGE SYSTEM

The piece-rate system of wages constitutes the most important mechanism to regulate the labor process. The workers' earnings depend on their output. The piece-rate system has a built-in mechanism to motivate the worker to maximize output. But the wage system as it operates at KDB has become a hindrance to productivity and has given rise to conflicts between individual self-interest and the collective needs.

Wages are determined in three steps: attendance, basic wages, and dearness allowance. In 1993, these steps were as follows. First, the roller had to roll at least 600 beedis to register as present on a particular day. Second, Rs 14.5 per 1,000 was paid for rolling up to 800 beedis. In other words, Rs 14.5 times .8, or Rs 11.6, would be paid for 800 beedis per day. For the 801st beedi rolled, the roller received a one-shot cost-of-living payment called "dearness allowance" (D.A.). In 1993 the dearness allowance was Rs 19.8 (Haridasan Int: 1 April 1993; Raghavan Int: 23 March 1993). Above 801 beedis the rate of Rs 14.5 per 1,000 set in again. A worker rolling the expected 1,000 beedis per day thus earned the official wage of Rs 14.5 plus the dearness allowance of Rs 18.9, totaling Rs 32.4. Table 5.1 gives a few sample beedi-rolling numbers for 1993 and their associated wages.

From Table 5.1 we can see that, overall, workers earned more rupees for rolling more beedis. But the wage structure had an incentive mechanism that encouraged workers to roll about 801 beedis per day and then stop. The dearness allowance kicked in as a fixed amount at the 801st beedi and did not increase after that. As a result, workers producing high amounts of beedis got more money, but the incentives were actually negative in terms of marginal wages. An outstanding roller who produced 2,000 high-quality beedis in a day actually earned less per beedi than a worker rolling 900.

The Dearness-Allowance Debate

Why should the beedi industry have adopted this apparently irrational structure? The peculiar system of wage determination results from the struggles of the unions to limit self-exploitation by over-

Table 5.1. Beedi Rolling Wages for Selected Outputs: As of 31 March 1993

Beedis Rolled	Wage	D.A.	Total	Rs per Thousand
700	10.15	0	10.15	14.5
800	11.6	0	11.6	14.5
801	11.6	18.9	30.5	38.1
900	13.1	18.9	32.0	35.6
1000	14.5	18.9	32.4	32.4
1100	16.0	18.9	34.9	31.7
1500	21.8	18.9	40.7	27.1
2000	29	18.9	47.9	24.0

Source: Computed from KDB report for 1992–93.

work. Under the piece-rate system in the private sector, workers are overworked to produce enough to earn a meager wage. Unions have always fought for a minimum wage to be guaranteed to workers for a normal day's work. But under a piece-rate system, how can a minimum wage be set? One mechanism is to fix a certain output level as a day's work: this minimum piece-rate output should result in a livable wage. The D. A. is fixed with reference to this concept of a day's work. As the cost of living and consequently the D. A. rise, the built-in incentive to stop work before maximizing production has increased. Private employers seldom pay either the minimum wage or the D. A. according to the idea of a standard day's work. Only KDB is consistently hampered by this structure.

The trade union position was built in part on an ethical concept: a more skilled or more industrious worker already gets more pay for more production. This should not be compounded by giving more D. A. too. After all, the cost of living increases the same for the less skilled and the less industrious as for the hardest workers. The union commitment is thus to the greatest degree of equality and fairness possible given some differences in skill (Kannan Int: 21 June 1994).

Until the minimum wages committee decision of 1984, the D. A. had been tied to the piece-rate structure. Just like the basic wage, the dearness allowance was in proportion to beedis rolled. The trade unions were able to get the committee to accept the idea of a daily D. A. after 1984. Then the unions argued successfully for setting the minimum number of beedis at 800, apparently to compensate for the lower output of aging workers. Beedi rolling demands tremendous dexterity. After a few years, the skin on the tips of the workers' fingers begins to smooth off so that rolling becomes more difficult. Sometimes arthritis will also set in or muscle coordination will deteriorate. By age forty, a beedi worker loses up to 25 percent of his or her dexterity (Haridasan Int: 1 April 1993), meaning a big loss in output and thus wages.[3] The D. A. system with an 800-beedi minimum was designed to protect the older workers, who can always attain at least the 801st beedi. Younger workers thus subsidize them to some extent. Many younger beedi workers opposed the dearness-allowance mechanism and called for changing the wage structure. Some directors also wanted change; many of them argued for setting the allowance to kick in at 1,000 instead of 800. If workers beyond age forty can barely roll 801 beedis, however, setting the threshold at 1,000 would defeat the purpose. KDB Chairman G. K. Panikkar (Int: 20 June 1994) personally expressed a preference for a return to the piece-rated D. A.

The most severe critics of the wage structure dominant in the 1980s to early 1990s claimed that some of the best workers rolled their 801 beedis, left work, and went home to roll for private contractors. But most coop members interviewed seemed to feel this was rare. Another criticism was that the system encouraged uneven work patterns. A fast roller would take care of family or other matters on some days of the week, rolling just the 801 beedis required to get the D. A. Then on the last day or two of the pay week, he or she would roll feverishly and produce the high output that management wished he/she would roll every day (Raghavan Int: 23 March 1993). From the worker's perspective, however, this setup allowed less regimentation and greater freedom to mix work with other aspects of life.

The pattern of wages for labelers followed a logic similar to that for rollers. The D. A. was the same and the basic wage was Rs 16.5, with the D.A. kicking in after a hundred packets had been labeled. In 1993, packers and other miscellaneous workers received Rs 19.5 plus the D. A., while blenders got Rs 20.5 plus D. A.

Wage Rate Revisions: 1993–96

Stagnation in beedi sales (see table 3.1) and concern with KDB's long-term viability led to internal discussions in 1993 aimed at setting a higher output norm as an incentive to earn the D.A. After months of negotiations—within the context that the government minimum wages commission would set the new piece rate and D.A. rates from time to time to reflect cost-of-living increases and to improve the standard of living of the workers—KDB arrived at a compromise solution. In 1996, wages were set at Rs 30 per 1,000 plus a DA of Rs 20.1. The D.A. now kicks in at the 901st beedi. How have the older workers been protected? A compromise solution allows workers to carry over beedis from one day to the next within any particular workweek. Thus, a worker who rolls only 700 beedis on Monday can earn the D.A. on Tuesday with the 201st beedi and can continue that way through the week. On the following Monday, the count of beedis, however, goes back to zero. The result of this policy is that workers unable to roll 900 beedis per day lose only one or two days' worth of

D.A. in a week instead of losing all five or six days. It is likely that many workers are not happy with this compromise, but it does represent a compromise rather than a management-imposed edict to raise output. This norm has led to increases in the average output figures for the entire cooperative, as is shown in table 5.2, but may have other efficiency consequences (discussed below and in chapter 6). Another compromise resulting from sales stagnation was a two-months' delay in implementing D.A. increases in April 1994 and October 1995. By 1996, however, full D.A. was implemented at KDB along with the 900 beedis output norm. By maintaining the basic form of the D. A., KDB maintained its generally egalitarian wage structure. Strong intervention by the worker-elected directors was required, however.

Output versus Leaf and Tobacco Efficiency

Another conflict arises between beedi output per day and the efficient utilization of wrapper leaves and tobacco. Since wrapper leaf prices have risen substantially in recent years, the most efficient use of the leaves has become a priority. Despite this, leaf outturn (the number of wrappers produced from one kilogram—2.2 pounds—of tendu leaves) plays no role in the wage structure. The individual worker gains no direct benefit by maximizing the number of wrappers cut from the day's allotment of leaves. Instead, such maximization competes with the worker's time for output of total beedis, since wrapper leaf cutting has to be done at a slower pace for more leaf outturn. Thus, attempts to increase leaf outturn might adversely affect workers' daily output, unless they are willing to work longer hours.

Similarly with tobacco, an optimum amount leads to the best-quality beedis. Workers rolling too quickly may put too much or too little inside the wrapper leaf. Tobacco outturn (the number of beedis produced from one kilogram of tobacco) and beedi quality also do not figure directly in wage determination.

How have these conflicts been manifested in the quantity and quality of beedis produced? The data on average leaf outturn and tobacco outturn, along with the number of beedis produced per worker per day, are presented in table 5.2.

We see that the average tobacco outturn reveals a stable picture over the years. The variation across primary societies is also not large,

Table 5.2. Tobacco and Leaf Outturn and Beedi Output per Day, 1983 to 1995
(Combined Average of all Primary Societies)

Year	Tobacco Outturn: Medium Beedis	Leaf Outturn	Beedis per Worker per Day
1983	n.a.	1,752	813
1984	n.a.	1,644	852
1985	n.a.	1,553	800
1986	5,439	1,665	818
1987	n.a.	1,822	888
1988	5,536	1,904	861
1989	n.a.	1,886	855
1990	5,510	1,933	865
1991	n.a.	1,975	836
1992	5,512	2,185	867
1993	5,473	2,088	921
1994	n.a.	2,108	971
1995	5,488	2,109	941

Source: KDB records and reports.
Notes: n.a. = data not available. The fiscal year ending 31 March 1993 is the reference year for most of the statistical materials in this book.

ranging between 5,307 at Thottada to 5,660 at Kannur City in 1993. This was a difference of only 6 percent. The 1995 average figure was very close to that of 1993.

Despite the absence of a monetary incentive, leaf outturn rose from 1,665 beedis per kilogram in 1986 to 2,185 in 1992. The increase reflects the heightened efforts at more closely supervising leaf-cutting work and also the campaigns for greater worker awareness. Leaf outturn varies more across the primary societies. In 1993, the range went from a minimum of 1,971 at Valiannoor to 2,284 at Payyanur—a difference of 313 beedis, or 14 percent. The variations indicate a potential for improvements at some primary societies.

The efforts to raise beedi output per worker per day did not meet with comparable success until 1993. The data in table 5.2 show that in 1985—the year the daily-rated D. A. was implemented—output per worker declined by 6 percent from 1984. By 1987 it rose to an all-time high for the decade at 888 beedis. Then beedi output per worker declined. In 1994 it rose again, partly as a result of union and management campaigns and partly because of a change in the wage payment system enacted in December 1993. In 1995, output declined by 3 percent compared with that of 1994 but remained 6 percent above the highest figure for the 1980s. The 900 beedis threshold for D. A. wage structure is generating more beedis per worker per day. An investigation into its possible effects on the lives and health of the workers would be important.

THE MANAGEMENT STAFF:
SECRETARIES, MAISTRIES, AND FOREMEN

The discussion of wages underlines the need for managerial initiatives to ensure quality while raising output. These tasks are different from central society activities such as purchasing raw materials and distributing them to the workers, collecting and marketing the beedis, and filing reports. The management staff that carries on the day-to-day operations consists of secretaries, maistries, foremen, and their assistants. Their relationships to the workers on the shop floor illustrate how successful KDB has been at avoiding degeneration, but this success is not without its tensions and problems.

The primary society secretary is the key figure in the local management structure. He or she is in charge of the day-to-day functioning of the primary societies. The secretary reports activities and problems to the director board at its meetings. He or she supervises the primary society office and keeps a daybook of expenditures, raw materials received, workers' attendance, and output. In larger primary societies, the secretary has an accounting assistant, in keeping with the directive of the central society that there can be one clerk engaged for each two hundred fifty production workers. The secretary must also prepare the reports for the central society audits that take place every six months as well as weekly statements on wages, production, costs, and raw material inventories. Secretaries are hired by the local director boards and are responsible to them.

The maistry is the supervisor at the work centers and is paid by the primary society. Maistries are skilled and experienced beedi workers with proven leadership and management qualities. Many are also active trade unionists. The maistry distributes raw materials to the rollers and collects the beedis manufactured by the workers on the previous day. Maistries conduct quality-control checks both during production and at the collection of finished beedis. In addition, they keep records of the raw material and beedis produced by each worker and records of leaves taken. They submit weekly reports of average output and leaf and tobacco outturn to the primary society headquarters. These reports are circulated among all work centers of the primary society and are read aloud to the workers each week to keep them informed about the overall working of the cooperative relative to the performance of their particular work center.

Every primary society has a foreman who is in charge of production and particularly of quality control. Central society policy requires that there be one foreman for every fifteen hundred workers. The foreman is paid by and reports to the central society. He or she visits each of the work centers at least once a month. The foreman inspects the production work in progress at the work centers and also does spot checking on rolled beedis as they come to the primary society headquarters for drying and packing. He or she also inspects the labeling work. The foreman is usually an experienced beedi worker considered by fellow workers to be among the most skilled.

Staff Salaries versus Workers' Wages

We see from table 5.3 that secretaries are the highest-paid primary society staff personnel. Their salaries rise to a maximum of four times those of average production workers.[4] Table 5.4 shows that central society staff earn somewhat more than the primary society management and salaried workers, but most salaries remain within a range

Table 5.3. Primary Society Staff Salaries As of 1 November 1992

Job Titles	Annual Salary Range	Ratio of Highest Pay to Pay of Average Beedi Roller
Secretary	Rs 25,237–47,840	4.0
Accountant	Rs 21,690–42,670	3.6
Clerk	Rs 19,237–35,576	3.0
Driver	Rs 18,872–31,116	2.6
Maistry	Rs 16,825–28,762	2.4
Helper, Messenger	Rs 16,420–26,150	2.2
All-Year Beedi Roller	Rs 13,713	1.1
Average Beedi Roller	Rs 11,976	1.0

Source: KDB-Salaried Staff Agreement of 1 November 1992.
Notes: The average beedi roller income assumes eighty-one paid holidays, and forty-six unpaid days off, and includes the bonus of 16.5 percent. (See chapter 6 for details on attendance.) Dearness allowance is assumed on all workdays. The "all-year" beedi worker income assumes taking no unpaid leave days.
   Salaries are based on monthly figures multiplied by twelve to make them annual; then a 45 percent dearness allowance and 16.5 percent bonus has been added as per the KDB-Salaried Staff Agreement of 1 November 1992.

Table 5.4. Salaries of the Central Society Staff As of 1 November 1992

Job Titles	Annual Salary Range	Ratio of Highest Pay to Pay of Average Beedi Roller
Office Manager	Rs 35,576–69,023	5.8
Store Manager and Public Relations Manager	Rs 33,346–61,421	5.1
Chief Accountant	Rs 30,001–57,367	4.8
Accountant, Cashier,	Rs 25,237–47,840	4.0
and Inspector	Rs 21,690–42,670	3.6
Office Assistant, Electrician, Foreman, and Driver	Rs 18,872–39,833	3.3
Cleaner, Messenger, and Watchman	Rs 17,615–33,346	2.8
All-Year Beedi Roller	Rs 13,713	1.1
Average Beedi Roller	Rs 11,976	1.0

Source: KDB-Salaried Staff Agreement of 1 November 1992.
Note: For average and all-year beedi roller incomes, see note to table 5.3.

close to those of the production workers. In comparing these salaries to that of the average beedi roller, we have exaggerated the degree of inequality by presenting its maximum degree: most salaried workers are not at the top of their ranges.[5] Chairman Panikkar was a retired Indian Administrative Service (IAS) officer and received a pension from the Indian national government. KDB reimbursed him a few thousand rupees annually in travel expenses and other minor expenses. The secretary is a government officer but is paid by KDB.

Conflicts between Staff and Production Workers

Benefits and Status. Secretaries, maistries, and foremen are non-elected management staff, though they are appointed by worker-elected director boards. Being part of a permanent, salaried staff, they could become alienated from the production workers, a situation that may be inherent in all unequal wage structures; at KDB radical workers and their unions actively intervene to limit such developments. One example has been the struggle over the powers and privileges of the secretaries.

Initially, the secretaries were taken on deputation from government service in other departments. Conflicts soon arose. In 1970 the nongazetted (lower-salaried)[6] officers' union of which the government employees were members issued a public statement criticizing the central society management, much to the latter's embarrassment (KDBWCCS 1988: 6). The secretaries of the primaries resented the fact that nongovernmental employees of the central society were inspecting their work. Further, the government officers who were deputed to the primaries were often transferred back to their parent departments, creating instability of operations at KDB (Gopalakrishnan Int: 10 June 1993). The conflict was finally resolved when the central society decided to permit the primary society director boards to recruit their secretaries rather than use government employees on deputation. Here local empowerment worked better than centralized supervision.

The creation of a permanent cadre of secretaries as direct employees of KDB created new problems, however. A KDB staff union covering all the salaried employees of the cooperatives—secretaries, clerks, foremen, and maistries—was formed. Union members asserted that the Cooperative Act gave them a claim to parity in pay and working conditions with cooperative employees in other sectors (Secretary, Bediaduka Primary Int: 25 March 1993). Their attempts at collective bargaining resulted in occasional protest meetings, sit-ins, pendowns (refusal to lift pens off the desk), and even an indefinite strike called at the end of 1973 (KDBWCCS 1989: 13). The public reaction to the strike was so adverse that the staff unconditionally withdrew it on the fourth day. There has been no recurrence of such incidents, but staff salary and benefits have remained problem areas at KDB.

The production workers' unions, whose representatives make up the director boards of KDB, are not completely opposed to the demands of the management staff. They admit that KDB staff members receive lower pay than the cooperative employees in most sectors. But union leaders argue that staff pay and benefits have to be linked to the financial capacity of the cooperative and to improvements in the earnings of the production workers. As we have already noted, production workers' wages are determined by a government minimum wages committee. The same committee decided on minimum salaries for all staff except the top layer of management. KDB preferred to draw up independent pay scales that are significantly higher than those of the committee but still lower than for the staff of other cooperatives in Kerala. If staff salaries at KDB go as high as those of government cooperatives, worker alienation could develop.

Production workers' union leaders are totally opposed to treating all salaried employees as management staff. The union leaders accept the idea that administrators with higher educational qualifications should receive pay above the level of production workers. But the same union leaders insist that maistries and foremen, who rise from the ranks of production workers, should not be provided pay and benefits substantially higher than those of production workers solely for their superior craft skill and management abilities (Sahadevan Int: 9 June 1993; Vijayan Int: 7 June 1993), nor should cleaners, transport workers, watchmen, or others whose qualifications are no higher than those of the rollers and labelers. Instead, such workers should have pay and benefits in a constant ratio to production workers' wages. Otherwise, union leaders predict and fear worker resentment.

Fallout from this conflict was the failure for several years to draw up "standing orders"—the formal written work procedures and disciplinary norms required in industrial organizations with more than one hundred employees. The staff refused to be bound by the same set of standing orders as applies to the production workers. The production workers' unions were adamant that there could not be two sets of standing orders in the same establishment. Union leaders expressed fears that widening differentials between staff and workers could cause the relationship between the two to deteriorate. They argued for parity in increases in pay and benefits between management staff and production workers. Evidence of worker resentment surfaced in our interviews, while some of the staff openly admitted witnessing worker hostility (Secretary, Bediaduka Primary Int: 25 March 1993). A compromise agreement was not reached until February 1996. The atmosphere of resentment caused by this long-standing dispute could give rise to problems in the workplace, where the salaried staff have to supervise production. We can see the potential for these problems by looking more closely at the two kinds of supervisors who interact directly with the workers: foremen and maistries.[7]

Supervision at the Work Site. Empowerment and supervision often stand in a delicate balance on the shop floor. The most intense supervisory interactions are between the maistries and the beedi rollers. The maistry inspects the workers nearly every afternoon after recording the raw materials given out to each worker. Quality checks involve several factors. Too much water must not be sprinkled on the wrapper leaves; otherwise, the tobacco turns into a lump inside the rolled beedi and the beedi will not burn. The quantity of tobacco must be at the optimum level—neither too much nor too little. The tail end of the beedi must be closed so that a diamond shape is created, allowing the right air draft to pass through and create a good smoking draw (Ganapathy Int: 3 March 1993). If a worker is not making beedis of satisfactory quality, the maistry must initiate corrective measures.[8]

The most important private-sector regulatory device to ensure quality is a fine against the worker. As noted in chapters 1 and 2 KDB arose in part out of the unions' struggles against the tyranny of the fines. Persuasion and training from more skilled workers are much preferred at KDB; fines are considered unthinkable—a return to the past that the workers fought to overcome.

Awarding prizes to the best workers is an attempt to create a positive incentive system. Each primary society awards fifty rupees every three months to the worker with the highest output and twenty-five rupees for the second highest. The maistry for the work center with the highest average output also receives fifty rupees. The prize distribution ceremonies are attended by central society representatives. These ceremonies become company meetings to discuss output, quality, and other issues before the cooperative. The winners are held up as models for emulation; photographs of them receiving their awards from the central society chairman often appear in local newspapers.

The prizes initially played an important role in improving productivity. Over time, however, the competitions have effectively become restricted to a select group of the best workers. Less skilled workers have no real hopes of winning, so they can't be stimulated by the prizes. Strangely, KDB does not have a prize for the greatest improvement in output—one that might encourage improvement among the workers at the bottom of the output charts who are bringing down profits the most. There have been suggestions for increasing the number of prizes and making workers ineligible for winning more than a specified number of times per year. Another suggestion is to offer a cash award to all workers who meet a certain high level of output. Our interviews suggest, however, that director board enthusiasm for prizes has waned. "The prize scheme was never given a fair trial," said KDB Chairman Panikkar: "If there are problems with the present system, it can be modified. The real drawback has been the resistance of the maistries, foremen, and secretaries. Quarterly or monthly prizes would mean that they keep detailed records and make considerable calculations. No one wants to shoulder these responsibilities" (Panikkar Int: 20 June 1994). The prize scheme continued into 1996 with mixed results. Some primary societies have embraced it enthusiastically while others appear to find it tiresome.

One punitive deterrent KDB occasionally uses is nonpayment of wages for defective beedis—but no deduction is taken for the wasted materials, as is done in the private sector. The foreman may also direct a worker to receive smaller daily amounts of leaves and tobacco flakes in order to emphasize the need for better quality. Since wages are driven by output, this puts pressure on the worker to do better to get back to a higher amount of raw materials. The Payyanur secretary describes that cooperative's experiment with some of the toughest leaf controls: "Suppose a worker gets 400 grams of leaves a day but fails to achieve the average output norm [900 beedis at 2,250 beedis per kg]. Then the next day we will give him only 350 grams of leaves. But if he attains the expected rate for this year of 2,250 beedis per kilogram [i.e., 778 beedis for 350 grams], we will raise the amount back to 400 grams again the next day" (Haridasan Int: 1 April 1993).

Payyanur has raised leaf outturn from one of the lowest in 1991 to one of the highest in 1993. But the cost has been a spate of worker complaints about the harsh measures of the maistries (Raghavan Int: 23 March 1993). The staff members reply that they are considerate of worker complaints; for example, poor-quality leaf will be immediately rejected by the maistry and replaced with some that can meet the outturn norm (Haridasan Int: 1 April 1993; Raghavan Int: 23 March 1993).

Some primary societies are said to be lax in enforcing the work schedule, allowing workers to engage in other activities that undermine their productivity. Payyanur has also attempted to get maistries to insist that workers stay a full workday and not waste time on nonproductive activities. Again, the price is disaffection: "Then our workers will complain that only they are being strictly supervised while workers from other primaries are free to do what they like" (Raghavan Int: 23 March 1993).

Strict work timings can also become antithetical to the physical and psychological needs of the workers. The monotony of beedi rolling is broken only by the morning's leaf cutting—itself hardly a varied set of tasks. Only the reader or radio livens the shop floor, but this too can become tiring. Sitting in one place all day in a monotonous atmosphere means that workers need to take breaks intermittently for tea or to chat with other workers. Such needs—built into the nature of beedi production—create a situation in which the maistry is likely to suspect the worker of trying to stop production just at the D. A. level, while the worker is likely to feel the maistry is rigid and authoritarian—or that he is trying to win the maistry prize at the cost of the worker. Despite these tensions and problems, KDB's workers and maistries have maintained a mostly conflict-free environment that has kept production and productivity competitive with the harsh, exploitative capitalist firms nearby. One reason for KDB's success in mixing empowerment and supervision is the fact that the local cooperative director boards are made up entirely of workers elected by workers.

WORKER-STAFFED, WORKER-ELECTED DIRECTOR BOARDS

As we have just seen, management initiatives carry the danger of alienating workers from management. The fact that KDB is owned by its workers makes it possible for them to intervene in the workplace in a more democratic and participatory manner than they could in a privately owned firm. One mechanism for maintaining democracy while encouraging management initiative is the democratic election of local director boards.

The Makeup and Duties of the Boards

KDB primary societies are governed by seven-member director boards. As we observed in the previous chapter, director boards were appointed by the Kerala state government until 1986. Thereafter, they became elected bodies. Currently the directors are elected every three years by the worker members, on a one-person one-vote basis. The number of shares owned conveys no additional voting power. Retirees can vote, except at Manjeshwar primary society, where the worker-members voted to compel retiring workers to sell back their shares. Sympathizers are allowed to vote but make up a maximum of only 5 percent of the membership. Staff members are prevented by KDB regulations from voting for directors, except for a small cadre of technical personnel—some of them previous shop floor workers who received technical training and who also have little statistical effect on the elections.

Director boards meet at least once a month to discuss the income and expenditure accounts of the primary society, to approve expenditures and records submitted by the secretary, and to respond to directives or requests for information from the central society. A major topic is the approval of thrift loan (credit union) requests by primary society members (see chapter 4). Other topics include requests by workers for transfer to another unit—usually because of marriage or other family reasons—and discussions of the output figures and any problems the primary society has, such as buildings in need of specific repairs. The director board has to respond to the comments of the central society's inspection teams and to consider the reports of the foreman concerning quality and productivity. The board makes decisions on disciplinary actions and intervenes in work site disputes. The elected directors thus play important roles in diffusing conflicts at the work sites. Each director board elects a president from among its members. The president calls and presides over meetings. According to director board member interviews, however, the board meetings are informal with consensus reached on most issues. Presidential power is irrelevant most of the time.

Formal elections alone are no guarantee against bureaucratic entrenchment. The origins, lifestyles, and political commitments of the directors also play a role. To ascertain these variables, in January 1994 we conducted a questionnaire survey of the 154 KDB primary society director board members. The most prominent feature of the director board members is that nearly all are or were beedi workers themselves. The survey showed that 81—nearly 60 percent of them—have been beedi workers for more than twenty years. On average, they have been in the cooperative for eighteen years, and nearly a third of them were founding members of KDB. Most important, nearly a quarter of them were elected to the director board for the first time. Only eleven (8 percent) had been on the pre-1986 appointed boards. The survey showed that KDB is not creating a permanent, entrenched bureaucracy at the director board level. Bureaucratization—one possible first step toward degeneration or the assertion of the iron law of oligarchy—does not show up in the election patterns.

Director board members do differ from workers as a whole, however. Table 5.5 shows that director board members are more heavily male, a bit older, and slightly less educated than average workers. Table 5.5 shows that workers elect older members of the coop to the director boards, especially workers aged thirty-one and above. Director board members emerge from among the beedi workers at the workplaces with many of the same qualities as their shop floor counterparts. As older workers, they have lower formal educational levels, but they make up for this with their years of work experience and organizing skills.

Can director board members derive economic privileges from their position? We asked them to identify the main sources of income for their household. The responses appear in table 5.6.

Table 5.6 shows that 111 of the director board respondents (94 percent) roll beedis as their primary or secondary source of income.[9] We see from this list that the director board allowance does play some role in the support of members, according to their own perceptions.

Thirty-seven respondents checked director board allowance as their main or secondary source of income; twenty-nine of them also listed beedi rolling, other work in the cooperative, other household members' income, or income from land. This leaves eight members who live only from their director board allowances. Seven of these

Table 5.5. Age and Education of Workers and Director Board Members

Characteristic	Percentage of All Workers	Percentage of Director Board Members
Sex		
Male	43	90
Female	57	10
Age		
Less than 20 years	1	0
20–30 years	37	14
31–45 years	47	50
Above 45 years	15	36
Education		
Illiterate	3	0
Below high school	71	83
High school	24	14
Above high school	2	3
N = 143		

Source: Director Board Survey, January 1994.
Note: The age breakdown of the workers comes from the primary society secretaries' reports. Several gave precise numbers of workers in each age category, while others gave percentages that might be estimates. See tables 6.4 and 6.6.

Table 5.6. Primary and Secondary Sources of Household Income:
Primary Society Director Board Members

Income Source	Number
Beedi rolling	111
Other KDB jobs	7
Work outside the coop	2
Income of other household members	20
Farming	9
Director board allowance	37
Trade union allowance	7
Other	2
N = 118	

Source: Director Board Survey, January 1994.
Notes: Responses total more than the number of respondents because several people checked more than one item. While 143 directors responded to the questionnaire, only 118 gave answers regarding their income sources. This raises the possibility that members with higher incomes might have been more likely to leave these questions blank.

eight are director board presidents, and one is a retired beedi worker with thirty years' experience. In some primary societies, the president works full time in the society headquarters along with the secretary. The president signs papers, sees to it that deliveries are received and made on time, resolves disputes among workers, monitors accounts, and arranges and oversees building repairs. Being primary society president can thus be a full-time job beyond the frequent primary board meetings over which he or she also presides. On the basis of the 1992 "sitting fee" (for working a whole day on director board activities) of Rs 35 per meeting (with travel costs reimbursed where appropriate), presidents could receive Rs 35 per day, meaning a maximum of Rs 9,450 per year, about 13 percent above the expected wage level of a beedi roller who rolls a thousand beedis per day. Sitting fees do not include the other benefits production workers receive, however: Sunday wages, pension, and paid holidays. When these benefits are added to the workers' wages, the total income for rolling a thousand beedis per day in 1993 came to Rs 60. From this perspective, the presidents and board members received less than the workers. On 1 January 1994, KDB raised the sitting fee to Rs 55, making it about even with a worker's daily wage and benefits. Three respondents who cited trade union or political party allowances receive amounts almost twice the wages of a beedi roller. These full-time activists constitute only about 2 percent of director board members. One director appears to receive an income from trade union officerships as well as director board sitting fees; he is the only person answering our survey at KDB who may be in a position to reap an extensive income from managerial type activities.

KDB's Invisible Women

The most dramatic inconsistency concerning director board members is the absence of women. As table 5.5 shows, in 1994 women made up 57 percent of the workforce but only 10 percent of the primary society director board members. By 1995, 60 percent of KDB's workforce was female, but the number of women on director boards had not increased. No women are members of the general body, the central society director board, or the pension and welfare committee. To some extent this discrepancy reflects the younger relative ages of the women workers. Deeper social and cultural forces are also at work.

One primary society foreman bemoaned the fact that women's household chores prevent them from attending trade union meetings in the evenings or on Sunday. He claimed the present leaders are discussing the problem (Kunhappan Int: 1 April 1993). Another primary society president noted in our interview that women workers have more household chores both before arriving and after returning home from beedi rolling. This limits their production and also their participation. We shall see in chapter 6 that the statistics seem to show women workers to be bringing down efficiency. The president continued:

> We have asked that more women workers be involved with trade union activities so that they would have the necessary experience to handle the directors' functions. However at present it has not happened. The women are not very active on the trade union front. . . . The women workers think that men should take such responsibilities. Earlier a lot of women used to get involved with the activities of the Communist Party. They had confidence and abilities. There are a few women workers like that, but not many are in the beedi industry. (Raveendran Int: 2 April 1993)

It could be argued that a traditionally male occupation has recently been entered by women who are just starting to work their way into union roles. This argument can be supported by the fact that many women have come into KDB through the northernmost primary societies, where left-wing traditions are weak.

The invisibility of women is not limited to the beedi industry, however. In other industries, such as cashew and coir, women constitute more than 90 percent of the workforce and 90 percent of union members but have hardly any presence in the union leadership. The Center for Indian Trade Unions (CITU), the trade union federation to which a majority of the beedi workers belong, admitted:

> Neglect of women and their problems, failure to fight discriminatory practices against them and defend their interests, the indifference towards recruiting them as members of trade unions and virtual resistance to promote them to responsible positions in the organization indicate the male feudal outlook inside the Indian trade union movement and especially inside the established leadership of the trade unions. This is nothing but a projection of the neglect of woman and her inferior status in Indian society. (Ranadive 1987: 40)

CITU has displayed some sensitivity to women's invisibility in the trade unions. In 1979 it formed an All-India Co-ordination Committee of Working Women (AICCWW). Similar coordinating committees have developed at lower levels to lead agitations on women's issues and to constantly review the status of women in the federation. When the Tellicherry and Kannur beedi unions celebrated their fiftieth anniversary in 1984, not a single woman could be found in their eighty-three-member executive committee. The situation has changed somewhat: at the Payyanur primary society union executive committee of the CPM-oriented CITU Federation, women made up 20 percent of the members by 1986. It seems a paradox that in Kerala, where achievements for women have included high educational access, low birth rates, and other indicators of better lives, the participation of women in public life still remains at a very low level. Several studies by women in the state show that no fundamental transformation has taken place for gender relations in the household. Working women continue to bear the double burden of the workplace and the household,[10] an issue we shall discuss further in chapter 6.

KDB's work center structure encourages women to come out of their homes, by contrast with the policies of private-sector employers that encourage in-the-home putting out of beedis. By coming to work in centers with many other workers, the women who work at KDB reduce their isolation, learn to share experiences, and broaden their horizons. They also set a precedent in their homes that they—just like their husbands—have lives outside as well as inside, and that, like their husbands, they earn money outside to bring into the home. By itself, this change is very small, but it provides an opportunity for conscious intervention to promote greater gender equality.

The 1987–91 Left Democratic Front Ministry initiated a program to propel more women into the sphere of public life. Elected district councils were established, with a 30 percent set-aside for women. Twelve of the fourteen councils ended up with LDF majorities, and 35 percent of all members were women. The 35 percent figure indicates that some women ran in nonreserved electoral districts and won against male candidates (Mathew 1991: 1320). This experience suggests that forceful policies can bring women into positions of leadership while pronouncements and explanations for failure to bring women in may be inadequate. In this context it is interesting to note that the one-third reservation for women in local government bodies has been mandated throughout India by the seventy-third and seventy-fourth amendments to the national constitution, ratified in 1993.

Improving Efficiency: Director Board Views

As experienced beedi workers, director board members should clearly understand the shop floor workers' perspectives on issues that bring them into conflict with management. As trade union activists, they should have a sophisticated understanding of the workers' overall needs. But as policy-making managers, they also have to protect the cooperative against a possible drift toward inefficiency by the workers. There are thus several central points at which empowerment and supervision intersect.

What are the views of director board members on these issues? Our survey showed that director board members favor economic incentives as the main device to improve daily output, but they also desire the use of worker awareness and giving more power to the maistries to compel workers to be at work at all required hours. To increase leaf outturn, 113 members (79 percent of respondents) favored stricter control of the leaf supply by the maistries, but 114 members (80 percent) also favored raising worker awareness. Thirty-six board members (25 percent) advocated giving prizes to all workers producing above a specified level of outturn, and only four (3 percent) supported the fine system of private-sector beedi companies. But one could argue that reducing leaf supply amounts to an indirect fine on the worker. KDB's 1995 annual report bemoans the stagnation in leaf outturn since 1992. The report calls for more effective implementation of prizes as a means to raise leaf outturn to what management believes is an attainable 2,500 beedis per kilogram.

To increase daily beedi output, 106 (74 percent) of the directors want a significant reform in the wage payment system, one that would merge the current D. A. with the basic pay and raise the minimum number of beedis a worker must roll in a day to be eligible for the D.A. Twenty-three (16 percent) suggested a return to the piece-rate D.A. For reasons discussed earlier, the trade unions oppose a piece-rate D.A. Raising the minimum output requirement creates opposition among older workers. During the negotiations in the 1993 minimum wages committee, KDB's top management supported the thousand-beedi minimum for D. A. (Panikkar Int: 20 June 1994). The final decision on nine hundred beedis and a day-to-day carryover represented a compromise with the unions, described earlier in this chapter. Some primary societies are said to allow workers too much flexibility in arriving, leaving, and taking breaks, and 88 directors (62 percent) supported the idea of giving maistries greater power to enforce working hours. Eighty-six (60 percent) thought raising worker awareness would help, and 27 (19 percent) advocated giving prizes for high output.

THE FUNCTIONS OF TRADE UNIONS
IN THE PRIMARY COOPERATIVES

Collective Bargaining and Dispute Resolution

The above discussion shows that electing management from the ranks of the workers does not remove management-worker conflict at KDB. As we have already explained, wages and D. A. are set by a government-appointed state minimum wages committee. Therefore, there is no collective bargaining over wages and D. A. directly with KDB management. All the major trade unions, however, have representatives on the committee. As noted earlier, in 1993, the committee set the D. A. threshold at nine hundred beedis, 13 percent higher than the previous level. It could not have made such a recommendation without the support of the trade unions.

The workers allege that the new threshold undermines the incomes of older workers and perhaps some new and less experienced workers who find it difficult to reach the nine hundred-beedi output per day. When we confronted central society directors with this issue, they replied that nine hundred beedis per day means cutting nine hundred leaves in the first two hours and rolling one hundred fifty beedis per hour for six more hours. They insisted this was quite a reasonable task. Reports indicate that many workers are unhappy with what they regard as a management-imposed speedup. As might be expected, the small unions, including the Congress Party-oriented INTUC—which was a signatory to the committee recommendation—have taken up the cause by criticizing the decision of the Communist-oriented, CITU-dominated director board. Kerala and KDB's main union federations are presented in table 5.7

The bonus is an item in the annual round of collective bargaining between the trade unions and KDB management. Trade union pressure has been responsible for the steady rise in the bonus. In 1993, the discussions almost stalemated. KDB had faced three years of losses, and many in the upper levels of management wanted to reduce the size of the bonus. Firm intervention by union leaders restored the bonus to its 16.5 percent level; they argued that sufficient accumulated profits allowed the cooperative to continue to keep its workers paid according to their expectations.

Similarly, trade unions have been the initiators of most of the benefits that workers enjoy. Even KDB's much acclaimed death benefit was not a gift from management. As the coop was being founded in 1969, the unions proposed collecting a voluntary small amount from each member to help the family of a deceased worker, to which the cooperative also made a small contribution. This gesture is the origin of the death benefit now paid from company funds with workers' contributions. Union pressure also paved the way for the "welfare cum pension scheme." All union representatives were actively involved in drawing it up and implementing it (Panikkar 1988). New

Table 5.7. Beedi Worker Union Federations

Acronym	Name	Political Party Link	Main Regions of Strength	Strength among KDB Workers
CITU	Centre for Indian Trade Unions	Communist Party of India (Marxist)	Kerala, West Bengal, and Indiawide	60–70%
INTUC (I)	Indian National Trade Union Congress (Indira)	Congress	Indiawide	15–20%
AITUC	All-Indian Trade Union Congress	Communist Party of India	Indiawide	5–10%
INTUC (S)	Indian National Trade Union Congress (Socialist)	Congress (S)	Kerala-based	1–3%
HMS	Hind Mazdoor Sabha (Indian Workers' Assembly)	Janata Dal	Bombay and Indiawide	1–3%
BMS	Bharatiya Mazdoor Sangh (Indian Workers' Association)	Bharatiya Janata Party	Indiawide	1–3%
NLO	National Labor Organization	Janata Dal	Kerala-based	1%
STU	Swatantra Tozhilali Union (Independent Workers' Union)	Muslim League	Kerala-based	3–5%
UTUC	United Trade Union Centre	Revolutionary Socialist Party	Kerala West Bengal	1%

benefits issues will probably arise from within the unions in the future. KDB's "invisible" women may be emerging from the shadows. Failure to provide full maternity benefits as laid out in the 1966 Beedi and Cigar Workers' Act is an issue among many women and will become more critical as the percentage of women workers increases. Demands for day care facilities are also being heard (and will be considered further in chapter 6).

The day-to-day functioning of the unions in the cooperative mainly involves mediating disputes at the work sites. The basic unit of the unions is the factory committee formed at each work center. The leadership of the factory committee initially takes up disputes. There may also be informal consultation with leaders of all trade unions at the work centers. In certain centers where workers are entirely CITU-affiliated, only a CITU committee exists. If more than one union is present, there will be a joint council with a representative from any union with at least one member at the work center. This principle of inclusion promotes democracy and tolerance, but it does not completely prevent interunion rivalries from sometimes upsetting the cooperative's daily work routine, as we shall see below.

The factory committees mostly take up worker grievances against the maistries, which make up most shop-floor grievances. Union activists and leaders we interviewed insisted that because most major disputes have been solved by the very fact of worker ownership and worker electoral power, informal and collegial processes dominate over structured and antagonistic ones. Workers have several avenues through which to pursue grievances. They can ask the union factory committee to take up the issue with the primary society president. They can go directly to the functionary with whom they have the dispute, with or without a union presence. In both cases, union activists see their role as mediation more than unquestioning advocacy of the worker's point of view. If these avenues fail, workers can go outside KDB to a Kerala labor court.

The most common dispute occurs when a maistry reduces the amount of wrapper leaves and tobacco given to a worker to a level the worker finds unacceptable. The argument centers around whether the worker is wasting raw materials or whether the maistry is being punitive. Most disputes are settled quickly through mediation by the worker's chosen union representatives, but a few cases have gone to the labor courts. Other disputes involve the transfer of workers to other primary societies because of marriage or for other reasons, hiring of part-time labelers to compensate for fluctuating labeling needs, fights between workers—sometimes a result of interunion rivalries, sometimes for personal reasons—and reinstatement of workers who were absent for long periods and had been dropped from the rolls.

New Roles:
Transmitting Policies and Maintaining Worker Enthusiasm

The role of the trade unions at KDB is not confined to traditional collective bargaining and intervention in workplace disputes. Because KDB is worker-owned, the unions have taken on new roles: (1) transmitting policies to the shop floor, (2) providing elected policy makers, (3) providing staff to implement policy, and (4) acting as watchdogs over management decisions.

Transmitting Policies to the Shop Floor. Union leaders take responsibility for aiding management in transmitting unpopular policies to the workers, a function sometimes referred to as the "transmission belt" role of unions.[11] This role was put to the test in January 1992 when KDB had to delay payment of an increase in the D.A. for three months to smooth its way through a temporary financial crisis without raising the price of its beedis. Getting the workers to forgo a raise for three months fell to the union activists (Kunhappan Int: 1 April 1993). Other emergencies may also arise. For example, sometimes during the monsoon season, a lull in beedi smoking by consumers forces a day or a few days' shutdown to avoid a buildup of stocks.[12] Persuading the workers to use their personal leave days at such times is the job of the union activists.

Union leaders consider the formation and success of the cooperative a great achievement for the workers and for the union movement in Kerala. They use their prestige with the workers as much as possible to promote KDB and to keep workers from making what the leaders consider impractical demands. As one beedi union vice president put it, "We cannot insure the workers' rights without the growth of the cooperative. . . . We don't make any unrealistic demands on the cooperative, only what it can pay. Even then, we have the best standards in the whole industry" (Vasu Int: 7 June 1993). A primary society foreman and CITU area president adds, "This cooperative is a model for the whole country and the trade unions have a duty in safeguarding it" (Kunhappan Int: 1 April 1993).

Providing Policy Makers. The unions provide the training ground for the main policy makers of KDB and play a major consultative role in the development of policy. The director boards discuss major policy decisions with the unions before implementing them. These consultations have the effect of amplifying KDB's internal democracy because regular consultation brings in the views of the smaller unions.

Providing Management Implementation Staff. In addition to facilitating election to the director boards, union experience has helped move some workers into positions to implement management policy in the cooperative: maistries especially, but also foremen and some primary society secretaries. Foremen and maistries can succeed in their roles partly because of how they get the jobs: through recognition of skills and respect by the elected representatives of the workers on primary society director boards. At both the policy and implementation levels, union activists have determining influence on KDB. The dual role of union activist and manager is explained by one primary society president as follows: "Here the worker is himself the owner of the enterprise. I am only an administrator elected by the workers. . . . As long as I carry their trust it is easier for me to fulfill my function of administration of the cooperative" (Raveendran Int: 2 April 1993).

Acting as Watchdog over Management. Even though the trade unions provide a large proportion of the policy makers and implementation staff, that staff could develop management sympathies. Therefore, the unions play the role of watchdog over some of their own most successful members. A recent example illustrates this need. In 1992, the cooperative's top management called together the trade unions committee to explain that much unsold beedi stock was piling up. This would require a slowdown in production and some involuntary leave time. When informed of this, workers and some union activists immediately checked and found a shortage of beedis in some retail outlets. They demanded immediate union meetings to discuss the problem and accused the central society of a management lapse. They then sent their union leaders to the central society to demand restarting production and giving attention to the marketing errors. Management acceded (Vijayan Int: 7 June 1993). The union leaders, however, also had to explain to the workers what had happened. Special Beedis, the smaller type sold mostly in southern Kerala, had indeed built up unsold stocks while a shortage was developing in the northern districts, where the traditional Medium Beedi is most popular. Because of the low fixed capital investment in beedis, it was not difficult to switch over the production line at several primary societies from Specials to Mediums.

TRADE UNION RIVALRIES

Morale and production at KDB are occasionally hampered by disputes among Kerala's many unions and union federations. One source of the rivalry is the unequal membership pattern. As we saw in the previous chapter, from the formation of KDB in 1969 until 1985, all the union federations were represented by one member each on the director board of the central society and—with a few exceptions—on the primary society boards as well. In 1969 the CPM-affiliated, CITU-federated union represented 70 percent of beedi workers, but held only 45 percent of the director board seats. Six different union federations were represented, four of them—HMS, INTUC(S), INTUC(I), and STU—with very limited worker support. A list of the main federations, their party connections and their influence in KDB appears in table 5.7.

The director board elections that began in 1986 eliminated the smaller unions from the director boards. Of 130 directors who responded to the union portion of our questionnaire, all are trade union members; 84 hold officerships of various levels in their unions. Beedi workers heavily favor CITU, the union of the CPM. The 1993 elections gave CITU 77 percent of the director board positions, with another 20 percent won by AITUC, the CPI (the other Communist Party) labor federation. The HMS union of the Janata Dal Party had held 10 percent of the appointed directorships, but this was reduced to 3 percent in the elections. The Congress-affiliated INTUC(I) and INTUC(S) and the Muslim League's STU federation that had accounted for a combined total of 20 percent of the directorships before 1986 were completely shut out with the elections. The right-wing BJP-affiliated BMS union has almost no support among KDB workers. Even the AITUC representation may be larger than its numbers among the workers would suggest. The two Communist Party unions had an understanding to vote together after making a combined list of candidates to prevent a split that would give right-wing parties positions they didn't deserve. This agreement seems to have facilitated AITUC representation much larger than the union's strength among beedi workers.

In KDB's early years, CITU leaders were hesitant to move to elected boards. They had raised the issue of elected director boards in 1977, after which they got KDB general membership meetings to pass resolutions calling for them. But even when the CPM was in power in Kerala's state government in 1980–82, no elections were held. CITU's leadership was apprehensive about taking nearly complete control of the director boards, fearing this would increase the number of nuisance demands from the smaller unions who would be in opposition with no management responsibility (Sahadevan Int: 9 June 1993). As we saw in chapter 4, a partial solution to this problem has been to keep the pension and welfare committee open to all unions.

Union rivalries take several forms. Some of the most bitter are between activists of CITU and AITUC, the two main Communist Party union federations. Following the 1964 split in the Communist Party of India into the CPI and the CPM (Communist Party of India-Marxist), the CPM took most of the support in Kerala and later in West Bengal, Tripura, and some other parts of India. The CPI retained major strength in the other Indian states and in its All-India Trade Union Federation (AITUC).[13]

From time to time, especially at certain primary societies where AITUC retains many followers, jockeying for power goes on between the two Communist federations. At Bediaduka primary society in 1992, a compromise had reportedly been worked out allowing one federation the presidency while the other would have the majority of directors. At the last minute, the compromise collapsed with both sides claiming treachery. This conflict soon developed into a major political confrontation at the district and state levels. CITU withdrew its candidates. AITUC ran unopposed (Balakrishnan Int: 27 March 1993; Sahadevan Int: 9 June 1993). During the incident and for some time afterward, output at the primary society declined. It currently has one of the lowest outputs, as we shall see in chapter 6.

A second kind of rivalry involves INTUC. Although its influence among KDB workers is small, it is related to the Indian National Congress, until 1996 the major political party at the national level. The president of Payyanur primary society recounted an incident that occurred in November 1992, when CITU had led a procession in the area for caste and religious harmony. INTUC and the Indian National Congress did not oppose the concept but probably preferred to lead their own procession. Since most of the Payyanur primary society workers belong to CITU, management closed the work centers for that day. A dispute arose over whether the few INTUC workers had been given adequate notice of the society's plan to offer employment for the day at an alternate primary society. We do not know whether this incident resulted in sufficient friction at the work centers following the day of the procession to affect production (Raghavan Int: 23 March 1993), but it illustrates how near to the surface the Congress-Communist rivalries are.

A third rivalry involves the more marginal unions. In the view of CITU and AITUC leaders, the small unions are always looking for some toehold in the KDB workforce. This causes them to take up trivial or anticoop causes simply to win members. At Chala primary society a complex dispute developed over the hiring of temporary labelers. Different types of beedis are packed in different-sized hanks (tied bundles). Because production of various kinds of beedis is not precisely even, owing to market fluctuations, the number of packages and labels, and thus the number of labelers, can vary somewhat at the primary societies, producing a mix of beedi types. When the Chala primary society hired and then laid off some part-time labelers, a Naxalite union took up their cause and demanded that KDB take them on as permanent employees, even though it had insufficient permanent work for them (Nanu Int: 2 April 1993).[14] While refusing to negotiate with the Naxalite union on the grounds that the workers were not in any way covered by KDB rules, the director board decided to put the workers at the top of the list to be hired when a vacancy came open (Raveendran Int: 2 April 1993). One Naxalite leader went on a brief hunger strike in front of the primary society headquarters, but the Chala primary society secretary claims that production was not affected (Govindan Int: 7 April 1993).

While noting union rivalries, we should not overstate their importance. The joint factory committees reduce tensions by incorporating all the unions in union work, but this is far from a perfect solution. Perhaps some tension and disputes are inevitable in such a situation. Simultaneously with the rivalries, we see in KDB a remarkable degree of political tolerance, as militant workers with major differences usually unite to keep the cooperative functioning. The Chala primary society secretary reflected:

> We implement all decisions through a broad mutual understanding. Even if the secretary and the director board belong to mutually hostile political parties or ideologies, there are no fights. I know of many primaries where this is the case. Earlier Kannur City primary society was headed by a Muslim League director board while the secretary was a Marxist [CPM] sympathizer of the CITU. Similarly the Kakkad primary was headed by a Muslim League president while the secretary was a Marxist. (Govindan Int: 7 April 1993)

COMMITMENT OR SUPERVISION?

At the outset, KDB set itself the task of providing enough supervision to ensure business success while maintaining the democracy and worker participation to which it was committed. But the very success of KDB seems to be undermining political consciousness. The director board survey revealed that these most experienced worker members consider raising worker consciousness to be paramount to its success. A common refrain of the older generation of activists is the decline in beedi worker consciousness. As veterans of decades of revolutionary struggles and commitment, they perceive the new workers not living up to past traditions. Is degeneration setting in? Will the iron law of oligarchy assert itself?

The Kannur Tobacco Workers' Union president offered the following appraisal: "It frightens us. The beedi workers at one time were the most politically conscious of all workers. . . . But young workers of today . . . have no idea of what is happening. . . . The new cultural values are making heavy inroads into their minds" (Kannan Int: 6 June 1993). He continued:

> Before the cooperative came, everything was different in the beedi industry. Every day was a struggle against fines, illegal deductions, low

wages, and so on. But now the workers in the cooperative get their full wages and benefits with periodic upward revisions as stated in the law. Everything can be settled through negotiations. This is true to an extent even in the private organized sector. The new workers have no experience of struggles. They don't know how history was made. They take everything for granted. Because they didn't have to fight for it. (Kannan Int: 21 June 1994)

In the past, as workers rolled beedis, readers would inform them of world events, the struggles for independence, and union organizing from the pages of nationalist and Communist newspapers. "Today the focus is more on pulp literature like *Mangalam* and other such periodicals" (Raveendran Int: 2 April 1993). *Mangalam* is a weekly magazine featuring serialized mysteries and soap opera romances.

Union leaders insist that they are trying to educate the workers who have not experienced strikes, struggles, and deprivation, but they could offer no specifics on what they are doing or plan to do. Holding meetings is helpful only for those who attend. Attendance at primary cooperative general body meetings is between 20 and 30 percent. At Chala primary society activists and director board members tried convening meetings at all the work centers and convinced workers to take classes on union history. They also held two-hour long meetings with workers to hear their views and to exhort them to raise output: "For two weeks there was some effect. After that everything came back to the earlier level. So whatever we do does not really convince the workers in the long run" (Raveendran Int: 2 April 1993).

Lax workplace discipline and waning commitment to the cooperative are widely reported. Some union activists and director board members and staff complain that more and more workers roll beedis up to the D.A. but save energy to roll them at home for private manufacturers. In that way, they may be able to double their daily wages (Raveendran Int: 2 April 1993). Using their own or other children as assistants, they undermine the gains for which the unions and the cooperative have struggled for so many decades.

Other workers frequently absent themselves to take care of small businesses or other skilled seasonal work such as cashew trading and construction work (Govindan Int: 7 April 1993). According to one primary society president, about five to ten workers are typically on leave at any work center on any day (Raghavan Int: 23 March 1993). Some workers are also accused of taking advantage of easygoing staff in some primary societies by leaving unfinished rolling materials in their baskets at the work centers through the night (Vasu Int: 7 June 1993).

G. K. Panikkar, KDB chairman from its inception until his death in December 1996, felt the workers had gained much but had failed to fully absorb the cooperative ideal:

> Our workers have a better life. Better food, better medical care. Their children are being taught. They even get scholarships. But I can't say they have achieved the objective of each for all and all for each. They have not started doing something for one another. No. They work for their own betterment. I say this because you ask me about the philosophy. (Panikkar Int: 18 January 1993)

We should not exaggerate the problem of waning commitment and lax discipline at KDB. Despite all the problems, it continues to be a sound business. Even though attendance at general meetings is only 20 to 30 percent, 90 to 95 percent of the workers turn out for the director board elections. The almost immediate worker response to the layoff crisis in 1992 also reflects a high level of grassroots vigilance. There has not been a single serious corruption charge yet in a business with an annual earnings of Rs 600 million.

Despite the problems of lax discipline and low meeting attendance, KDB workers remain substantially more aware of and better satisfied with their workplace than do private-sector workers. In an attitude survey, N. Mohanan (1982: 53–55) found that 90 percent of Dinesh Beedi workers understood the organizational structure of the cooperative, while 80 percent of private-sector sample workers answered "don't know" about the ownership or structure of the company they worked for. Results of the survey revealed the other differences shown in table 5.8.

A larger and more recent survey indicated similar worker perceptions favoring KDB as a place where job satisfaction is high except with regard to wages, which nearly all workers in all sectors of the beedi industry would prefer to have raised. These data appear in table 5.9.

**Table 5.8. Attitudes of Workers at Dinesh Beedi and
in a Kannur Private Sector Beedi Firm, 1981**

Attitude	Percentage Answering Yes	
	KDB	Private
Satisfied with organization	83	30
Believe in its ability to assist them	73	17
Satisfied with overall performance	77	20
Satisfied with working conditions	83	30
Derived job satisfaction	80	29
Satisfied with existing wage rate	13	10
Getting stable employment	75	20
N = 30		

Source: Mohanan 1982: 55.

EMERGING ISSUES

From the discussion in this chapter, four major issues emerge. They all pose potential threats to KDB. First, there are tensions between the staff and the production workers. How will the cooperative resolve this potentially divisive and harmful issue?

Second, interunion rivalries remain a potential danger to the cooperative. Can the unions find a reliable mechanism to set limits on these rivalries so that they are either healthy disagreements or at worst minor annoyances?

Third, what are the ways by which workplace democracy can be extended and deepened so that management becomes truly participatory and discipline more voluntary, so that less dependence is laid on supervision and regulatory mechanisms? Can the workers move to a higher form of democracy while keeping the business competitive in a capitalist economy?

Finally, how can the unions and coop activists instill in the younger members the sense of commitment born of a struggle those younger workers have not experienced? Can KDB make a successful transition from mobilization to institutionalization? This question faces all institutions born of mobilization and sacrifice.

The major barriers against bureaucratization and degeneration at KDB so far have been the effective functioning of the trade unions and the high public esteem in which KDB is held. Bureaucratization is also restrained by the fact that most of the shop floor supervisors as well as all of the director board members rise from the ranks of the

Table 5.9. Workers' Perceptions about Their Workplaces:
1989 (Kannur Area of Kerala)

Item	KDB	Private Organized	Private Unorganized
	Percentage of Workers Agreeing with the Statements		
Satisfied with the setup	85	28	12
Satisfied with the purpose of the system	77	20	10
Satisfied with working conditions	83	30	8
Having job satisfaction	80	29	7
Believe in stability of employment	78	21	9
Satisfied that the system can help them	74	17	3
Dissatisfied with the existing wages	90	94	98

N = 600

Source: Aziz 1990: 155.

workers through the trade unions. This does not hold true of the clerks and administrative staff, who, as we saw in this chapter, initially came from the state bureaucracy but today are separately recruited by KDB. The conflicts that have developed between the staff and the workers could threaten the long-term interests of the cooperative.

The workers on the whole have taken a resolute and united position to maintain a consistent relationship between shop floor and administrative salaries. The compromises obtained so far have been achieved largely through political mediation, which has been further facilitated by the fact that most of the recently hired staff are also leftist sympathizers.

To further arm KDB against degeneration, greater grassroots participation and more active democratic functioning of the trade unions are needed. The trade union leaders are aware of the need to maintain the high democratic consciousness at KDB. They view this consciousness as a key element in KDB's emergence and success—thus sharing a view held widely in the comparative literature.

Active trade unionism brings in its wake the interunion rivalries that have adversely affected production in some cases. But these are rare. The overall picture at KDB is one of consensus and compromise, processes that are reinforced by KDB's high prestige among its workers and among the public in general. This prestige derives in part from the high political consciousness of the beedi workers and of the radical culture in the Kannur area, and in part from the dramatic circumstances of KDB's birth—a David versus Goliath success drama—which created widespread public sympathy and then admiration for the victory of the struggling workers over their arrogant and exploitative capitalist bosses.

So high is KDB's standing with the workers and the public that antileft governments have not dared to try to dismantle its organization or restructure it by appointing managers hostile to its functioning. Left forces likewise have treated KDB with care: the CPM, which holds an overwhelming majority among the workers, never attempted to replace Chairman G. K. Panikkar, not a Party member, with one of their own. He remained chairman even after the retirement age, until his death in December 1996.

It may seem puzzling that state intervention did not result in the bureaucratic degeneration and clientism that pervades state-sponsored cooperatives in much of the developing world. This can be attributed partly to periodic left ministries but mostly to the strength of grassroots public opinion against interference and to the vigilance of the trade unions and shop floor workers themselves. The KDB mix of empowerment and supervision, participation and discipline, voluntarism and fair wages and benefits has been built up in its twenty-five years of struggle and growth. This mix makes substantial workplace democracy possible while allowing KDB to maintain a competitive position in a capitalist environment. Recent developments in KDB's workforce raise yet another challenge to the cooperative's competitive market position, however. We turn to this problem in the next chapter.

CHAPTER SIX

Efficiency and Profit in the Primary Societies: KDB's Market Dilemma

KDB's origin and its survival up to now have depended on a combination of many factors. But the cooperative's survival in the long run will depend on its ability to maintain itself in a hostile environment of mainly capitalist firms that can exploit their workers, pay bribes to government officials for favored treatment, and undertake other measures not possible for a worker-owned, radically oriented company.

Can KDB survive in such an environment? In attempting to answer this question, we must first consider whether KDB has the internal resources to maintain *efficiency* at a level high enough to compete with privately owned companies. We call this KDB's market dilemma. The dilemma is complex, and we can make only a partial analysis. The variation in profitability among KDB's twenty-two primary societies, however, provides some insights into the sources of efficiency and therefore the possible means of raising it, given the constraints under which KDB must operate. It cannot exploit its workers or lay them off as cost-saving measures. It cannot cut their pay to be more competitive and it can raise prices to only a small level above its competitors'. To be true to its own origins, KDB cannot reduce the benefits for which its workers have struggled so hard and sacrificed so much. Does the cooperative have any options?

In this chapter, we shall investigate the factors influencing the efficiency of the production of beedis at KDB. Such an investigation is facilitated by the structure of KDB: a central society and twenty-two primary societies that constitute production units, each with its own accounts. The variations in efficiency and the factors behind it among these primary production units lend themselves to comparative analysis. (The locations of the primary societies are shown on the map facing page 1.)

Our analysis of these factors will employ both case study data and statistics. Where information allows, we try to explain the efficiency of a primary society with specific historical information. Explaining most of the individual cases, however, as well as the differences across all the cases, requires statistical analysis. The statistics for this chapter come from the financial records of the twenty-two primary societies for the bookkeeping year ending on 31 March 1993. These records were kindly made available to us by the central society chairman and secretary of KDB in October 1993. Since most interviews were conducted in 1992 and 1993, the statistical analysis covers the same time period for which worker and management perceptions are available. Another data source was a three-hour discussion with the central society director board in June 1994 at which we were given their detailed responses to an initial version of this chapter. We include the KDB responses to our major points at appropriate places in this chapter. We begin with an overview of beedi output and sales for the reference year 1992–93.

PRODUCTION AND PROFIT

KDB workers produced 6.7 billion beedis in 1992–93, which the primary societies sold for 543 million rupees to the central society.[1] This means an average primary society price of Rs .08 per beedi, or about 12 beedis per rupee. The average 1992–93 retail price for medium beedis—the main type produced—was Rs .091.[2] After deducting the agents' commissions of Rs .0019 per beedi, the surplus at the central cooperative level was Rs 0.0091 (.091 – .08 – .0019). This calculation would result in a sales surplus of approximately 61 million rupees, from which the central society deducted its various costs and expenditures before registering a trading profit of 7.8 million rupees, about 13 percent of the sales surplus. The other 87 percent of the surplus went for worker bonuses (16.5 percent of wages in 1993), rebates to the primary societies (5.3 percent of the sales price from the primary societies to the central society), central society taxes (5 percent excise tax to the Indian central government), and primary society taxes (5 percent on raw materials and labels to the Kerala state government). In accordance with India's national Cooperative Act, the central society also contributed 3 percent of its profits (Rs 234,000 in 1992–93) to local hospitals, child care centers, schools, libraries, and sports and cultural clubs. The central society also has to keep rotating funds available to make the large-scale purchases of tobacco and leaves that were described in chapter 4.

As chapter 4 also showed, central society profits are skimmed off the top of the surplus created in the primary societies. Since all production occurs in the primary societies, they must be the main sources of profit, despite the assistance they receive from the large-scale purchases of raw materials and the marketing services of the central cooperative. Part of KDB's efficiency lies in the skills of the central cooperative's director board and management, but the main element must lie within the primary societies.

PRIMARY SOCIETY TRADING PROFIT:
THE MEASURE OF EFFICIENCY AND THE DEPENDENT VARIABLE

We have chosen a simple and direct profit figure for our dependent variable and indicator of efficiency. This figure is the total of raw material costs plus the major labor costs for each primary society subtracted from the rupees value of the total beedi sales to the central society.

The "Total Costs" column in table 6.1 includes raw materials, labor costs, and a few other costs. The other costs are medical payments, maternity leaves, and rents. Because the maternity leaves and building rents vary, they could influence profitability.[3]

To obtain the total profits, we subtracted the total costs from the total sales.[4] The total profit appears in the fifth column of table 6.1. To compute the profit per employee, we took the total profits and divided by the total number of employees—rollers, labelers, and support workers such as headloaders (carriers), sweepers, and drivers. We also included primary society office staff, since we wanted to see whether the variation in their numbers influenced profitability. The profit per employee appears in the last column of table 6.1. The primary societies are listed in order of efficiency from the highest to lowest on table 6.1 and all other tables in this chapter.

Table 6.1. Production Costs, Profits, and Profits per Worker by Primary Society 1992–93

Primary Society	Raw Materials	Labor Costs	Total Costs	Total Sales	Profit	Profit per Employee in Rupees
1. Kannur city	2,394	3,215	5,613	6,636	1,023	2,914
2. Kannur town	2,646	3,440	6,075	6,909	834	2,272
3. Azhikode	6,579	9,680	16,273	18,335	2,062	2,161
4. Chervathur	12,475	21,250	33,788	38,759	4,970	2,077
5. Thottada	6,786	8,912	15,703	17,585	1,882	2,023
6. Kakkad	5,139	7,279	12,402	14,079	1,677	1,989
7. Payyanur	8,104	13,332	21,457	24,388	2,932	1,974
8. Chala	20,141	27,615	47,943	53,746	5,803	1,966
9. Chirakkal	5,274	7,420	12,699	14,208	1,509	1,957
10. Chalad	2,857	3,941	6,784	7,603	819	1,820
11. Tellicherry	9,512	14,054	23,567	26,205	2,638	1,788
12. Pinarayi	19,873	29,049	49,049	54,522	5,473	1,730
13. Kottacherry	8,245	15,295	23,584	26,429	2,845	1,702
14. Manjeshwar	6,937	12,914	19,871	22,455	2,584	1,619
15. Kadirur	11,131	17,234	28,376	31,307	2,931	1,508
16. Valiannoor	16,227	22,142	38,396	41,907	3,511	1,497
17. Nelishwar	9,306	15,045	24,384	26,896	2,512	1,437
18. Dharmadam	10,973	13,825	24,782	26,708	1,926	1,205
19. Hosdurg	10,604	17,830	28,500	30,951	2,450	1,192
20. Kasargod	9,436	17,731	27,219	29,758	2,540	1,083
21. Bediaduka	3,828	7,321	11,161	12,055	893	862
22. Badagara	4,371	6,947	11,345	11,842	497	594
TOTALS	192,839	296,373	488,972	543,282	54,310	
AVERAGES	8,765	13,472	22,226	24,695	2,469	1,699

In Thousands of Rupees

Source: KDB primary society balance sheets for the year ending 31 March 1993.

Table 6.1 shows that efficiency measured in profit per employee among the primary societies can be broken into three major groups. The highly efficient primary societies range from Kannur city, which produced a profit of 2,914 rupees per employee, to Chirakkal, with 1,957. Kannur city primary society achieved a profit per employee 72 percent above the average of 1,699. Middle-efficiency primary societies run from Chalad, at 7 percent above average, down to Nelishwar, at 15 percent below average. Low-efficiency primary societies go from Dharmadam, at 71 percent, to Badagara, at a mere 35 percent of the average.

When we consider the causes of inefficiency within the KDB structure, one obvious candidate for examination is Bediaduka primary society. It has the second lowest efficiency at Rs 862 per employee, 51 percent of the average. Why should this primary society have such low output? We saw in chapter 4 that Bediaduka was involved in prolonged disputes with the central cooperative over its interpretation of autonomy and over investigations of bookkeeping irregularities. In chapter 5 we saw that the same primary society was a focal point of staff and production worker conflict and also rivalries among major union federations. The perceptions of workers and management, whose accounts were reported in those chapters, appear to be borne out in the independently gathered statistics: excessive turmoil within Bediaduka primary society resulted in substantial loss of production efficiency. The Bediaduka case shows that sectarian political mobilization and competition that turns into excessive rivalry can become harmful under certain circumstances. Because so many forms of turmoil existed at Bediaduka during the study period, we cannot say which are the most important, but the strikingly low efficiency figures suggest these factors must have played a role.

The efficiency figures for Badagara primary society are even lower than those for Bediaduka. Were similar forces at work there? Our research indicates no major political upheavals at Badagara. The forces limiting this primary society's efficiency appear to be of a different nature. Badagara was one of the last two primary societies to join KDB. It came into the cooperative in 1975 after intervention by trade union leaders among a small number of beedi workers in Badagara municipality. Badagara alone among the KDB primary societies has had some difficulties in recruiting sufficient numbers of skilled workers in its immediate area. As a result, the unions themselves have taken on responsibility for training the beedi rollers there.

Surprisingly, KDB chose Badagara to take up production of the more skill-demanding Special Beedis in the late 1980s. The low efficiency at Badagara may result from its historical background of low skills combined with a risky management decision to try to catapult it to a special position in the cooperative. Special Beedis are tied in hanks of ten instead of twenty-five, as is the case with other beedis.

The extra tying time creates a slightly lower daily output. This factor, however, does not seem large enough to account for Badagara's low output. For Special Beedis, union leaders demanded and got only a ten-paise (one-tenth of a rupee) add-on to the piece rate for a thousand beedis. Through the statistical analysis, we shall see that Badagara may also be a particular case of certain more general problems with efficiency at KDB.

THE INFRASTRUCTURE OF EFFICIENCY

Basic infrastructure should influence the efficiency of production. The available data allow us to consider average distance to work centers, rent for buildings and other items, and the percentage of work center buildings owned. To evaluate these infrastructural variables, we must employ statistical indicators. Two statistics lend themselves to the data at hand: correlation coefficients and multiple regression. We shall first consider individual factors that might influence efficiency using correlation coefficients. Then we shall combine these into a multiple regression analysis. We adopt the common social science practice of considering coefficients around 0.3 to be "low," those around 0.5, "medium," and those around 0.8, "high" (Downie and Heath 1983: 104).[5]

The primary societies are spread across about sixty kilometers in Kannur town, north to the Karnataka state border, and south into Kozhikode (Calicut) district. Each primary society has a headquarters from which its director board and management operate. The societies in turn branch out into work centers, the smallest units of the cooperative. Table 6.2 shows the main features of the primary societies. Each one has between four and twenty-nine work centers with between 70 and 123 workers at each center on average.

The spread-out nature of the work centers results from the fact that most of the workers are themselves spread over rural areas. As we have seen, private employers use this feature to manipulate beedi workers and to try to keep their unions weak. Under the coop, decentralization of workplaces has been maintained as a positive working condition: most beedi rollers can walk to work centers that are less than two kilometers from their homes; the greatest distance is five kilometers. The effects of transportation costs that the primary soci-

Table 6.2. Indicators of Infrastructural and Organizational Efficiency

Primary Society	Total Workers	Number of Work Centers	Distance to Work Centers (km)	Staff as Percentage of Workers	Rent (Rs)	Percentage of Work Center Buildings Owned
1. Kannur city	340	5	2.2	3.2	10,800	40
2. Kannur town	356	4	0.0	3.1	2,500	100
3. Azhikode	936	10	6.4	1.9	36,170	30
4. Chervathur	2,349	21	6.0	1.9	47,600	48
5. Thottada	912	10	2.8	2.0	34,185	20
6. Kakkad	819	8	4.4	2.9	9,825	63
7. Payyanur	1,456	15	5.6	2.0	27,830	33
8. Chala	2,900	29	8.0	1.8	95,440	38
9. Chirakkal	750	11	2.9	2.8	27,492	27
10. Chalad	435	6	2.2	3.4	3,150	83
11. Tellicherry	1,449	16	4.9	1.8	13,165	63
12. Pinarayi	3,116	29	3.5	1.5	37,496	38
13. Kottacherry	1,644	15	8.3	1.6	49,993	33
14. Manjeshwar	1,555	13	4.9	2.6	45,840	15
15. Kadirur	1,912	22	4.4	1.7	22,005	55
16. Valiannoor	2,310	23	7.5	1.5	57,760	43
17. Nelishwar	1,709	16	4.4	2.3	35,539	44
18. Dharmadam	1,585	16	1.9	0.9	15,750	38
19. Hosdurg	2,017	18	7.6	1.9	70,077	28
20. Kasargod	2,298	20	12.6	2.1	27,456	50
21. Bediaduka	1,014	10	11.4	2.2	9,022	80
22. Badagara	820	9	3.6	2.1	24,213	44
AVERAGES	1,486	15	5.3	2.2	31,969	46
TOTALS	32,682	326			703,308	

Source: KDB primary society balance sheets for the year ending 31 March 1993.
Note: The average distance to work centers refers to the distance from the primary society headquarters.

eties pay between their headquarters and the rolling sites vary with the distance from a society's headquarters to its work center and must be taken into account. Buses, vans, cars, and loads carried on heads, are all used to transport the raw materials and rolled beedis to and from the work centers. We see in table 6.2 that the average distance varies from 12.6 kilometers at Kasargod, with its widely dispersed work centers, to zero kilometers at Kannur town, where the entire primary society is physically located in one building.

How much difference does work center distance make? It correlates with profit per worker with a medium coefficient of −0.44. As we would expect, the sign is negative: greater average work center distance lowers profitability. Some primary societies own or rent vehicles, which use costly fuel, need repairs, and have to be insured. Kannur town primary society has no transportation costs at all; several societies have only a few costs. But some primary societies with spread-out work centers save on transportation by sending out supplies and retrieving beedis with headload workers who ride the Kerala State Transport and Road Corporation (KSTRC) buses. For Rs 2, almost any distance within a primary society area can be covered. Because the headload workers' wages are not solely for transportation costs and are not marked separately on the account sheets as transportation charges, we cannot add these figures in. Our analysis therefore probably underestimates the effects of these costs. We should keep in mind that dispersed work centers lower costs to workers and increase convenience. By keeping their workplaces near their homes, KDB absorbs part of the transportation costs as an indirect nonwage benefit to workers in the more dispersed primaries.

Variations in rent paid for use of work center buildings and other necessary facilities might also influence efficiency. In table 6.2 we can see that rent varies from a minimum of Rs 2,500 at Kannur town to Rs 95,440 at Chala. We might assume that this great difference in rent would produce a comparable difference in levels of efficiency between the two primaries. For buildings owned, we also see a large range, with the minimum of 15 percent at Manjeshwar and the maximum of 100 percent at Kannur town. This range of 6.7 to 1 also suggests possible effects on efficiency. Rent and percentage of buildings owned correlate with each other at only −0.56, suggesting that they are measuring at least one additional infrastructural element. This is most likely the variation in the rental price of land and buildings in the various locations where KDB primary societies are established.

Neither rent paid nor percentage of buildings owned has any meaningful correlation with profitability, however. Rent correlates at −.07 and percentage of buildings owned at −.02. KDB's central society policy of constructing new buildings based on workers' needs rather than primary society efficiency—a policy described in chapter 4—has offset any link that might otherwise have developed.

ORGANIZATIONAL COMPONENTS OF EFFICIENCY:
PRIMARY SOCIETY SIZE AND MANAGEMENT STAFF
AS PERCENTAGE OF EMPLOYEES

The primary society workforce is composed almost entirely of members of the cooperative. Rollers make up 94 percent of the total workforce that is shown in table 6.2. Labelers comprise another 3 percent, and other workers (transportation, cleaning) account for 1 percent. Managerial staff members make up 2 percent of the total. In table 6.2 we see that primary societies vary greatly by number of work centers and employees. The larger primary societies have larger overall profit figures. But does that mean their profitability is higher? The figure for total workers has a low negative correlation of −0.26 with profit per worker. This suggests that the smaller societies may be more profitable. The idea is reinforced by the higher negative association of −.41 for number of workers per work center.

The size of the management staff might also play a role. It seems logical that the smaller the ratio of the nonproductive staff to the entire workforce, the greater the output per worker and thus overall profitability. This would be especially true of the primary societies, since many essential managerial functions such as purchase of raw materials and marketing of finished beedis are handled by the central society, which has a single profit/loss account covering all the primary societies collectively. On the other hand, too few supervisors could lead to lax worker discipline (discussed in chapter 5) or to ineffectiveness in handling the essential bookkeeping, transportation, and management functions of the production units. Table 6.2 shows the variations in the numbers of primary society staff workers such as foremen, secretaries, and bookkeepers as a percentage of the total workforce. We see that Dharmadam has the smallest staff percent at 0.9 percent, while Chalad has the largest at 3.4 percent. This is a range of 3.7 to 1.

The staff percentage correlates with profit per worker at +0.43. This figure is consistent with KDB's policy of keeping staff to a minimum: a strong negative association would suggest that the primary cooperatives are overstaffed. The medium positive correlation of staff percentage with profit per worker corresponds with the late Chairman Panikkar's belief that maistries and primary society secretaries considered themselves overworked.

The statistical associations among total workers, average workers per work center, and staff percentage reveal a further component of efficiency at KDB. Staff percentage correlates +.68 with total workers but −.45 with average numbers of workers per work center. These correlations seem to indicate a shortage of management at the larger work centers: lower profitability at the primaries with larger work centers corresponds with lower staff percentages. This set of correlations seems to support the views attributed in chapter 5 to some of KDB's experienced union leaders and others that work discipline can become lax in the absence of adequate supervision. Further research is needed to confirm whether this or some other factor is at work.

WORKER CHARACTERISTICS AND EFFICIENCY

Worker Skill

Daily Output of Beedis. Throughout the beedi production process virtually no machinery is used except transportation vehicles and tobacco drying ovens. As we described in chapters 1 and 5, wrapper leaf cutting and beedi rolling—the most important parts of the production process—are done entirely by hand. Worker skill is therefore the most important factor in producing surplus value.

Since 94 percent of all primary society employees are beedi rollers, almost all value produced by the societies derives from the rollers' speed and skill. The number of beedis rolled per worker per day correlates with profit per worker at +0.67, making it the most important single direct factor in determining the profitability of the primary societies. As we saw in chapter 5, the mechanism by which worker speed contributed to profitability in 1993 was complicated by the wage structure that seemed to encourage stopping after eight hundred beedis. Despite the vagaries of the wage structure and its piecework orientation, speed still comes out first among the skill variables.

From table 6.3 we can see that the average number of beedis produced per worker per day in 1992–93 was 921—about 15 percent above the D. A. threshold discussed in chapter 5.[6] In table 6.3 we see that the average number of days worked varies considerably among the primary societies. Kakkad registered the lowest average attendance, with 216 days, while Hosdurg had the highest, with 248. This is a range of thirty-two days, or 13 percent. All the figures are well below the presumed work year of 284 days.[7]

KDB workers get eighty-one paid leave days per year—24 percent

Table 6.3. Components of Worker Skill 1993

| Primary Society | Average Days Worked | Beedis per Worker per Day | Beedis per Kilogram | |
			Leaf Outturn	Tobacco Outturn
1. Kannur city	227	929	2,130	5,660
2. Kannur town	232	1,032	2,060	5,507
3. Azhikode	232	1,115	1,989	5,475
4. Chervathur	235	898	2,160	5,444
5. Thottada	239	1,011	1,972	*5,307
6. Kakkad	216	1,005	2,054	5,499
7. Payyanur	233	907	2,284	5,501
8. Chala	237	970	2,051	5,501
9. Chirakkal	247	969	2,028	5,491
10. Chalad	234	942	2,017	5,507
11. Tellicherry	232	993	2,052	5,494
12. Pinarayi	234	933	2,101	5,478
13. Kottacherry	245	878	2,161	5,491
14. Manjeshwar	227	860	2,221	5,440
15. Kadirur	229	911	2,102	5,511
16. Valiannoor	234	968	1,971	5,359
17. Nelishwar	227	895	2,136	5,425
18. Dharmadam	227	885	2,034	5,499
19. Hosdurg	248	811	2,036	5,453
20. Kasargod	231	761	2,186	5,497
21. Bediaduka	223	724	2,138	5,390
22. Badagara	222	866	2,054	*5,474
AVERAGES	232	921	2,088	5,473

Source: KDB primary society balance sheets for the year ending 31 March 1993.
* All figures are for Medium Beedis except those for Thottada and Badagara. See note 8 for explanation of the figures for these two primary societies, which did not produce Medium Beedis.

of all calendar days of the year. Nonetheless, they take on average another fifty-two days off without pay—22 percent of the remaining work year. These additional days off represent illness, family emergencies, and possibly days used to take advantage of higher-paying work such as construction or cashew trading. The high number of unpaid leave days also suggests that rolling beedis is so monotonous that workers take advantage of KDB's high wages and benefits to meet psychological needs. This is a subject worth further investigation.

The missing workdays represent lost profits for KDB. A worker does not generate any profit when not rolling beedis. Table 6.1 showed that the average profit per worker across 1992–93 was Rs 1,699. That means the average profit per worker came to Rs 7.3 per day (1,699/232). The fifty-two lost days mean Rs 380 lost profits per worker in 1993. This would mean 22 percent more profits than recorded in that year, or 12.1 million rupees. If even half the unpaid leave days were transformed into workdays, KDB would see a big increase in profits, assuming the extra beedis could be marketed.

Variations in attendance rates appear to have little effect on variations in profitability among the primary societies, however. Average days worked correlates at only +0.15 with profit per worker. The harmful effects of worker absence apparently hit KDBs primary societies with almost equal force.

Leaf and Tobacco Outturn. Efficiency in the use of wrappers and tobacco shows up in wage efficiency and in lower costs of raw materials relative to numbers of beedis and thus to sales. The central society accounts include leaf and tobacco outturn figures for each primary society based on data from monitoring by maistries and foremen and by central society quality improvement teams that sometimes inspect the work centers. Outturn means the number of beedis produced per kilogram of leaf or per kilogram of tobacco.

In table 6.3 we see that leaf outturn varies from 1,971 beedis per kilogram at Valiannoor to 2,284 at Payyanur, a range of 313 beedis, or 14 percent. Tobacco outturn ranges from 5,307 at Thottada to 5,660 at Kannur city, a difference of 353 beedis, or 6 percent.

One problem in ascertaining outturn is the different mix of beedis produced by some primary societies. Altogether KDB manufactures four kinds of beedis: Medium, Small, Special, and Rajadhani. The percentage breakdown is as follows: Medium, 57 percent; Special, 39 percent; Small, 1 percent; Rajadhani, 3 percent. The Medium Beedis are the historical mainstay and still the most important product. Special Beedis are sold in the southern Kerala markets, while Rajadhanis are manufactured for outside markets such as Keralites in the Middle Eastern Gulf States and for promotion among non-Kerala smokers there and in states of India outside Kerala. For our analysis, we have standardized the figures in terms of Medium Beedis.[8]

Tobacco outturn correlates at the medium level of +.41 with profit per worker. Leaf outturn, however, which we had predicted to be a major element in profitability, shows a correlation coefficient of only −.03 to profitability. This number suggests no relationship at all between the two variables. When we use a multiple regression analysis (see below), we can establish that leaf outturn is an important element in profitability. There is also a medium negative relationship of −.54 between leaf outturn and beedis per worker per day. This relationship fits our expectations as described in chapter 5; rolling more beedis comes partly at the cost of wasting the expensive wrapper leaves that do not get cut as efficiently. Tobacco and leaf outturn correlate with each other only at the low level of +0.26, consistent with other evidence noted in chapter 5 that tobacco outturn is not as difficult to maximize as is leaf outturn.

Workforce Composition

Another set of variables we would intuitively expect to influence profitability consists of aspects of workforce composition. Age and experience of workers should both be factors: very old workers experience smoothing of the fingers, which reduces their ability to roll beedis quickly. Very young workers may not have developed their skills to the highest level.

Worker age and experience are tied in with gender: the youngest and newest workers are mostly female. Fifty-seven percent of the rollers and 57 percent of the total workers in 1993 were female.[9] But the proportion of female workers varies among the primary societies. It tends to increase as one moves away from traditional beedi industrial centers like Tellicherry and Kannur toward Kasargod in the north. Most of the workers are between the ages of twenty and forty-five. Only 1 percent are below age twenty and 15 percent are above age forty-five. The average age of women in nearly every society is lower than that of males. This is consistent with our observation in the previous chapter that women have been recent entrants into beedi work in Kannur. Table 6.4 shows substantial variation in the gender makeup of the beedi rollers among the primary societies: the percentage of females runs from 10 percent at Kannur town to 96 percent at both Kasargod and Bediaduka. Such a range suggests that gender makeup might account for differences in profitability among the primary societies.

Seventy-seven percent of male workers and 70 percent of females are literate but lack education beyond the seventh grade. Only 2 percent of men and 6 percent of women are illiterate. Educational levels are lower in the northern primary societies. Female workers are gen-

Table 6.4. Characteristics of Primary Society Workers

Primary Society	Number of Rollers		Percentage Female	Average Age		Percentage with Seven Years' Education	
	M	F		M	F	M	F
1. Kannur city	294	50	15	37.9	24.5	72	68
2. Kannur town	299	35	10	40.6	29.4	80	60
3. Azhikode	694	193	22	35.3	35.3	79	79
4. Chervathur	766	1,495	66	42.3	40.5	90	95
5. Thottada	620	248	29	36.0	31.1	82	73
6. Kakkad	586	195	25	36.9	30.6	83	63
7. Payyanur	599	819	42	36.4	30.5	85	90
8. Chala	1,619	1,167	42	36.4	29.2	75	62
9. Chirakkal	485	231	32	39.4	29.3	76	41
10. Chalad	328	87	21	43.9	29.5	92	31
11. Tellicherry	799	600	43	38.8	29.7	91	89
12. Pinarayi	1,545	1,478	49	36.3	30.6	83	83
13. Kottacherry	291	1,307	82	35.4	34.6	50	43
14. Manjeshwar	106	1,411	91	38.6	33.6	59	98
15. Kadirur	714	1,148	62	36.3	31.9	80	74
16. Valiannoor	1,610	606	27	35.6	32.2	90	90
17. Nelishwar	538	1,098	67	37.4	35.2	93	92
18. Dharmadam	774	752	49	36.8	36.8	65	60
19. Hosdurg	535	1,481	73	39.8	33.2	81	85
20. Kasargod	99	2,145	96	36.9	31.4	60	48
21. Bediaduka	44	943	96	29.8	29.5	83	93
22. Badagara	184	597	76	41.9	31.3	71	58
AVERAGES	615	822	57	37.4	32.1	77	70

Source: Computed from survey of primary society secretaries, 1994.
Note: The average ages of male and female workers are available for all the primary societies except Azhikode, which gave the data for both genders combined. For purposes of the analysis in this chapter, we considered the percentages based on age for Azhikode to be equal for men and women.

erally 5.3 years younger than their average male counterparts, and the age differential varies somewhat from primary society to primary society. We shall take average age as one stand-in for experience; we will also consider the age distributions as possible factors in explaining profitability. In addition, the numbers and percentages of new rollers recruited in the past six years can indicate the level of experience. Table 6.5 gives the totals of new rollers for the years 1988–93 for each primary society and the percentage of that six-year total to the number of rollers in 1993.

Workers over age eighteen join the primary societies by purchasing at least one share at Rs 20. They are encouraged to eventually purchase up to the maximum of ten shares. Today the primary societies hold recruitment when sales increases or retirements justify the hiring of new workers. Competition to join the coop is so keen that ex-

Table 6.5. Work Force Composition, Age and Length of Employment

Primary Society	New Rollers Since 1988	As Percentage of All Rollers in 1993	Males Years of Age <20	20–30	30–45	>45	Females Years of Age <20	20–30	30–45	>45
1. Kannur city	124	35	0	18	61	21	11	82	5	0
2. Kannur town	112	31	0	25	25	50	0	70	25	5
3. Azhikode	171	18	3	29	52	16	3	29	52	16
4. Chervathur	284	12	0	1	60	39	5	2	60	33
5. Thottada	119	13	0	30	56	15	2	56	34	8
6. Kakkad	316	37	0	28	49	23	4	59	27	10
7. Payyanur	300	20	0	24	61	15	0	50	48	0
8. Chala	623	21	0	27	55	18	1	65	34	0
9. Chirakkal	338	44	0	14	57	29	8	58	30	4
10. Chalad	144	32	0	2	45	53	2	65	29	4
11. Tellicherry	256	17	0	25	40	35	5	60	30	5
12. Pinarayi	616	19	0	27	56	17	1	55	43	1
13. Kottacherry	220	13	0	28	57	14	0	28	71	2
14. Manjeshwar	650	41	0	11	73	17	1	37	55	7
15. Kadirur	444	23	0	30	50	20	0	55	35	10
16. Valiannoor	500	21	0	30	55	15	0	50	40	10
17. Nelishwar	335	19	0	22	57	21	1	29	62	9
18. Dharmadam	409	26	2	18	65	15	2	16	69	13
19. Hosdurg	353	17	0	11	64	26	2	45	39	14
20. Kasargod	900	38	0	28	53	20	1	53	36	9
21. Bediaduka	457	44	0	62	38	0	2	59	37	1
22. Badagara	184	22	0	15	35	50	4	50	44	3
TOTALS	7,855									
AVERAGES	357	26	0	23	53	24	3	49	41	7

Source: Computed from survey of primary society secretaries, 1994.
Note: Percents not adding up to 100 are due to rounding errors.

aminations are held in which prospective worker members display their beedi-rolling skills before a recruitment panel. Following announcements on primary society notice boards and word of mouth in March of 1993, for fifty openings, 600 people applied (Ganapathy Int: 12 March 1993). Table 6.5 shows that the number of new workers in the years 1988 to 1993 varies from 112 at Kannur town to 900 at Kasargod. As a percentage of rollers in 1993, it varies from 12 percent at Chervathur to 44 percent at Chirakkal and at Bediaduka. In all, 7,855 new workers were hired to replace 8,588 who left or retired. About 4 percent of workers retired annually during the six-year period. About 1 percent of workers transfer within the coop each year. Most of the transfers are for women, who by custom move to their husbands' homes after marriage.[10]

Recruitment and departures do not precisely match up because the central society holds recruitment competitions only after a certain number of vacancies have arisen. As we saw in chapter 4, this sometimes results in tensions with primary society director boards. Although KDB holds competitions for the best younger workers at its recruitments, we can still assume that new workers would produce fewer beedis and would be less skilled at leaf and tobacco outturn than more experienced workers. We thus predict that number or percentage of new workers should correlate negatively with profitability.

To consider the older end of the spectrum, we use the age distribution from table 6.5. We see that almost no male workers are below age twenty, while 3 percent of females are in that age category. By contrast, only 7 percent of females are over forty-five, compared with 24 percent of males. Since—as noted in chapter 5—workers over forty begin to lose their rolling skills, we would predict that primary societies with higher percentages of workers over age forty-five should have lower profitability. In both Kannur town and Badagara 50 percent of the male workers are over forty-five, but Badagara has only 24 percent male workers, suggesting that the male age distribution may be only a minor factor. Kannur town has 90 percent male workers, so their age distribution could well play a role.

Work Force Composition Variables: Correlation Coefficients

The strongest single correlation with profitability among all the variables we could measure was the −0.74 association with the female percentage of the workforce. The highest single coefficient among all the independent variables is a −0.84 association between female percentage and beedis per worker per day. These two associations strongly suggest that women workers are not producing nearly as many beedis per day as men are and that this low output is the major factor limiting the efficiency of the primary societies. The +0.54 association of female percentage with leaf outturn indicates that women workers are fairly efficient in leaf use. Female percentage displays a medium coefficient of +0.41 with overall size, meaning that women are more represented in the larger primary societies. The +0.67 correlation with average size of work center also indicates that there are more females in the larger centers.

Surprisingly, the female percentage of rollers bears no relation to attendance levels. Central society director board members strongly asserted that women take more days off beyond the eighty-one paid leaves than do men because women are more likely to take care of visiting relatives, to take off work if children are sick, or to attend to other family matters. The argument makes sense in the Kerala context, where women—as in most societies—are expected to bear more of the burden of family responsibilities than men. The insignificant −0.04 coefficient between female percentage and days worked, however, suggests that men are taking just as many extra days. Their reasons may be different, but the effect on primary society profits is apparently the same.

The number of new workers associates negatively with profitability at a medium level of −0.42 and with beedis per worker per day at −0.49. These coefficients suggest that new workers are indeed less skilled at producing large numbers of beedis per day. New workers and female percentage correlate at +0.55. The effects of being new workers and being female workers may be difficult to disaggregate. Are the new workers all women, or are all the women workers new? Or are other factors influencing both these variables? A correlation of −0.37 for number of days worked with percentage of new workers suggests that newer workers are slightly more likely to take off extra days without pay.[11]

The age-by-gender breakdown produces both expected and unexpected results. The percentage of females below age twenty correlates with profitability at +0.41, while the percentage older than forty-five has a −0.40 association. Contrary to our prediction, the percentage of males over forty-five associates at 0.09, essentially no relationship at all. Our prediction of a negative association is not even borne out for beedis per worker per day, which correlates +0.24 with males over forty-five. If older males are not rolling enough beedis to keep up profitability, they are apparently localized in primary societies where other workers are compensating. The correlations do not prove that the older workers are achieving their D.A.—only that primary society average output and profits are not suffering.

FEMALE WORKERS AND MATERNITY BENEFITS

As we have noted in earlier parts of this book, one of KDB's most impressive achievements is its implementation of maternity leaves. KDB is committed socially and politically to maternity leaves, but the cooperative has not been able to grant the full amount prescribed in the Beedi and Cigar Workers' Act. The pattern of rupees spent on maternity leaves associates −0.35 with profitability. But maternity leaves display a varied impact on the different primary societies—an impact that combines both female percentage and the age distribution of the female workers. This can be seen on table 6.6.

In Dharmadam, which shows a 9 percent use of maternity leave, 82 percent of the female workers are older than thirty—that is, mostly beyond the child-bearing age for Kerala women. By contrast, in Kannur city 11 percent of the female workers are below age twenty and another 82 percent are between twenty and thirty. This means that 93 percent of the females are within the main child-bearing ages and probably explains the 36 percent maternity leave usage at Kannur city, which is by far the highest percentage of all the primaries for 1993. Overall, the age groupings correlate with the percentage of females using maternity leaves in 1993 as follows:

females less than twenty   +0.44
females twenty to thirty   +0.20
females thirty-one to forty-five −0.33
females older than forty-five −0.01

The higher maternity use correlation with females below age twenty is surprising in the Kerala context. The figure suggests that KDB women workers are marrying younger and having children ear-

Table 6.6. Female Workers and Maternity Leaves, 1992–93

Primary Society	Total Female Workers	Percent Female of Total Workers	1992–93 Maternity Leaves Used	Percentage of Females Taking Maternity Leaves
1. Kannur city	50	14	18	36
2. Kannur town	54	15	8	14
3. Azhikode	235	25	43	18
4. Chervathur	1,571	66	208	13
5. Thottada	286	31	27	10
6. Kakkad	223	26	23	10
7. Payyanur	631	42	103	16
8. Chala	1,268	43	167	13
9. Chirakkal	260	34	28	11
10. Chalad	107	24	7	6
11. Tellicherry	643	44	101	16
12. Pinarayi	1,558	49	165	11
13. Kottacherry	1,347	81	122	9
14. Manjeshwar	1,398	88	85	6
15. Kadirur	1,189	61	137	11
16. Valiannoor	688	29	137	20
17. Nelishwar	1,155	66	132	11
18. Dharmadam	800	50	72	9
19. Hosdurg	1,470	72	155	11
20. Kasargod	2,181	93	215	10
21. Bediaduka	962	93	80	8
22. Badagara	630	75	67	11
AVERAGES	850	57	84.7	11.6

Source: Computed from KDB primary balance sheets for the year ending 31 March 1993.

lier than women in Kerala generally. This raises the possibility that women who gain employment at KDB are able to consider having children earlier because of the cooperative's benefits during their pregnancies and its guarantee of getting one's job back after giving birth. If the maternity leave program is the reason for the young mothers, KDB might be paradoxically helping to maintain features of northern Kerala society that most observers praise the Kerala Model of development for overcoming: early female marriage and its associated higher birth rates. In 1981, the average marriage age for Kerala women was 21, compared with an all-India average of 19 (Franke and Chasin 1994: 88). Along with lower birth rates, higher age at marriage correlates statistically with lower infant mortality and higher educational levels. The 1991 average age of marriage for females in Ernakulam district, considered one of the state's most advanced on these indicators, was 22.9 years. In Malappuram, a district bordering Kozhikode and closest of those with available data to Kannur and Kasargod, where most KDB workers are, the average female marriage age was 19 in 1991 (Zachariah 1992: 6:6). The Malappuram data coincide with the apparently lower age of marriage suggested by the KDB maternity data. Even so, the figure of only 1.9 children per household in the age cohort 15–29 in a central Kerala village (Franke [1993] 1996: 236) makes the Kannur city primary society figure of 36 percent of women having children in a single year seem unusually high. Unofficial estimates of birth rates per thousand by district for 1988 give 20.3 for Kerala as a whole, 26.4 for Malappuram, 25.2 for Kannur, and 26.8 for Kasargod (Zachariah 1992: 4:5). These higher birthrates for the KDB areas do not seem enough to explain the unusual Kannur city figure but would be consistent with a generally high usage of maternity leaves by KDB female workers in the age groups below 20 and 20 to 30.

Surprisingly, the use of maternity leaves seems to have no impact on average days worked. Number of days worked correlates at only +0.22 with rupees spent on maternity leaves. Number of days worked correlates at only −0.03 with percentage of women taking leaves and +0.27 with number of maternity leaves taken. Apparently, women not having babies and male workers are taking almost as much unpaid leave as are women who take leave to have children. Since KDB gives only partial maternity leave payment, women may be taking only part of the leave. The fifty-two days of general unpaid leave workers take averages 58 percent of the ninety days' paid leave for maternity. Women taking half their maternity leave would be taking about the average leave but getting some money for it. The dynamics of leave taking and of maternity leaves and benefits deserve further research, especially since KDB wants to make good on its promise to fully fund maternity leaves in the near future.

MULTIPLE REGRESSION ON THE VARIABLES

The correlation coefficients provide much useful information. For this study, we can add three valuable elements by also conducting a multiple regression analysis on the data. The multiple regression adjusts the variables in their relation to one another; the correlations only measure the association between two variables at a time. The multiple regression also gives us outcomes in the actual units of the dependent variable—in this case, rupees of profit per worker for the year 1993. The correlation coefficients, by contrast, are units of relationship—more abstract and difficult to interpret. Finally, the multiple regression procedure lends itself to creation of simulated significance figures. The correlation matrix cannot have statistical significance figures associated with it, since it is the entire population rather than a sample from a population. The same is true of the multiple regression, except that we can employ a computerized randomization technique that generates a pseudorandom sample within which the regression statistics can be placed. We have employed this technique with a randomization run of ten thousand to produce the significance numbers shown on table 6.7.[12]

Table 6.7 shows the results of an unweighted ordinary least-squares stepwise regression. We see in the first column the "raw regression coefficients." These raw coefficients are in units of the dependent variable, rupees per worker, per units of the independent variables—aspects of the primary cooperatives and their workforces.

We see from table 6.7 that the most powerful component of primary society efficiency is the percentage of female rollers. Each 1 percent increase in female percentage of rollers causes a decline of Rs 18.94 in profit per worker. We also see that leaf outturn has a positive and statistically significant effect on profit of Rs 3.20 per extra beedi per kilogram, even after the effects of female rollers have been

Table 6.7. Partial Regression Coefficients

Variable	Raw Regression Coefficient	Standardized Regression Coefficient	Significance	R-Square	R-Square Change
In the equation					
Percent female	−18.94	−1.01	.0000	.54	.54
Leaf outturn	3.20	.51	.0037	.73	.19
Intercept	−4050.61		.0365		
Adjusted R-square			.0080	.68	
Not in the equation					
All other variables					

Source: Computed from data in tables 6.1 to 6.6.
Notes: Some elements of this table are not discussed in the text but are presented in accordance with widely accepted statistical practice. The adjusted R-square corrects the R-square downward to compensate for the number of variables in relation to the sample size.

taken into consideration. These two variables account for 68 percent (the adjusted R-square times one hundred) of the variance in primary society profits.

Aside from the particular problems of statistical interpretation raised by our analysis in this chapter, what can we learn generally from the correlations and the multiple regression that will help us understand efficiency at Kerala Dinesh Beedi? The analysis points to three issues: leaf outturn, daily output, and women workers.

Leaf Outturn

Leaf outturn appears as statistically significant in the multiple regression (table 6.7). Table 5.2 indicated that leaf outturn increased from an average of 1,665 per kilo in 1986 to 2,185 in 1992. This is an increase of 35 percent. The average of 2,088 in the reference year 1992–93 means a drop of 4 percent from the previous year, but still a 25 percent increase over 1986. Leaf outturn may be nearing its practical maximum. If not, the regression equations tell us that KDB can increase its profits by Rs 3.2 per worker for each extra beedi per kilogram of leaves. If the price of leaves goes up, the efficiency effect of leaf outturn will increase. It is contained in the price of raw materials to the primary societies, which will be raised by the central society if their price goes up.

Daily Output

The medium negative association of –0.54 between leaf outturn and daily beedi output suggests that attempts to increase output could be largely undercut if these attempts cause declines in leaf outturn. The correlations and the regression equation suggest the need for some experimentation to see how close a relationship will exist at daily output levels above eight hundred. A D.A. threshold of eight hundred fifty beedis could result in more output with improved leaf outturn. But a threshold of nine hundred, for example, might bring on decreased leaf outturn. The thresholds might affect different age and gender groups differently. The data and the relations thus imply complex internal issues for KDB's future survival.

At our June 1994 presentation of these data, central society director board members disputed the negative daily output/leaf outturn relationship. As longtime beedi workers themselves, the directors argued that the amount of leaf given by the maistry each day controls both the worker's leaf outturn and beedi output. At the level of the individual worker, higher outturn should correlate positively with higher output. Is the negative statistical association spurious? Or are maistries more flexible in giving out wrapper leaves than the best workers—those represented on the director board—realize? Maistries could feel pressure to give out extra leaf for two reasons: to help workers reach the D. A. and to help raise output. The experience at Payyanur primary society, discussed in chapter 5, suggests that maistries have to be pushed by higher management to be strict in giving out wrapper leaf bundles in the morning. One result of this approach appears to be Payyanur's first rank in leaf outturn efficiency at 2,284 beedis per kilogram for 1993 as shown in table 6.3. Tobacco outturn was also above average, but daily output was slightly below average (table 6.3), lowering the overall efficiency rank to seven of twenty-two (table 6.1). Payyanur also had only average attendance (table 6.3). These various findings suggest that strict maistry control over leaf supplies to the rollers cannot by itself ensure the optimal combination of high leaf outturn, high daily beedi output, and high attendance that KDB management presumably desires.

Women Workers

The significance of leaf outturn seems intuitively obvious: it is a direct component of worker skill and efficiency in the use of raw materials. The percentage of female rollers, however, is an indirect variable. What is it about female rollers that results in lower profits for their percentage of the workforce? From the correlation coefficients, the interviews, and from our experience with the KDB data, we conclude that female workers are not producing as many beedis per day as are male workers. We can see this in the correlation coefficient of −0.84 between percentage of female rollers and beedis per worker per day. Since percentage of female rollers correlates positively with leaf outturn, it is difficult to attribute lack of leaf-cutting skills to the women rollers. The fact that leaf outturn remains significant in the regression equation after female percentage has been entered, means that the leaf outturn variable worth Rs 3.20 includes male and female rollers and might be mostly a result of lack of leaf outturn skill of the male rollers.

Why do women workers produce fewer beedis per day than their male counterparts? We posed this question at the KDB central society director board meeting. They gave two responses. The first was that women workers miss more days of work. As we have seen, the data on attendance by gender do not seem to support such a view. Their second response was that women are not able to stay sufficient hours or to concentrate adequately while at work. They arrive late because of household chores and child care responsibilities that Kerala men are not accustomed to assuming and leave early for the same reasons.

Our data do not directly support or contradict this idea. It could be tested with time allocation and output studies on men and women workers. Do women often arrive late and/or leave early? Do women with young children produce fewer beedis than other women? Do women produce fewer beedis than men of comparable age and experience? How much more time do women spend on child care and on other household tasks than do male beedi workers? Do the households have servants, older children, grandparents, or other family members to take care of household tasks?

Given KDB's board members' explanations, we asked why they do not invest in day care centers. This met with several objections from KDB management staff and elected director board members. They argued that although the primary societies appear to concentrate adequate numbers of women to justify day care centers, the spread-out work centers actually have too few women with children of the right ages to use the day care centers. We were told that the priority of building day care centers fades when compared with the urgent need for building well-ventilated new work centers, with adequate space and infrastructural facilities to provide necessary conveniences to the workers, both male and female, old and young, who work for KDB. Since KDB is in the middle of major work center construction, however, we see the possibility that day care centers could be planned right into the building program, cutting their cost. Wouldn't their staffing provide additional employment in the Kannur area? And couldn't they attract some paying middle-class customers in a society in which socialized day care is not very available?

As we showed in chapter 5, KDB's director board positions are filled with the most experienced workers. Because of the coop's history, the experienced workers are all men. We also saw that 50 percent of its workers now are women. KDB is thus at an awkward stage in its development where its democratic structures are possibly inadequate to deliver input about certain needs from the very workers who may experience those needs. The absence of significant numbers of women in the upper and even middle levels of KDB's elected management and their total absence on the director board or other upper layers of the central society staff make it difficult to know whether the reluctance to build day care centers is based on genuine knowledge of KDB's best interests or is the result of male prejudice. We heard one unsolicited statement of the need for day care from a female union activist. We also saw several women workers with young children at the work sites.

EMERGING ISSUES: WOMEN, EFFICIENCY, AND SOCIAL JUSTICE

Our findings seem to pose a dilemma for KDB. The cooperative has become an attractive employer for young women in the Kannur region, but it appears that profitability is adversely affected by this change in the composition of the workforce. High wages, guaranteed year-round work, maternity leave, and the other benefits at KDB are drawing more women into the coop, sometimes with their husbands, other times perhaps to provide a salary base while the husbands look for higher-paying local work or try their luck in the overseas Gulf labor market. KDB's success has thus partly engendered a new challenge. This challenge arises because daily output for women is lower than that for men. As we noted, the data show women are not absent from work more than men; therefore, it is likely that the director board members' second explanation is correct: women work fewer hours because of their household burdens. The double shift is thus a practical production problem for KDB as well as a burden on the individual women workers. KDB's competitors in other states also use high proportions of women workers. As we noted in chapter 1, 56 percent of beedi workers nationwide are female. The capitalist com-

petitors may try to undermine KDB's market success by their traditional methods: they pay the women low piece-rate wages and allow
them to work unlimited hours at home, where an effective "self-
exploitation" occurs. KDB pays a price in lost daily output caused by
oppressive institutions outside the workplace; private employers
simply attach themselves to those oppressive institutions.

To continue to survive in a market economy in which its competitors have advantages through exploitation, KDB must make use of
whatever organizational and policy options it can muster. In respond-
ing to the growing female proportion of its labor force, drawing on its
tradition of social justice measures might be such a weapon. The specific measures will have to be new. Day care services for women
workers are a cost of production that might pay for itself in the increased efficiency of an increasingly female workforce.

We also saw the importance of maximizing leaf outturn to improve
profitability and competitiveness. The possibility of a tradeoff between leaf outturn and daily output suggests the need for stricter supervision to ensure greater leaf outturn. We saw the possibilities and
problems associated with this in chapter 5, especially in terms of the
ongoing issue of participation versus supervision. KDB's powerful
mix may need adjustment from time to time.

As a worker-owned business, KDB exists somewhere along a con-
tinuum where one extreme is the unregulated capitalist system that
dominates most beedi production in India. In the absence of strong
unions and progressive political movements capitalism's tendency is
to push down workers' wages and benefits to the level at which
workers can just reproduce themselves while leading miserable lives
and to reduce them to powerless, alienated victims at the workplace.
In this way, workers maximize profits for owners. Most of the Indian
beedi industry currently fits this description. At the other extreme
KDB could theoretically develop into a business in which workers are
so lazy and complacent that they waste resources on a colossal scale.
Such a business would last only by burdening some other sector of
society, which would suffer exploitation to keep it afloat. Neither the
elected management nor the workers at KDB give any indication of
seeking such a position. KDB must maximize efficiency while fulfill-
ing its mission to provide the maximum possible benefits to its workers who are its owners. Finding the best mix of the two is KDB's
market dilemma.

CHAPTER SEVEN

KDB and the International Movement for Workers' Cooperatives

In the previous six chapters, we saw how Kerala Dinesh Beedi was born from a long history of working class formation and the development of high worker consciousness. We saw that much sacrifice and struggle were required to build the cooperative and that particular conjunctions of events helped shape the cooperative's origin and growth, along with the democratic consciousness of the workers and the support of many talented and principled individuals. Today KDB stands as a rare international example of a successful worker cooperative.

But, as we suggested in chapter 1, KDB faces many of the same challenges faced by cooperatives worldwide. Can workers fully own and manage a large industrial enterprise? Do they succeed in gaining better pay and working conditions? Can they make a profit? Will they invest for the future? How do they boss themselves? What kinds of decision-making procedures do they set up to manage the long-term needs of the company? What kinds of conflicts arise between workers and their elected managers and among workers themselves? Can unions continue to function meaningfully in a worker-owned business? In this chapter, we also speculate on two larger issues: Does the experience of workplace democracy affect workers outside the workplace? Does it affect people outside the cooperative?

These several issues can be reduced to two underlying questions: Are workers' cooperatives practical, and are they desirable? In this chapter, we take up these questions as posed in the history and comparative literature on cooperatives and based on the material we have presented concerning KDB. Because KDB never existed in a socialist economy, our discussion emphasizes the literature on workers' cooperatives in capitalist or mixed economies.[1]

THE GENERAL STRUCTURAL REQUIREMENTS
OF A WORKERS' COOPERATIVE

Workers' cooperatives are usually associated with three characteristics: profit sharing, employee ownership, and significant worker participation in decision making—including the appointment of management (Bonin et al. 1993: 1291). The weakest form of a workers' cooperative involves profit sharing only. Capitalist firms have experimented with profit sharing without giving employees power to control the workplace. A second form of cooperative includes worker ownership. This form is found in a number of companies in the United States in the form of the employee stock ownership plan, or ESOP (Poole 1989; Krimerman and Lindenfeld 1992). ESOPs give formal, legal ownership to the firm's employees but do not necessarily encompass egalitarian ideals, since different workers are allowed to own more or fewer stocks and vote according to the capitalist principle of more stocks more votes. Such firms do, however, introduce the concept that workers, voting as stockholders, are responsible for their decisions as voting members of the firm's directorship, thus reaping benefits or accepting losses (Bonin et al. 1993: 1292).

In our view, true workers' industrial cooperatives are of the third type: *owned and managed* by the workers themselves.[2] Ownership here refers to business and not necessarily to capital. Capital may be borrowed; the means of production may be leased. What is important is that the ultimate control of the business decisions rests with the worker members or their elected representatives. Worker ownership also implies that workers must be members; nonmember workers must be avoided. Self-management by the workers does not obviate a separate managerial staff; this may be unavoidable in any medium to large-scale enterprise. But the cooperative's management must be appointed by and accountable to the workers or their representatives. The management structure should also facilitate direct or indirect participation of the workers at various levels. The workers receive wages for their work and also share in the net income of the firm according to their work contribution.

A true workers' industrial cooperative is distinct from a capitalist firm, in which the surplus is privately appropriated. In a private capitalist firm, workers receive the lowest possible wages the owners can get away with paying. Only special market circumstances or the political strength of the workers through unions or labor parties can offset this tendency. The owners share in the net income according to their contribution to the firm's capital. Money invested can bring more return than work performed—this is the classic precondition for exploitation. Opposition to exploitation and the hope of a more just and democratic workplace have fueled many movements for workers' cooperatives over the last two hundred years.

EQUALITY AND DEMOCRACY

One of the major arguments for and against workers' cooperatives concerns equality and democracy. Ethical considerations have been a major motivational force among promoters since the days of Owen. Cooperatives were considered the most ethically desirable form of industrial organization for three major reasons: (1) achieving a more egalitarian income distribution, (2) making the workplace more democratic to make work more meaningful, and (3) creating more democratic individuals to improve overall life satisfaction and to support democracy in society more generally.

Egalitarian Income Distribution

Workers' cooperatives should have an egalitarian impact on incomes at the level of both the macro economy and the firm. The entire net income of the cooperative is either distributed among the worker members or collectively accumulated for future investment (see chapter 4). By contrast, in a capitalist enterprise the surplus generated by the workers belongs to the employer and thus contributes to the concentration of wealth in a narrow stratum. Among small producers, workers' cooperatives can eliminate middlemen's profits—a major source of unearned income. Avoidance of middlemen's profits is an important reason for the state sponsorship of producers' cooperatives in rural handicraft industries in the third world. Given the scattered nature of the petty production units, these industries are characterized by a long chain of middlemen who, through their manipulations in the raw material and product markets, appropriate not only the surplus but more often even a part of the subsistence of the petty producers. As we saw in chapter 1, this has been a powerful tendency in the beedi industry with devastating consequences for noncoop workers and their families. Most reports of the minimum wage committees in cottage industries appointed by different state governments in India have emphasized the importance of producers' cooperatives to facilitate the implementation of minimum wages.

The worker-owned cooperatives are likely to distribute wealth and power more equally among their members than are private capitalist firms. Since private owners want to maximize their profits, they may hire middle and upper management at whatever salaries they think will result in the highest profits. Highly paid executives in turn often become semi-independent powers within the corporations and can raise their incomes far above what is justified by their performance. The managerial elite thus becomes a second layer of exploitation within private corporations. This seems to have happened in the United States during the 1980s, when corporate executives gave themselves enormous raises derived from the output of workers, who were not proportionally compensated. The result was a growth of economic inequality within the United States.[3]

Egalitarianism in Theory and Practice. In chapter 1 we pointed out the substantial wage differentials between KDB and the private beedi sector. This wage difference between cooperatives and private employers largely holds for the entire cooperative sector in India. Statutory minimum wages are normally fully implemented within the cooperative sector, while the private sector ignores them. As we showed in chapter 3, however, KDB has extended this principle by distributing additional surplus in the form of extensive benefits, and, as we showed in chapter 4, it has accomplished this while maintaining adequate investment for the future.

KDB's wage and benefit structure tends toward John Rawls's philosophical principle of justice. Rawls (1971: 62) argued that "all social values—liberty and opportunity, income and wealth, and the bases of self respect—are to be distributed equally unless an unequal distribution of any, or all, of these values is to everyone's advantage."[4]

The justification for any divergence from pure equality Rawls (1971: 76–80) labels the "difference principle."[5] Applying the difference principle to cooperatives, we can predict that workers would support higher incomes for some technical and managerial specialists if they could reasonably expect that the overall performance of the cooperative and thus the workers' own wages, benefits, or job security would improve as a result. Democratic control of power within the cooperative should lead to a wage structure in which only inequalities producing benefits for all would be allowed.

Cross-cultural evidence from worker-owned cooperatives suggests that workers agree with Rawls's principle of justice. The plywood cooperatives in the United States insist on equal incomes for equal amounts of work (Stephen 1984: 171). The Spanish-Basque Mondragón cooperatives limit wage differentials within a particular unit to a ratio of three to one, with the differences going to reward different skill levels (Alleva 1983: 160). In 1990, 1991, and 1992, Mondragón management introduced measures to increase the pay differentials to seven and even ten to one. Workers voted overwhelmingly against the proposals; at one factory the speeches from the floor were so vociferous that the measure did not even come up for a vote (Kasmir 1996: 189–90).

Egalitarianism at KDB: The Ongoing Struggle. Tables 5.3 and 5.4 show that KDB maintains a low level of inequality between production workers and staff. The cooperative maintains no formal ratio between the salaries of managerial staff and those of workers. It appears that insufficient thought was given to leaving pay scales for the managerial staff independent of the earnings of the workers and to including the pay scales of supervisory staff, who are recruited from the workers as part of management. KDB's worker-directors insist that managerial emoluments keep parity with the workers' earnings. In chapter 5 we saw how this led to conflicts between workers and the nonelected management staff. Whereas the workers' earnings are largely determined by the recommendations of the minimum wages committee, the aspirations of the managerial staff are linked to the salaries enjoyed by the employees of the cooperative department of the government. The cooperative department has no direct link to

KDB's business performance. If the staff members' aspirations are met, the result could be significant widening of earning differentials within KDB. The resistance of the worker-directors to this demand has been a major internal source of tension at KDB. Ad hoc compromises are put together from time to time, but no clear policy has developed.

Given the piece-rate system prevalent in the beedi industry, KDB workers receive wages in proportion to their output. As a result there can be significant differences in the daily earnings by gender and age. A more egalitarian wage distribution would be a time rate without reference to output, but this would remove the main material incentive for improving productivity. As we saw in chapter 5, the trade unions opposed changing the daily dearness allowance into a piece-rate system. We discussed at length how the peculiar system of piece-rate basic wages and daily dearness allowance on completion of a minimum quota of output have become a built-in disincentive to achieving maximum daily output by the workers. The problem was aggravated with the decision to reduce the minimum quota of output, a measure introduced with an egalitarian vision, to facilitate higher incomes for older workers. Despite the resulting production crisis, KDB did not consider a piece-rated dearness allowance as an option. It was feared that such a reform would elevate the earnings differentials among the workers to unacceptable levels. Instead, as we described in chapter 5, management and union leaders put more emphasis on moral and political persuasion combined with stricter supervision by maistries to overcome the productivity problem. From 1994 to 1996 the wage system was altered, but the basic structure of the wage and dearness allowance has been retained. Although workers in 1996 had to produce 12 percent more beedis to gain the D.A., they can carry over production from one day to the next for up to one week. The fastest beedi roller can get only one D.A. per day, and the slowest roller is likely to lose no more than one D.A. in a week under the new system. The trade unions, both at KDB and industrywide, have fought to maintain the concept of a day's wages for a day's work despite heavy pressure from the private sector. We saw in chapter 5 that only 16 percent of KDB primary cooperative director board members—made up mostly of veteran trade union activists—favored a piece-rated D.A. that would have introduced significantly greater levels of pay inequality among workers.

Though minimum wages are set by the state government for the whole beedi industry, nonwage benefits are fixed at KDB locally in consultation with trade union representatives. So far care has been taken to ensure a steady improvement in nonwage benefits both in real terms and in relation to wage earnings. These benefits have become a key method of transferring a part of KDB's net income to the workers. The rest of the net income is accumulated for expansion of employment and creation of fixed assets for the benefit of future generations of workers. No dividends are paid on the shares held by the workers.

KDB's worker directors and trade union leaders share a near obsession with egalitarianism in the distribution of nonwage benefits. The annual bonus is uniformly awarded to all workers irrespective of the profit or loss of their particular primary cooperative.[6] Similarly, as we showed in chapter 3, the construction of new work sheds is undertaken on the criterion of need of particular cooperatives without reference to their financial performance. There is virtually no material incentive for any primary cooperative of KDB to perform better than the others. Reliance is on the workers' sense of solidarity and on their political consciousness.

Making the Workplace Democratic

Democracy is the second major ethical principle underlying arguments in support of workers' control. If democracy is the ideal in politics, where people spend little of their time, should it not be even more desirable at work, where people spend around half of their waking hours? Opponents argue that democracy should be limited to the domain of political activity because its extension to the workplace would adversely affect efficiency.

In any large-scale enterprise, labor requires some directing authority. In a capitalist firm this authority is exercised by the capitalist owners or the managers they appoint. It has been argued that the basic objective of the capitalist hierarchical work organization is not technical efficiency but subordination of the labor process to accumulation (Marglin 1974: 34; cf. Braverman 1974). The managerial pursuit of profit maximization, or of sales or growth—ignoring the material and spiritual needs of workers—renders the workplace a contested and often unhappy terrain.

Workers' participation in management should theoretically reduce alienation and enhance labor productivity. John Stuart Mill (1909: 791–92) argued the case from classical economics:

> The other mode in which cooperation tends, still more efficaciously, to increase the productiveness of labor, consists in the vast stimulus given to productive energies, by placing the laborers, as a mass, in a relation to their work which would make it their principle and their interest—at present it is neither—to do the utmost, instead of the least possible, in exchange for their remuneration.

Empirical studies have reported positive correlations between the level of worker participation and economic performance (Estrin, Jones, and Svejnar 1987; Jones 1980; Bellas 1972; Espinosa and Zimbalist 1978). Despite these correlations, most classical economists consider the workers not well equipped for self-management by either talent or training (Jones 1976). They argue that workers do not appreciate the importance of entrepreneurial roles and that excessive egalitarianism may fail to attract talented management: the most popular manager need not be the most efficient one. Webb and Webb (1920: 67) go a step further, arguing that the very concept of labor's hiring the management is self-contradictory: "The relationship set up between a manager who has to give orders all day to his staff, and the members of that staff who, sitting as a committee of management, criticize his action in the evening, with the power of dismissing him if he fails to conform to their wishes, has been found by experience to be an impossible one." A worker-appointed management may shirk its monitoring duty, a situation that outweighs any advantage gained in the incentives for the workers to raise productivity (Alchian and Demsetz 1972: 315). It has also been argued that worker ownership would require a near consensus among members for successful functioning. It further requires designing efficient methods of information flow and consultations among members, which results in additional cost (Arrow 1974: 70).

Thus there appears to be a trade-off with increased labor productivity balanced against declining managerial efficiency with the introduction of workers' control. A major objective of the various labor participation projects, quality improvement, job enrichment experiments, and profit-sharing schemes in capitalist economies is to realize the benefits of increased productivity without yielding capitalist managerial control. Claims of "industrial democracy" through reforms that leave capitalist managers in place have been challenged by radical trade unionists (Clarke 1977). They argue that such experiments are meant to create an illusion of democracy while depending on "manufactured consent" (Burawoy 1983) for increased productivity according to a managerial agenda. Genuine industrial democracy requires worker ownership.

The empirical evidence on the *net* impact of worker control on efficiency, narrowly defined in terms of a technical input/output relationship, is inconclusive (cf. Pencavel and Craig 1994). Therefore, it must be argued that efficiency alone cannot be the criterion for industrial democracy. The argument for workplace democracy has to be rooted in moral grounds. Work has to be viewed as an expression of human creativity and a source of freedom and satisfaction. Therefore, control of workers over their labor is central to human happiness—a goal that is good in itself (Street 1983).

Satisfaction versus Alienation. Making work more meaningful requires overcoming the alienation and regimentation of daily work routines. This makes jobs more satisfying and less oppressive. Cross-cultural data support the idea that this can happen. Coop workers at Mondragón, Spain, feel less inhibited in expressing opinions than do private-sector workers. They also feel that they participate more in making decisions and sense less division between themselves and management than their private-sector counterparts (Whyte and Whyte 1988: 209–10).[7] Canadians in worker-owned coops also express greater feelings of participation than do private-sector hierarchical company workers. The effects are not important among top managers, become noticeable among middle managers, but are especially strong for Canadian shop floor workers (Nightingale 1982: 90, 93, 102). Peruvian peasants underwent rapid attitude changes during the cooperative experiment there between 1969 and 1974. Unions and assemblies met often, and feelings of efficacy increased (McClintock 1981: 325).[8]

The data from Mondragón and the Canadian coops support and expand the findings from the classic study of U.S. worker alienation conducted by sociologist Robert Blauner. Blauner (1964: 32–33) tried to measure the concept of alienation by breaking it down into four components. He labeled the first of these *powerlessness,* whereby workers on assembly lines have no control over the pace of work or other important decisions. The second component he called *meaninglessness,* whereby workers cannot see any relation between their work and their lives. *Isolation* captures the feeling of being a member of society but not really a part of it, of feeling remote from events affecting other people. Finally, Blauner identified *self-estrangement* as a state in which work is only a means to a paycheck, and the individual cannot derive feelings of self-worth from his or her job.

Though he did not study worker-owned coops, Blauner found a range of personality types within U.S. industry strongly suggesting that the degree of participation in and control over workplace decisions contributes significantly to each of these four components of alienation. Printers (now largely replaced by computerized typesetting equipment) displayed the least alienated work-derived personality characteristics, consistent with their high pay, high skill, low degree of supervision, variety of tasks, and pride of accomplishment in their product. Chemical workers, while more alienated than printers, exhibited high pay, low supervision, high skills, and fairly non-alienated characteristics. By contrast, auto workers on assembly lines, though well paid, were intensely supervised or controlled by the pace of the technology and complained of boredom and feelings of worthlessness. The most alienated workers in Blauner's study were in the textile industry, where even the pay was low. Blauner's overall findings suggested that industrial work settings tend to intensify the components of alienation. He did not consider worker ownership and control as a means to attack alienation.

Workplace democracy has to be viewed as a complex and incremental process. Paul Bernstein (1980) identified six dimensions of workplace democracy: participation in decision making, fair remuneration to workers, guaranteed individual rights, a formal judicial process, participatory consciousness, and sharing of managerial knowledge. Participation is the most vital component. Bernstein (1976: 493–95) also developed a list of sixteen types of decisions against which workplace democracy can be tested, from physical working conditions, safety rules, layoffs, and promotions, through investments in new buildings and division of the profits to raising capital, establishing a policy toward other firms, banks, and the government, and research and development. Bernstein suggested that the degree of worker control can range across a seven-point scale, from the suggestion box (the weakest form of participation) through selective veto power over management decisions to the highest form: the workers' council or assembly, which has power superior to that of the management staff. Bernstein also pointed out that different types of worker participation may occur at different levels of an enterprise.

Other scholars have suggested similar indicators of the level of participation. Warner and Peccei (1978: 81–82) listed eighteen types of decisions that determine the direction and ambience of a company and its associated workplaces. These include recruitment, transfer, dismissal and layoff of employees, level and structure of pay, overtime emoluments, holidays, safety measures, restructuring and reorganization of work task, job evaluation procedures and practices, organizational changes such as creation of new departments, work-time rules, selection and appointment of managers and supervisors at various levels, disciplinary measures, and investment policy.

All these studies point to similar conclusions: workplace democracy requires that worker owners have major input or final decision-making power in all areas of policy and implementation and that they have equal voting power in those decisions. Actual mechanisms for the decisions could vary from representative to participatory. A more representative form would consist of an annual meeting at which management is elected, reelected, or replaced and major decisions are ratified or rejected. More participatory control might require that certain decisions be subjected to immediate vote in special elections preceded by informational meetings. The choice of form is probably a mixture of practical and ethical considerations. A satisfying mix of shop floor participation and delegation of authority to elected and accountable representatives depends on the overall cultural and political traditions of the workers as well as the unique economic and historical circumstances of each worker-owned cooperative.

Workplace Democracy at Kerala Dinesh Beedi. KDB would rank in the category of high worker participation and control among all the major cross-national studies cited above. KDB's workers have direct or indirect decision-making power from working conditions at the shop floor through distribution of the surplus at the top management level to building of new work sheds to the cooperative's role in the community. As we saw in chapters 4 and 5, KDB has a three-tier structure: work centers, primary cooperative headquarters, and the central cooperative. The individual worker members elect boards of directors of the primary societies and delegates to the general body of the central society. The twenty-two-member general body elects five of the seven director board members of the central society. The day-to-day managers of the central and the primary cooperatives are appointed by their respective boards of directors. Thus, in principle the cooperative structure is federal. As we saw in chapter 4, however, in practice there has been a tendency toward centralization. The central society sets most of the policies of the managers and the supervising staff of the primary cooperatives. It is the sole purchasing and sales agency and the custodian of all surplus funds, including those of the primary cooperatives. The primary cooperatives thus do not enjoy financial autonomy. The capital investment policy is the sole prerogative of the central society. The salary structure, benefits, holidays, and the like are determined at the central society level through collective bargaining. The individual primary cooperatives may undertake disciplinary actions and devise their own work-time rules and job procedures to some extent. The layoff policy is determined at the central society. Some decision-making power at KDB is thus indirect, through representatives rather than through participation at the level of the shop floor. We feel that insufficient thought has been paid to the elements that could contribute to greater direct participation and democratization of the workplace at KDB.

Making Work Meaningful at Kerala Dinesh Beedi. Beedi rolling is a repetitive, boring activity. Improvement of the working environment and the reading and discussion sessions during the working hours contribute to livening up the atmosphere. The high degree of absenteeism that we reported in chapter 6 is probably an indication that the workers do not always enjoy their work. However, given the craft nature of production and the virtual absence of a division of labor, the beedi rollers exercise a high degree of control over the labor process. The variations of output per day among workers and for the same worker across working days has been a serious managerial problem. A managerial response was the attempt to enforce stricter working hours, but no deterrent punishment was instituted. A major achievement of KDB has been the abolition of the fine system that is universal in the rest of the beedi industry. Instead of fines, a positive incentive for better performance in the form of competitive prizes has been instituted. There is much more scope for further experimentation in this direction, which we feel has not been adequately considered. Moral persuasion through peer group pressure and political campaigns have been the chief means of improving quality and productivity and of ensuring compliance with collective norms. The strong collective feeling within KDB—in part the outcome of the long and painful struggles described in chapters 2 and 3, to achieve the cooperative—give these political incentives a meaning and power absent in private companies and in many cooperatives. Comparative studies of beedi workers in private and cooperative sectors—as indicated in tables 5.8 and 5.9—seem to confirm a greater sense of participation and lower self-estrangement (to use Blauner's term) among workers at KDB.

Workplace Democracy As a Means of Health and Happiness. How much of KDB's worker satisfaction is due to the structure and democratic participation at the cooperative and how much to the higher wages and better working conditions than those of private-sector beedi workers? The interrelations among the various components of worker satisfaction make this question difficult to answer. Worker ownership has been the main mechanism for raising the incomes of beedi workers. Opinion research in the United States consistently shows that workers with higher incomes are happier than those with low incomes (Bok 1993: 230).[9] Kerala's average per capita income in 1993 was Rs 5,065 (at current prices). In Kannur district, the figure was only Rs 4,620 (Government of Kerala 1994: 13). By contrast, the average KDB roller in that year made Rs 11,796. If the roller is his/her family's only source of income, a beedi worker's standard family with four members has only Rs 2,994 per capita. If husband and wife both worked at KDB, their per capita incomes would rise to 5,988, 30 percent above the Kannur average and 18 percent over the Kerala statewide average. Even though KDB workers complain of low wages, they are probably doing about as well as the average Kerala household and probably much better than many workers in other rural industries.

In terms of general health and happiness, job security must be one of the most important benefits.[10] Research in Finland, Sweden, and the United States shows that unemployment leads to social isolation, anxiety, and stress, all of which are associated with deteriorating health. In times of retrenchment, those who still work labor under the fear they will be next to go. Competition among workers increases, also raising stress levels.[11] We cannot say for certain that all these factors work in the same ways in Kerala, with its different cultural context. But the likelihood seems great and would certainly warrant in-depth research. KDB workers have not faced the threat of unemployment since 1969. The occasional cut in the workweek during the monsoon means that all workers share equally in the slowdowns and that the stress-inducing factors such as fear and increased competitiveness that harm workers in capitalist enterprises are thereby minimized.

Beyond wage levels and the threat of unemployment, the nature of the workday exerts an influence on health and happiness. Studies in the United States show that the incidence of heart disease, psychosomatic illness, psychiatric disorders, and social pathology are partly attributable to job dissatisfaction (Mason 1982: 129). Studies in Scandinavia indicate that workers who participate more in constructing their workdays suffer fewer stress-related illnesses than others (Karasek and Theorell 1990).

KDB workers benefit from a general sense of community in their workplace. Voting for director board members, contributing hanks of beedis to the day's reader, hearing reports of achievements in other work centers and of political developments, and belonging to sporting clubs and other community associations supported financially by KDB—all these activities help to reinforce social ties among many workers. With its nonthreatening, noncompetitive environment, KDB may be indirectly encouraging the development of social networks like those that, in studies in Finland, have been found to lower stress and reduce mortality, at least among men (Kaplan et al. 1994). Further research into these economic and structural features of KDB might yield worthwhile information.

Workplace Democracy As a Means of Mobility. We noted in chapter 2 that some Tiyya caste families benefited from the rise of beedi production in the early decades of this century. The problem with mobility through entrepreneurship is that very few can succeed. In a capitalist society they usually succeed at the expense of fellow caste or class members. KDB provides an alternative mechanism for mobility, open to a fairly large cross-section of workers. Through worker ownership, elections, and trade union policies, workers themselves can aspire to salaried and management positions. Rising from the shop floor, the secretary of the Payyanur primary society was trained in necessary clerical skills at cooperative cost, allowing him to move into a permanent position requiring more education than beedi workers usually get, even though Kerala has a high overall literacy rate.

We saw in chapter 5 that the qualities leading to advancement at KDB are experience, dependability, and a record of commitment to fellow workers. The trade unions promote workers through their ranks. Activists who prove their commitment, responsible work habits, and abilities in union leadership are those most likely to be put forth as candidates for primary society director board positions. After gaining experience at this level, some of them can go on to the central society where they will broaden their knowledge and horizons. Neither level of director board position offers much in the way of direct financial rewards, but the exposure to major responsibilities and the experience of seeing one's ideas and skills actually working to solve problems must surely have an impact on the workers' self-perception and eventually on their aspirations for their children. By contrast with the extremely low incomes and limited opportunities for advancement of beedi workers in the past, KDB represents a major new avenue for job mobility. And, as we saw in chapter 3, KDB workers' children do not have to assist their parents in the factory but can attend school. It would be interesting to compare the achievements of KDB beedi workers' children with those of children whose parents work in the private sector: would the KDB children demonstrate more consistent upward mobility?

Workplace Democracy As a Check on Corruption. Corruption and excessive privileges of top management characterize many Indian cooperatives. Kerala Dinesh Beedi has achieved a reputation for a virtual absence of corruption coupled with few privileges for executives at the top. We saw in chapter 5 that in the primary societies, the secretary, foreman, and other staff earn only slightly more than the workers. Director board members receive only minimal sitting fees for meetings and some travel costs. These do not amount to even one-tenth of 1 percent of KDB's operating costs. Such practices were instituted at the demand of the workers' organizations, the trade unions, at the inception of the cooperative. Central society staff members also earn only a few times as much as the production workers.

One traditional capitalist argument for exceptionally high management salaries is the idea that low salaries will only encourage corruption. At KDB worker empowerment and workplace democracy help to limit corruption. Well-designed and well-managed reporting procedures help to check any tendency for dipping into the cooperative's till, but as one primary society secretary explained: "It is very difficult for us to make any falsification of accounts [but] the main reason for the absence of corruption is not these weekly reports or inspections by the central cooperative but rather our commitment. More than that we know that we are keenly observed by the thousands of eyes of our workers. So we have thousands of these observers monitoring us" (Govindan Int: 7 April 1993).

Corruption is limited not only by the structure of the coop but also by its particular history leading to the creation of the radical workers' culture that we outlined in chapter 2. The same secretary evoked this culture when further explaining the checks on corruption: "If I indulge in corruption I won't be able to come out of my house. I won't have any social existence if I am found to be corrupt. Such social pressures prevent the occurrence of corruption and not the statements and queries of the central society" (Govindan Int: 7 April 1993).

Workplace Democracy As a Barrier to Dictatorship. The relation between workplace democracy and overall democracy has historical origins in research on the emergence of fascism. A leading thinker in this area is the psychologist Erich Fromm, who argues (1973: 259–72) that humans have five essential psychic needs. These are (1) a frame of orientation, (2) rootedness, ties to others, (3) a sense of unity, (4) a sense of effectiveness, and (5) stimulation or excitation to avoid boredom.

Fromm's list is very similar to Blauner's psychic features of the work experience. The difference is that Fromm argues further that these needs can be met either in a life-affirming way—through cooperation, equality, participation, developing love and respect for others, and self-respect—or in a destructive way. The destructive way requires the exercise of power over others along with submission to an authoritarian leader or structure. This process led to the popular support for the violence of the Nazi regime. Indeed, Fromm ([1941] 1965) titled one of his earlier contributions to this problem *Escape from Freedom.*

Fromm argues that common features of modern capitalist society predispose people psychologically to fascist movements and dictators. These features include alienation of workers from their jobs and their products—a set of features much like those investigated by Blauner—the boredom of an overly individualistic life combined with expectations for complete happiness and the dependence on consumption as a substitute for interpersonal satisfaction of the basic psychic needs.[12]

Creating More Democratic Individuals: Spillover and Proximity Hypotheses. To the extent Fromm's list is accurate, worker ownership and participation could have consequences beyond the workplace. John Stuart Mill ([1909] 1965: 792) described the "moral revolution in society" that would follow the spread of production cooperatives:

> the healing of the standing feud between capital and labor; the
> transformation of human life from a conflict of classes struggling for
> opposite interests, to a friendly rivalry in the pursuit of a common good
> to all; the elevation of the dignity of labor; a new sense of security and
> independence in the laboring class; and the conversion of each human
> being's daily occupation into a school of the social sympathies and the
> practical intelligence.

Despite his conviction regarding the beneficial moral impact of cooperatives, Mill shared the liberal vision of a dichotomy between civil and political spheres. Modern advocates of the beneficial "spillover" impact of democracy at the workplace would end this dichotomy (Pateman 1970). The extension of the principles of political democracy to industry is justified by the "proximity hypothesis" (Mason 1982: 77–78). Since both industrial and political experience "approximate one another," they may be organized on the same principles. Workplace democracy should lead to values and behavior of workers that make them more active in political life and more supportive of humane, democratic political goals.

To other advocates of industrial democracy (Gorz 1973; Horvat 1982), the struggle for workplace democracy holds the key to the transition to a socialist and democratic society through a process of escalation from democracy at work to democracy in the entire economy. According to Greenberg (1986: 21–22):

> The theory suggests that the experience of democracy in the most immediate work environment is an essential educative tool in the growth of socialist consciousness because in such an environment a person comes to appreciate cooperative and collective efforts, cultivates confidence in productive skills, and develops a sense of power as a member of a class; here, too, human talents and abilities become sufficiently developed that the absurdity of capitalist social relations becomes clear.

Greenberg (1986: 22) continues by noting that "as workers gain a sense of confidence in their abilities through the practice of democracy, the desire to control their own destiny begins to escalate to higher levels, first to the level of the enterprise and eventually to the entire economy."

Industrial democracy advocates received a rude shock from Greenberg's evidence showing that in the celebrated plywood cooperatives in the United States the workers were more conservative and less egalitarian in attitude than private-sector workers. His evidence pointed out that the political impact of workplace democracy depends upon the social context of the experiment. He distinguished between capitalist societies that are "mediated" by social forces opposed to capitalist social, political, and cultural domination—like Italy and France—and those that are devoid of any such mediation—like the United Kingdom and the United States. In the latter two "unmediated" societies, industrial democracy tends to reinforce the dominant value system. The spontaneous workers' self-management that springs up in revolutionary situations could have an altogether different impact (Greenberg 1986).[13]

Here our study of KDB runs into a problem. Beedi workers are known throughout Kerala for their political awareness and activism, and they continue to be a strong support base of communists. But how much of this can be attributed to their experiences in the cooperative? Have beedi workers become more democratic because of KDB, or did KDB succeed because they were so democratic and activist?

It is difficult to answer this question fully from the research we have conducted. The most desirable approach would be a study of levels of democratic belief and participation at the time of the founding of KDB and in a recent year. In the absence of such studies, we can say that the long experiences of beedi workers in politically active unions, the independence movement, and Kerala's democratically oriented communist parties have probably created strong feelings of activism instead of passivity, participation instead of apathy, and questioning instead of automatic obedience. KDB benefited from the activist, democratic experiences of its workers.[14] During the 1930s to 1960s and for a period during the "Emergency" of the late 1970s, beedi workers distinguished themselves as self-sacrificing advocates of democracy. In chapter 2, we described their role in fighting for an independent and democratic India. Following proclamation of the Maintenance of Internal Security Act (MISA) in the 1970s—the main implementing device of the Emergency—hundreds of beedi workers were arrested. Pandiyala Gopalan Master, the president of Pinarayi primary society, and director board member A. T. Rajan were among those arrested. Kannur Tobacco Workers' Union Secretary N. Abdulla died in custody at Kannur central jail—probably from maltreatment (Chandran 1984: 89–90). Beedi workers not only fought government repression but also successfully resisted RSS attacks (see chapter 3) that increased during the emergency. The price was seven workers killed, including a leading activist, Kolangaroth Ragavan, who was murdered at work (Pandakal 1984: 55–56).

At the same time, KDB's success seems from our data to have led to some increase in worker passivity, part of the feeling that the workers have already attained as much as they can hope for. Since the cooperative works reasonably well and the paychecks tend to improve, what are the reasons to be more active? The challenges facing KDB in the near future—especially the need to diversify from tobacco to other kinds of production—will clearly put the democratic and activist potential of KDB's beedi workers to a severe test. We will return to this problem in the afterword.

KDB, DEGENERATION, AND THE KERALA MODEL

In chapter 5 we examined the shop floor at KDB in relation to the idea that cooperatives naturally tend to degenerate into capitalist firms. For structural as well as political reasons, KDB seems largely immune from this. KDB's membership is not open to "producers" in general—including wage-labor-employing petty capitalists—but is exclusively confined to its own workers along with a few sympathizers. This contrasts with many other industrial cooperatives in India that consist of both workers' cooperatives and general producers' cooperatives. Of late the tendency has been to reorganize cooperatives on the principle that all or nearly all workers must be members and all or nearly all members must be workers. In Kerala, this gradual transition is nearly complete.

At KDB workers are directly employed in common work sheds owned by the cooperative. Although nonmembers may be employed for temporary casual work such as transportation, membership is a precondition for employment in the main production process of beedi manufacture. The virtual prohibition of wage employment for nonmembers is a guarantee against degeneration. The history of KDB's expansion—as outlined in chapter 3—verifies the cooperative's acceptance of the social function to generate employment for as many workers as possible even after the official target of rehabilitation of the original 12,000 displaced workers was met. KDB's other direct contributions to the social welfare of its immediate community and of Kerala generally are noted in chapters 5 and 6.

In chapter 5 we saw that KDB offers complex mixed evidence on the applicability of the iron law of oligarchy. The cooperative's creation and survival have depended on a strategic mix of three elements: *mobilization, efficiency,* and *justice.* The beedi workers' mobilization—based on decades of commitment and struggle—gave them extraordinary capacities to sacrifice and work together in the early years as well as the ability to inject their product into the market in a novel way—through class solidarity. The efficiency of their structure, which involves a delicate balance of participation and delegation of authority, gave them short-term parity with capitalist firms in the same sector. The justice they have achieved makes their lives better and has improved the economies of their nearby communities as well. As we have seen, however, justice and security do threaten to lead to complacency that could undermine the very forces that made success possible in the first place.

KDB was born and survived for another reason as well. Like the beedi workers' militant unions, the class-conscious consumers, and the early sympathizer members, KDB has been a component of the larger phenomenon now called the "Kerala Model," to which we referred in chapter 1. Indeed, at the very moment that KDB was being born in Kannur in 1969, peasants in Malabar and other parts of Kerala were culminating a century of land reform struggle by occupying plots and planting red flags to indicate their willingness to fight physically if necessary to make the land reform law of 1969 a reality.[15] Education, activism, optimism, and democracy combined in Kerala for many reasons that lie outside the scope of this study.[16] Like other social movements, the forces that built KDB influenced, and were influenced by, developments in the larger society of which they have been a part.[17] KDB's survival thus depends on further developments in the Kerala Model, and the model in turn may depend on what KDB—with its size and resources—can do to further it.

KDB's continued and active identification with larger movements may insulate it from the dangers of the Weber-Michels "iron law." In chapters 2 and 3, we saw how KDB emerged from the radical, activist workers' culture in Malabar that was itself a key component of the Kerala development model. Rothschild and Whitt (1986: 128) hypothesized in their comparative study of cooperatives that *"the more a collectivist organization* [such as a workers' cooperative] *remains identified with and oriented toward the broader social movement that spawned it, the less likely it is to experience goal displacement* [oligarchical tendencies]."[18] This hypothesis grows out of the attempt by sociologists Zald and Ash (1966) to generalize the Weber-Michels iron law. They discovered that the founders of movement organizations tend to arise from the movement's ideology and idealism, while the next generation of organization members tends to be more involved with maintaining the organization. By participating in the larger movement for change and development in Kerala, KDB members could avoid this tendency and renew their commitment to the general struggle that gave birth to their cooperative—only now they would be participating in that movement's next generation of activities. Actions seem more promising as recruiting devices than wistful speeches by older union activists about a glorious heritage of struggle the younger workers view from an increasingly distant time.

KDB's recent involvement with Kerala's Left Democratic Front and its associated popular movements gives reason for optimism that activism and participation will continue to hold back degeneration.

One example took place in 1989–90, when Kerala's left government joined with mass organizations and the Kerala People's Science Movement (KSSP) to mobilize thousands of teachers and college students to conduct a "Total Literacy Campaign." This campaign succeeded in bringing basic literacy to nearly all adults in Kerala (Kerala Sastra Sahitya Parishad 1991; Tharakan 1990). Many units of KDB participated actively in the campaign. At Bediaduka primary society, literacy activists identified 7 percent illiterates among the male workers and 29 percent among the females. These percentages represented about two hundred workers who had traditionally signed for their wages by pressing a thumb onto an ink pad and putting a thumbprint onto the ledger book. The primary society held lunch hour literacy classes at work for several weeks. The Bediaduka primary society secretary even told the illiterate workers he would eventually refuse them their salaries unless they could sign their names properly. He says it was only a threat; the wages, of course, would have been paid. But after several weeks, nearly all the workers achieved the ability to write their names and many other words and to read in Malayalam at the campaign target speed of thirty words per minute (Secretary, Bediaduka primary society Int: 25 March 1993).

STATE SPONSORSHIP AND WORKER SOLIDARITY

A basic constraint on the performance of industrial cooperatives in India has been the nature of the industries these cooperatives were to have promoted. Most of the traditional and cottage industries are under severe pressures from raw material and product markets. Promotion of industrial cooperatives in this sector was itself a response to the failure of private-sector manufacturers and traders to guarantee a minimum living to the workers. In this respect KDB was more fortunate. It operated in a buoyant demand market. The workers' beedi cooperative, paying all the statutory wages and benefits to the workers, could compete with the cheaper products of the private sector because it had deep and widespread solidarity in Kerala based on two significant factors. First, the struggles we referred to in chapter 1 that created the Kerala Model meant that people were not only skilled in writing letters and sending around petitions, but they were also keenly aware of the need to respond to them. When union activists sent around their sales brigades, as described in chapter 3, enough people understood the political need to switch immediately to Dinesh beedis. The cooperative thus did not have to build brand loyalty according to a normal market timetable. Second, the tremendous energy, enthusiasm, and optimism unleashed by the decades of struggle gave the cooperative's founders the means to overcome their limited technical and financial resources.

KDB's early rush of energy and solidarity has waned but is still impressive; it plays an essential role in the cooperative's continuing success. This helps to explain why KDB has done better than other Indian industrial cooperatives even though the others have often received more government support and have had less hostile competition. State sponsorship—despite its positive effect in expanding the number of cooperatives—has also introduced extreme bureaucratization that stifles member initiative. A typical producer cooperative in India is formed from above by the government department concerned, often mechanically within a set plan target. The cooperative bureaucracy thus created tends to become a management structure alienated from the workers. Though nonmembers are generally not employed in the cooperative, in most of the cooperatives the majority of members are nonworkers. Therefore, the elected worker representatives in the management may not genuinely represent the workers. The advantages of the cooperative form of production over that of capitalist firms, springing from the solidarity of the cooperative's workers, is thus lost.

In contrast, as we saw in chapters 2 and 3, the formation of KDB was the outcome of a genuine workers' initiative from below; the role of the government was more that of facilitator. The politically charged circumstances of KDB's origin have left a distinct birthmark on the cooperative. As we noted above, corruption is limited in part by the radical workers' culture of northern Kerala. We have seen how, despite an adverse incentive system, the productivity of both leaf outturn and per-worker output has been improved through moral persuasion and peer scrutiny. The ability of the cooperative to maintain product quality has been an important factor in strengthening consumer loyalty to its brands.

The Accumulation Debate

The accumulation process within KDB has belied the usual notions of long-run inefficiency of workers' cooperatives. We showed in chapter 4 that Vanek's model of self-extinction does not apply to accumulation at KDB. KDB has been pursuing a strategy not only of maximizing earnings per worker but of combining a steady improvement of workers' earnings with expansion of employment. The short-run objective was to maximize the surplus after meeting the guaranteed payout to the workers. Since the wages are set industry-wide within the state, the improvement in workers' earnings can be achieved only through improvement in the nonwage benefits. Worker members have no claim on the accumulated assets. Only the face value of the share can be claimed on retirement. Chapters 3 and 4 indicate that KDB's accumulation facilitated a fully self-financed employment expansion and improvement in working conditions. Adjustments in output have been achieved through changes in the days of employment of the existing workforce rather than through retrenchment. These adjustments have resulted from the combined factors we described earlier: worker sharing and solidarity, trade union idealism and egalitarianism, and efficient and nonexploitative management.

The financial management system devised by the central society has contributed significantly to KDB's success. As we saw in chapter 4, financial surplus is not allowed to accumulate in the primary cooperatives. It is held by the central society either directly as its undistributed profit or indirectly in accounts of the primary cooperatives. Decisions about how to invest or allocate the surplus are also made at the central society level.

The Politics of Workers' Cooperatives

The support extended by the trade unions and the political parties to central society decisions reached with active participation of the worker representatives constitutes rejection of a narrow populist notion that the entire surplus created belongs immediately to the current workers. As we saw in chapter 4, the present undistributed surplus accrues not to the current workers but to future workers. The trade unions—instead of being merely the protectors of the immediate interests of the workers—have taken a longer vision of the growth of the firm. It is difficult to evaluate KDB independently of this political process.[19]

The Limited Role of Nonworker Sympathizers

KDB has shown flexibility in using the funds and political support of sympathetic members of the Kannur community. In addition to the production workers, up to 5 percent of a primary society's membership can come from outsider "sympathizers." Sympathizer members were important in the early years of KDB. They provided the full Rs 20 payments to join, lessening dependence on the state government. Many were well-known professionals such as doctors and artists whose support also provided valuable encouragement to the struggling laid-off beedi workers. At first, a few accepted appointments to positions in KDB to give publicity and support to the beedi workers' cause. In keeping with KDB's worker-oriented democracy, they have receded into the background and play little if any role in the affairs of KDB today. The 5 percent sympathizer option, however, does make it possible for KDB to offer membership to a few technical specialists whom the director boards want to involve in coop activities in addition to paying them salaries.

SOCIALIST DEBATES ON WORKERS' COOPERATIVES

Most of the trade union leaders and a large body of the membership of KDB have been inspired by Marxist ideas. What theoretical basis does Marxism provide for the formation of a workers' cooperative within a nonrevolutionary, capitalist society? The political significance of workers' cooperatives under capitalism caused important differences of opinion among the various schools of socialism.

In chapter 3 we referred to the New Lanark experiment set up by Robert Owen and his followers. This utopian experiment was followed in England by the Fabian socialism of the Webbs, emphasizing consumer cooperatives, which eventually became dominant. The Chartists moved the English working class movement away from utopian socialist experiments. It was in the Chartist newspaper, *Notes to the People,* that Marx, in collaboration with Ernest Jones, carried out his polemics against Christian Socialist cooperative supporters. Marx criticized the utopian cooperative movement for what he saw as fallacious claims. He also criticized its paternalistic character, devoid of connection with working class struggles (Jones 1978a and 1978b: 573–82). Marx ([1866] 1973:27–28) considered workers' cooperatives "spontaneous movements of the working classes" and urged workers "to embark in cooperative production rather than in cooperative stores."

Marxist revolutionary socialism saw the cooperative movement "as one of the transforming forces of the present society based upon class antagonism," which demonstrated the practical possibility of transcending capitalism. However, in Marx's view, individual cooperatives of workers in themselves were incapable of bringing about the social transformation:

> Restricted, however, to the dwarfish forms into which individual wage slaves can elaborate it by their private efforts, the cooperative system will never transform capitalistic society. To convert social production into one large and harmonious system of free and co-operative labor, general social changes are wanted, changes of the general conditions of society, never to be realized save by the transfer of the organized forces of society, viz., the state power, from capitalists and landlords to the producers themselves. (Marx [1866] 1973:27–28)

Capturing political power thus held the key to the revolutionary transformation of society. Here the anarchists parted company with the Marxists. The anarchists stood for destruction of the state rather than seizing it. They expected that the removal of tyrannical state power would spontaneously give rise to a cooperative order from below through a process of improvisation and experimentation by the workers (Ward 1972; Guérin 1970). The 19th century Russian anarchist Kropotkin called for an extensive network of mutual aid institutions, arguing that such "mutual aid" was a natural tendency of working people. The influential French anarchist Pierre Joseph Proudhon further developed the ideas of mutualism that the French trade unions carried forward. To the syndicalist the general strike was the weapon to disrupt the capitalist order and the trade unions the agents of industrial governance. With their emphasis on decentralized participation, anarchists were a fertile source for individual cooperative experiments (Rothschild and Whitt 1986: 14–18). As we noted, anarchist ideals continue to influence the cooperative movement to the present, especially in first world cooperatives inspired by the New Left. In Kannur, anarchism has had little influence. Marxist ideas and Communist Party organizations have the loyalty of most workers, who believe that socialist transformation is not possible without the revolutionary capture of state power, which alone would create a socioeconomic framework facilitating full development of cooperative enterprises on a national scale. Isolated cooperative enterprises within the capitalist mode of production are circumscribed by the conditions of their birth and are likely to degenerate in the long run. Many Marxists, such as Ernest Mandel, have emphasized this aspect of Marx's analysis and adopt a negative attitude toward cooperative experiments (Coates 1976: 16–19). These thinkers neglect the question, can workers' cooperatives, despite their limitations, also be an instrument to raise awareness and mobilize workers for social revolution?

The study of KDB points out the need to put workers' cooperatives in their proper social context. Marx criticized the cooperative experiments of the utopian socialists for their isolation from the actual struggles of the workers (Marx and Engels [1848] 1972: 359–61). He enthusiastically approved of the advance over the English cooperatives—set up by the paternalistic utopian/Christian socialists—made by the cooperatives on the continent that were "in fact, the practical upshot of the theories, not invented, but loudly proclaimed, in 1848" (Marx [1864] 1972: 380). The latter were spontaneous working class organizations arising from the struggle. Therefore, Marx recommended that workers join producers' cooperatives and went on to discuss certain vital principles that maintain the democratic character and the incipient socialist orientation of such cooperatives (Marx [1866] 1973: 28).

The most comprehensive Marxist treatment of the political role of workers' cooperatives has received little attention in recent scholarship. Lenin's "The question of cooperative societies at the International Socialist Congress at Copenhagen" in 1910 (Lenin [1910] 1967b: 275–83) is a concise statement of the contending ideological trends among the international working class movement. Lenin identified three major beneficial contributions of cooperatives: (1) they improve the conditions of workers by restricting middlemen and influencing working conditions, (2) they can render assistance to the struggles of workers in times of strikes, lockouts, and victimization, and (3) they can teach the workers independent management and organization of distribution, preparing them for the future socialist society. At the same time, Lenin emphasized that the improvements secured by cooperatives under capitalism are confined to very narrow limits. There exist severe competitive pressures for degeneration. Not being organizations of direct struggles against capital, cooperatives may create illusions among the workers. Therefore, he put the following program of action before the socialists:

> (a) to join proletarian co-operative societies and promote their development in every way, directing their organization along strictly democratic lines (a low entrance fee, one share per person etc.); (b) by untiring socialist propaganda and agitation within the societies to help spread the ideas of class struggle and socialism among the mass of the workers; (c) with the growth of socialist understanding in the co-operative societies, to develop and strengthen organic ties between the co-operative societies and socialist party and also the trade unions; (d) at the same time the Congress points out that producer co-operatives can contribute to the struggle of the working class only if they are component parts of the consumer co-operatives. (Lenin [1910] 1967a: 266)

The last point is at variance with Marx's attitude toward the consumer cooperative movement in England, which had become a major barrier to the development of production cooperatives. Marx's recommendation to the workers ([1866] 1973: 28) had been "to embark in cooperative production rather than in cooperative stores." Lenin may have had the continental context in mind. His emphasis was on linking the two cooperative movements. Rosa Luxemburg ([1899, 1908] 1970), whose polemic against Bernstein made her an ardent advocate of the degeneration thesis, also pointed to the importance of insulating the production cooperatives from market pressures through the buffer of consumer cooperatives.

How does KDB measure up to the political expectations discussed above? KDB's organizers have no illusions that a single beedi cooperative constitutes socialism. However, even the rank-and-file workers consider the cooperative qualitatively distinct from private-sector beedi firms, a distinction that has been confirmed by their experience. It may be considered a hybrid variety, a democratic enterprise but functioning to a large extent according to the market rules set by the larger capitalist economy. Knowledge of the potential degenerative tension between the micromanagement and the macroenvironment was the reason for the initial hesitation of many trade union leaders in 1969 to opt for a workers' cooperative rather than a government-owned corporation.

Trade Unions and Cooperatives—Uneasy Alliance?

The antipathy of trade unions to workers' cooperatives has a real basis. The cooperative renders the traditional adversarial role of trade unions ambiguous. They are forced to be crisis managers and watchdogs of productivity. The self-exploitation within the cooperative in the struggle for survival may undermine union standards; the firm's success can undermine union influence. Therefore, unions do not consider workers' cooperatives an alternative to collective bargaining; they are adopted in self-defense against unemployment.

Such trade union initiatives even for self-defense cooperatives have been rare in the United States and the United Kingdom. We noted earlier that the producer cooperatives in the United Kingdom are isolated from the mainstream working-class movement by their middle-class roots. A great proportion of them were offshoots of consumer cooperatives or creations of paternalistic reformers rather than the outcome of trade union initiatives (Cornforth 1983; Jones 1976). In the United States, most mainstream trade unions were involved only peripherally in workers' cooperatives, but there were some exceptions, such as the Knights of Saint Crispin or the Knights of Labor (Aldrich and Stern 1983). By contrast, in many European countries production cooperatives and trade unions had close relationships. The association of cooperatives and trade unions has contributed to the greater vitality of the cooperative movements in France and Italy. The workers' enterprises of France, originating from the mutual aid societies of the 1848 revolutionary period, exhibited a pronounced socialist orientation (Batstone 1983; Oakeshott 1978). In Italy the major cooperative federations are affiliates of trade union/political formations. Lega, the cooperative federation, is dominated by (former) Communists and by socialists (Thornley 1983).

The Mondragón cooperative network in Spain is an example of a cooperative that was successfully created and run with virtually no trade union involvement. The cooperative had been formed during the fascist regime when all trade union activity was banned. The church became the social organizer of the working class; the cooperative offered an alternative solidarity center to the workers under fascism. The radical politics and republican, antifascist sympathies of the Basque people were important elements of the social environment that nurtured the Mondragón cooperatives (Oakeshott 1982; Kasmir 1996). But even today at Mondragón—one of the most successful of all workers' enterprises—workers remain nonunionized.

What is the role of trade unions in a worker-owned and -managed firm? The debate on the roles of unions in cooperatives is reminiscent of a controversy that raged in revolutionary Russia in the early 1920s on the role of trade unions in a workers' state. While Trotsky argued for trade union subordination to management, Shlyapnikov urged the subordination of management to the trade unions. Lenin criticized Trotsky's opposition to union power (Lenin [1921] 1970b) as well as Shlyapnikov's call for trade union control of the industries (Lenin [1921] 1970a). Lenin ([1923] 1970c) took an intermediate position, attempting to improvise as the situation evolved. He thought that trade unions and management, though no longer adversaries as in the past, would continue to have distinct roles in the transitional society. Lenin realized that trade unions in a workers' state involved contradictory roles and therefore that "special tact" was required for the successful conduct of trade union activities. He advocated interventions of the Communist Party in the disputes that would inevitably result from these contradictory roles (Lenin [1922] 1970d: 471).

The traditional trade union role of protecting the workers' interests would continue to have relevance even in a cooperative owned and managed by the workers themselves. To begin with, a separate managerial cadre is required in any medium- to large-scale enterprise. Workers' participation in the management would necessarily have to be representative. There is every possibility that over time the workers' representatives might become alienated from the workers—the management might develop its own vested interests. Further, to survive the competitive pressures of the market, management would have to adopt strategies to increase labor productivity. This would create situations of conflict. The imperfect democratization of management and the nature of the market economy make the presence of trade unions desirable even in a workers' cooperative. In Mondragón, in the absence of trade unions, a new institution—the social council—had to be introduced to represent the members of the society as workers (Thomas and Logan 1982: 28–29; Whyte and Whyte 1988: 213–16). A recent study of Mondragón, however, strongly suggests that workers might prefer unions to what they apparently see as a paternalistic structure not able to represent their interests (Kasmir 1996: esp. 190–92).

The Trade Unions at KDB

In KDB one of the primary functions of trade unions is to negotiate with management for wages and benefits. The unions participate in industrywide collective bargaining for wages. The wages are eventually set by minimum wage committees appointed by the state government. At KDB, the nonwage benefits are fixed through local negotiations with management represented by the central society. We have seen how many of the welfare and social security measures grew out of trade union initiatives. The bonus is the major item of annual negotiation. The trade unions directly participate in implementing the social security scheme. The decisions of the pension and welfare committee are considered mandatory. Another traditional function performed by the trade unions concerns disciplinary actions taken against the workers by management. On rare occasions, when a settlement cannot be negotiated within the cooperative, recourse to legal measures is taken by some unions. Management also consults the unions with regard to limiting production, recruitment of new workers, etc. The multiplicity of trade unions gives the workers a genuine choice of organizations to represent them and puts pressure on the unions to be vigilant in protecting their members' rights. The price for the genuine choice is interunion rivalries and the consequent problems that we described in chapter 5.

In chapter 5 we also noted new roles played by the trade unions in the cooperative. From their ranks emerge the member directors and a majority of the supervisory staff. The trade unions are effectively a school for leadership in the cooperative. They also try to maintain worker enthusiasm for KDB. They are the main feedback mechanism between management and the shop floor. The demands of the trade unions within KDB have always been tempered by considerations of profitability. Accumulation of a major share of the surplus could not have occurred without conscious trade union support. Interunion rivalries have so far not led the unions to make irresponsible demands.

The temptation for leaders of the small unions to make irresponsible demands must be great. By appealing to the workers to demand more of KDB's surplus, they could conceivably undermine the CPM-dominated unions and strengthen themselves, even at the long-term expense of the cooperative. At least four factors probably hold them back. First, worker loyalty to the CPM-oriented unions is sufficiently strong to make opportunistic appeals difficult to carry off. Second, the non-CPM-oriented workers have enough understanding of the history of their cooperative and the sacrifices and dedication of the CPM leaders to be wary of attacks on those leaders. And third, the general political culture of Kerala in recent years has encouraged unity and cooperation among workers, farmers, and middle-class persons in such a way as to limit the capacity of strident opponents to make much headway. In chapter 3 we noted the similarities between KDB's record of cooperation among groups otherwise hostile to each other and the CPM's approach to development recently fostered by party leader E. M. S. Namboodiripad (1909–1998). The creation of an attitude of compromise among as many organizations and individuals as possible in place of sectarian political struggle surely helps create an environment in which minority party or minority union sectarianism appears out of touch with the needs of the people. A fourth reason for small unions to curb their demands is that the workers are undoubtedly politically sophisticated enough to understand the consequences of consuming all the surplus.

The unions' self-restraint within the cooperative and the new roles expected of them make their functioning much more complex. Thornley (1983: 336–41) has drawn attention to the failure of the Italian trade unions to adapt to the roles as worker representatives within the cooperatives despite the close historical relationship between the two and the active role of the unions in founding the workers' cooperatives during the 1970s. Within KDB an effective approach has evolved over time. The management and trade union roles have remained fairly distinct even though union militants often become director board members. The style of functioning of both the management and the unions ensures that conflicts are mostly kept within limits. Serious conflicts have been resolved through mediation of the Communist Parties. Both the main Communist Parties—CPM and CPI—have party-level committees with representatives in such groups as staff unions, trade unions, and worker directors. These committees meet periodically to sort out contentious issues. However, there have not been sufficient efforts by the political parties or the trade unions to formally theorize about their experiences.[20]

Dual allegiance to the firm and the union and the muted class struggles at the point of production adversely affect trade union morale. The cooperative gives the workers a false sense of security that makes them complacent. In chapter 5 we saw that experienced unionists consider complacency a problem especially among new workers who have not had the experience of the struggle for creation of the cooperative. The decline in class consciousness and solidarity undermines the success of the cooperative. There is no easy solution to this problem. The emphasis of the trade union leaders has been on political education, which, as we saw in chapter 5, has satisfied neither workers, who apparently prefer their "pulp literature," nor union leaders, who decry the workers' tastes but seem to have no alternative ideas.

Against signs of apathy, we should balance the positive contributions of KDB toward mobilizing beedi workers. It was the formation of the cooperative in 1969 that saved the beedi trade union movement in Kannur from collapse when the majority of union members faced permanent layoffs. The expansion of the cooperative slowed the decentralization of beedi production into the households of workers under the putting-out system. A major reason for the union demand for cooperatives in the cottage industries is to reorganize production from the household to common work yards where the workers become conscious of their collective identity.

Despite fears that the workers' cooperative would undermine union standards, the wage and nonwage benefits at KDB have become reference points for wage bargaining in the private sector. KDB proves in practice that beedi firms can work profitably even after paying all the statutory benefits. Thus, KDB has become an inspiration to emulate on a national scale as part of a larger trade union strategy to mobilize beedi workers in India. The national conference of the Federation of Beedi Trade Unions held at Kannur in 1993 devoted a special session to the relevance of the KDB experience to the problems of workers in the unorganized sectors in India (All-India Convention of Beedi Workers 1993). The late KDB chairman G. K. Panikkar was formally honored at the workers' conference. The conference resolved to organize model workers' cooperatives in major centers of beedi production. The expectation is that KDB's success in providing the workers with statutory benefits could be a powerful stimulus for the national mobilization of beedi workers.

But can KDB survive in present-day India as more than an oddity produced by the unique circumstances of Kerala's history and development? Will it be just another cooperative incorporated as a minority feature into a larger capitalist economy? Will its workers become increasingly less democratic and involved—more like workers in the more traditional, private sector? Can KDB expand its influence beyond beedis?

Tobacco Production and Diversification at KDB

Even the most sympathetic observer of KDB's many accomplishments will sooner or later raise the question whether it is ethical for workers to produce a produce that harms others. To readers outside Kerala, the health effects of smoking seem personally more immediate than the wage and benefits struggles of workers in a faraway place. At the same time, the high literacy rates in Kerala and among KDB workers mean that this book will be read by KDB's workers and worker-directors.[1] For them, the problem of smoking may seem more remote than the need to maintain the jobs for which they have fought and sacrificed so much. In this brief afterword, we propose to survey these difficult issues.

THE ETHICS OF TOBACCO PRODUCTION

Concern with the ethics of tobacco production derives from the mounting scientific evidence that tobacco—whether smoked, chewed, or inhaled secondhand—brings on diseases that cause suffering and premature death. Consequently, how can a workers' cooperative justify the continuation of such production? There are several dimensions to this issue. Let us first consider the main medical data that have come out of Western and Indian sources.

Since the U.S. surgeon general's report of 1964, smoking has increasingly become a public health matter in the United States. Scientific evidence from over seven thousand studies prior to the 1964 report implicated several of the components of tobacco smoke in causing lung cancer, other respiratory and circulation system diseases, and a wide variety of other health problems, including low birth weight in babies. In 1989, the U.S. government estimated that 390,000 Americans died from diseases caused by smoking (CDC 1990: v). The risk of developing lung cancer is twenty-two times higher in men and twelve times higher in women who smoke than for those who do not (CDC 1990: vi). One result of the growing public awareness of the dangers of smoking has been a dramatic decline: whereas 50 million Americans continued to smoke in 1989, 38 million had quit (CDC 1990: i). By 1991, 28 percent of American men and 24 percent of women smoked (Shenon 1994), down from a 40 percent overall average in 1965 (CDC 1989: i). Despite the reductions, smoking cost Americans an estimated $50 billion in health care expenses in 1993 (Hilts 1994).[2]

What are the ethical implications of a worker-owned cooperative's making tobacco products? Before drawing the obvious conclusion, we think a few qualifying factors should be considered. First, smoking is more common among poor and working-class people in the Western countries. In the United States, blue-collar workers and low-income ethnic minorities are the heaviest users of tobacco products (CDC 1989: vii). One possible reason for this is that poor people's lives lack other sources of gratification available to persons who are better off. The tobacco habit gives a bit of consolation and satisfaction. In Kerala, beedis are known as "the poor man's smoke." If that smoke is not available, what will take its place? Would KDB workers help low-income Indians to stop smoking just by stopping their production of beedis?

Second, research shows that most of the effects of cigarette smoking, in the United States at least, show up in persons smoking more than twenty cigarettes per day. A KDB beedi has about half the tobacco of an American cigarette, so it is possible that the most serious health consequences would require smoking of forty beedis or more per day. This would be a significant expense for most Kerala laborers.

These qualifications, however, seem insufficient to counter the nearly certain health dangers of beedi smoking. In India, surveys suggest that 70 percent of men and 15 percent of women use tobacco (Kumar 1994: 1841), but the nationwide effects may not show up as clearly as in Western countries because so many people die in India before reaching their late fifties and sixties, when the effects of smoking are most likely to set in. Even so, beedis are apparently almost as dangerous as cigarettes, even if smaller, because their tar content ranges to about 30 percent higher per milligram of tobacco. Already one study in Kerala has indicated increased risk of early death in tobacco users, although it is not clear whether the data are statistically significant (Kumar 1994: 1841). As Kerala's people live longer, the risk of tobacco-induced cancers increases. The gains of KDB workers in wages and benefits thus come into conflict with the gains of the Kerala Model: Kerala Dinesh Beedi workers—despite their political idealism, sacrifices, and commitment to social justice—are manufacturing a product harmful to their class.

At the workplace, too, beedi production may be harmful. We observed in chapter 4 that blending the tobacco is done with wholly inadequate safety equipment. This behavior seems to exemplify the general failure of KDB workers and management to take seriously the dangers of the chemicals in tobacco. We are unaware of any systematic evidence regarding the dangers to workers who produce beedis but do not smoke them. Apparently neither KDB nor Kerala health officials have commissioned the necessary research. And it is ironic that one recent development program has installed high-efficiency stoves to reduce chemical pollution in Kerala's kitchens, where mostly wood fires are used for cooking. One goal of that program is to reduce the fire-caused airborne particulates because they contain benzoapyrene—known to be dangerous because it is one of the by-products of cigarette smoke strongly associated with cancer.[3]

DECLINING MARKET FOR BEEDIS?

It would be unrealistic to ask beedi workers to put themselves out of work on ethical grounds alone. But the dangers of tobacco are creating market trends that may force them to take action sooner or later in their own economic interest. One of the strategies U.S. tobacco companies are using to offset losses in their home market is to push cigarette smoking in the third world. The biggest market is in Asia (Shenon 1994), where U.S. brands carry status and can compete with local products such as beedis. The first threat to the beedi market may come from U.S.- and British-based multinational tobacco firms that have substantial resources to advertise and thus cut into local markets. Already several U.S. firms are aggressively pushing cigarettes in the New Delhi middle-class market, appealing to women to become "modern" by wearing skirts and smoking "mild, filtered" cigarettes (Crossette 1990).

Though KDB's main market of poor men is not immediately threatened, the multinationals have the economic resources to launch new campaigns with incredible suddenness and speed. In chapter 4 we noted that KDB's 1995 annual report bemoaned the introduction of small cigarettes that are now eating into the cooperative's sales and are partly to blame for some economic cutbacks, such as a delay in implementing the D.A. in 1994 and 1995 and the inability of the cooperative to continue its commitment to hiring new workers to replace all those who have retired. Despite its substantial reserves, KDB cannot afford to wait much longer before starting to diversify out of beedis.

ECONOMIC AND POLITICAL ASPECTS OF DIVERSIFICATION

Against the ethical and practical desirability of diversifying, KDB faces significant obstacles. First, the workers are making good money and have secure jobs. The threat of declining markets is still theoretical, and the ethical questions about smoking can still be met with the reply, if people want to smoke, someone will manufacture beedis for them. Why should they be manufactured only by underpaid, exploited workers in the private sector?

Second. diversification would mean substantial KDB investment in areas where it has little experience. Beedi rolling is skilled labor. The workers derive their pay and benefits from their skills and from the fact that beedi rolling does not lend itself well to mechanization. To diversify means to demand that workers learn new skills and be able to transfer these skills at a sufficiently high level to earn what they could at beedi rolling. If KDB subsidizes wages for the transition period, it will mean a substantial drain on the cooperative's resources.

Both of these problems point to the need for KDB's worker-elected managers and its union officers to rise to the occasion as the selfless and dynamic leaders they have been in previous crises facing the cooperative. Perhaps workers cannot be expected to remain in a state of constant mobilization, but meaningful participatory democracy implies that they can mobilize for occasions when their contributions are required. Diversification is surely such an occasion.

Are KDB's leaders up to the task? A few years ago, the late Chairman G. K. Panikkar made some initial attempts to interest the coop in dairy production, even making trips to some dairy cooperatives in Gujarat to learn how they are organized. KDB's work sheds and other infrastructural investments could be applied to dairy production with limited retooling. Panikkar found little response to his ideas at the time.

Soap manufacture is another industry that displays some of the technical characteristics that might make it suitable for production in the KDB manner with sufficient income-generating potential to appeal to the workers, who—it must be remembered—would face almost certain large-scale decline in their incomes if the venture failed and they had to go out into the job market dominated by the private sector.

Recently KDB management and union leaders have begun to awaken to the challenge of diversification. Our director board survey reveals that fifty-six respondents in 1994 (39 percent) thought diversification necessary, while another forty (28 percent) believed it should be given consideration. This makes 67 percent of the directors in favor of considering the issue. Only five directors of the primary cooperatives thought diversification was "not needed," while another eighteen felt it was "not presently needed," and nine others considered it "not practical."[4] The general body meeting of the central society in March 1994 adopted a resolution authorizing the central society director board to draw up proposals for diversification.

1996: NEW INITIATIVES IN DIVERSIFICATION

Sluggish sales and continuing discussions among union leaders and the elected management of KDB resulted in rapid movement toward diversification in 1996. Consultations have been held with a number of experts concerning possible areas for diversification. Throughout July 1996, KDB held a series of meetings in the primary societies to discuss the issue. On 30 August 1996, KDB held a day-long conference in Kannur with invited experts from research centers and institutes who had experience in agro-processing and animal production. Over five hundred scientists, technicians, and KDB union and management representatives attended from all twenty-two primary societies and the central society. Noting that most of KDB's workers are educated only to the primary level, the cooperative is focusing on low- and intermediate-technology projects. Among those currently being considered are processing of fruits into fruit juice, coconut processing, spice and pepper production and processing, pig, cattle, and goat farming, dairy production, and silkworm development.

With its small, dispersed work centers, combined into a large central marketing and financial organization, KDB has the infrastructure to realize some of its diversification plans. Relying on their assessment of the beedi market today and considering their resources, KDB leaders have set a goal of absorbing about 25 percent of beedi workers (8,250) into the diversified activities over the next ten years (KDB-WCCS 1996). The presence at the conference of the Left Democratic Front industries minister, Susheela Gopalan, the widow of Kerala's famous peasant leader A. K. Gopalan and herself a revered leftist leader, indicates likely government support and serves to tie the new struggle for diversification to the heroic days of the past.

A visit to KDB in January 1997 found the cooperative taking swift action. Four workers had already been trained in the manufacture of bottled coconut curry sauce, which is currently made by most Indian housewives with an electric grinder or a lot of hand grinding. In typical KDB style, management has dedicated its own central offices to be the site of an experimental hundred-worker production center for the coconut sauce; management will move upstairs to smaller quarters. If the technical and market factors work out, KDB hopes to expand the operation to several hundred workers. A number of workers have also been trained in the manufacture of pickle condiments that are widely used in Indian cooking. KDB has conducted an educational and attitudinal study to find out the skills and interests of its workers as they may apply to diversification. A January 1997 spot visit we made to a work center far from the Kannur headquarters—with no management staff present—revealed that shop floor workers are well informed of the diversification plans and have been asked to consider whether they want to volunteer to participate in a nonbeedi project.

Diversification constitutes a challenge very different from those that faced KDB in the past, however. There are no arrogant bosses throwing down the gauntlet, as in 1969. Farm workers are not planting red flags on landlords' plots, and talk of revolution is not so much in the air. But as we noted in chapter 1, Kerala's left political culture is renewing itself in the form of a village democracy campaign to involve people more directly in fashioning their own sustainable development. KDB's history of workers owning and managing their company is an inspiration for the People's Campaign for the Ninth Plan, underway in Kerala in 1996 and 1997 (Government of Kerala 1996a, 1996b). Diversification might offer great potential for democratic renewal within KDB, too. It could become a project involving the workers themselves, from the discussions on what to do and how to do it to the decisions and the implementation. Here KDB's "invisible" women might also become a force. With a new challenge, different from the one in 1969, women workers might come forward with ideas and contributions they are currently not offering. We noted in chapter 6 that KDB might become involved in providing social services such as day care centers. This could become a means to free women worker members to become more active, but it could also become a means of diversification itself. The voices of the women workers on this issue need to be heard.

Our study of KDB thus ends with a series of questions that only the future can answer. Can the workers and their leaders today muster the courage and perseverance their elders showed in 1969 in forming KDB in the first place? Will they show as much efficiency in production and skill at marketing the new products as they have shown with beedis? Will other unionists and sympathizers throughout Kerala help to find their new products the markets they will need? Will the village democratization campaign of 1996 infuse back into the ranks of KDB's workers some of the inspiration that KDB's earlier struggles and achievements have given the 1996–97 democratization campaign? Will KDB become a larger and more diverse example of workplace democracy within a renewed Kerala Model?

Notes

1. BEEDI WORKERS AND THE KERALA MODEL

1. Driving across Kannur district, one would be surprised to discover that its 51 percent urban population made it the most urbanized in Kerala in 1991. The statewide average was 26 percent (Bose et al. 1994: 185).

2. Details of da Gama's raids and conquests and of early Portuguese rule on the Malabar coast can be found in Hart 1950 and Jones 1978.

3. This account of beedi workers' conditions is a composite from Raghavan 1986:25–26, quoting a 1947 *Report of the Court of Enquiry into Labour Conditions in Beedi, Cigar, Snuff, Tobacco Curing and Tanning Industries;* Government of Kerala, 1958; *Economic and Political Weekly,* 1974; Avachat 1978; Abraham 1980; Basu 1977; Mohandas 1980; Government of India 1981b; Panikkar 1982; Government of India 1988; and Dharmalingam 1993. The more recent indicate that the earlier reports remain accurate descriptions.

4. Pertussis is known to many English-speaking people as "whooping cough."

5. Jeffrey (1993) offers a special focus on the strong sense of dignity developed through Kerala's century of struggles. Franke and Chasin (1994) and Franke (1996) also provide evidence on this issue.

6. The crisis of the Kerala Model was a major theme of the First International Congress on Kerala Studies, held in Thiruvananthapuram in August 1994. A summary of the several hundred papers and many debates appears in Thomas Isaac and Tharakan 1995.

7. Thomas Isaac and S. Mohana Kumar (1991) survey the debates in the context of Kerala's 1991 election.

8. Törnquist (1995) is critical from a political-organizing point of view, while Franke and Chasin (1994: xiv–xviii) see the experiments as an optimistic beginning of a new Kerala model.

9. An initial overview of the campaign appears in Krishnakumar 1996.

2. THE MAKING OF THE BEEDI WORKING CLASS

1. Tiyyas made up 21 percent of Malabar's 3.1 million people in 1921 (Government of India 1921: 122). Franke and Chasin (1994) give a simplified overview of Kerala's caste system.

2. Franke and Chasin (1994: 76–85) summarize the caste antidiscrimination movements in Kerala with emphasis on the role of the Ezhavas.

3. The boom in coir began as early as the 1870s in the southern Kerala region of Travancore. Another boom started about 1904 (Jeffrey 1976: 139–41) and presumably spread to the Malabar coast.

4. We could locate no written materials about Swami Sivaprasad's life and beliefs. Scattered references and the remembrances of some of those we interviewed suggest that his attachment to Annie Besant's philosophy led him in a conservative direction while the workers were drawn first to Gandhian principles and then to socialism (Anandan Int: 9 July 1993; Kannan Int: 6 June 1993).

5. This refers to the main Buddhist prayer, which includes three affirmations: "I take strength in the Buddha; I take strength in the Buddha's teachings; I take strength in the community of followers." The "Sangham Saranam" refers to the community of followers. The Ezhava Social Reform Movement contained powerful Buddhist influences because Buddhism rejects the caste system.

6. See also the memoirs of Velanti Kunhikannan (1984), a trade union activist from Tellicherry, who, with a band of workers, went to Mangalore to take advantage of the higher wages.

7. This comes from the Malayalam words *enna*, meaning oil, and *kettu*, meaning bundle, referring to the hanks of ten or twenty beedis tied together by the rollers.

8. Satyagraha became the primary means by which Mahatma Gandhi led followers of the independence movement to protest British colonial rule. It has since come to mean any form of nonviolent, passive resistance to illegitimate authority.

9. In India, the term "communalism" refers to caste, ethnic, or religious bigotry.

10. An overview of the Mappila, or "Moplah," Rebellion of 1921 appears in Miller 1976: 135–48.

11. Sathyamurthy (1985: chap. 5) gives a history of these movements in the context of the all-Kerala struggles. Additional details appear in Karat (1976).

12. The communists concentrated their fire against the Japanese rather than the British, thereby swimming against the nationalist tide. They experimented with various forms of propaganda to explain the political line of the party. The most successful of these were the Anti-Jap *melas*, or rural gatherings, where a mixture of speeches, theater, songs, and folk arts were presented to inculcate anti-Japanese sentiments among the masses.

13. Raghavan (1986: 36) gives detailed wage figures by year and district for 1939–46.

14. *Goonda* is a Hindi word for crook or rascal. It was used in Indian labor disputes as a word for thugs or terrorists hired by bosses to beat up and intimidate workers. The similarity with the English word "goon" may be coincidental, but the English word "thug" derives directly from the Hindi word "*thag*," which means "thief."

15. Under the commission system, the household worker is paid a "commission" for the beedis rolled for the middleman. It is only a camouflaged piece-rate system. Under the trade system, raw materials are sold and beedis purchased from the domestic worker by the middleman. The legal fiction is that the domestic worker is an "independent" petty producer.

16. The data were compiled from numerous census reports. Details and complete references appear in Raghavan 1986: 47.

17. Wage rates collected from various government and newspaper reports are reported in Raghavan 1986: 51.

18. See table 5.7 for identification of beedi worker unions and their political affiliations.

19. See table 5.7 for details.

20. Nossiter (1988) and Sathyamurthy (1985) give the specifics on the right-wing manipulations leading to the dismissal of the first left ministry of 1957.

3. SOLIDARITY VERSUS RETRENCHMENT: THE BIRTH OF KDB

1. Staber (1993) argues against this view with evidence from Maritime Canadian cooperatives. His article summarizes some of the substantial literature supporting the views we refer to in the text.

2. Bayat (1991), Hammond (1988), and Richman (1969) survey many examples of workers' demanding more control and participation during revolutionary upsurges. They also summarize some of the debates about why most of these experiments failed.

3. There have been other independent attempts from below to form beedi cooperatives, particularly by the workers after the failure of strikes. In 1964 at Vengara in Malappuram district, after the failure to gain wage increases, a thirty-five-member workers' cooperative was formed "on their own without any help from the government." The newspaper report on this cooperative suggested that there was public interest in the "Thozhilali [Workers'] Beedi" produced by the cooperative, which was sold at twelve paise, four paise lower than most of the brands (*Mathrubhumi* 12 April 1964). Another attempt was reported from Kondotti in Calicut district. For discussion of an early cooperative experiment at the end of the unsuccessful strike in 1938 at Palghat, see Alathur R. Krishnan (1993: 58–63). The workers allowed the cooperative to be taken over by a sympathetic entrepreneur on the condition that he would expand the production. It eventually became a very successful private firm.

4. Our discussion is based upon interviews with Panniyan Bharathan, the secretary of the Kannur union at the time of formation of the cooperative (Kannur, 9 June 1993); K. C. Kunhiraman, a director board member (Kannur, 9 June 1993); T. C. Kumaran, a former president of the cooperative (Kannur, 10 June 1993); and C. C. Balan, former president of the Tellicherry Beedi Workers' Industrial Cooperative (9 June 1993).

5. See the statement of the Youth Congress President, *Mathrubhumi* 15 October 1968, and the resolution of the opposition-dominated Kannur Municipal Council, *Mathrubhumi* 10 October 1968.

6. See table 5.7 for union identifications.

7. See the statement of E. K. K. Mohammed, leader of the Muslim League STU, *Mathrubhumi* 21 November 1968.

8. The 1991 Indian census breakdowns by specific worker categories have not yet been made available.

9. The 44 million figure probably includes children working significant hours on their parents' farms. The figure of 14 million would be the minimum number of children working in the industrial sector. Weiner (1991: 175) reports that in 1971, 88 percent of Kerala's six- to twelve-year-olds were in school by contrast with the figure of 38 percent for all Indian children in that age group. In 1975, 82 percent of Kerala children who entered school completed the fifth grade; the all-India figure was 26 percent. See also Srikantan (1991).

4. FROM MOBILIZATION TO EFFICIENCY: THE ROLE OF THE CENTRAL SOCIETY

1. Rock and Klinedinst (1992: 611) summarize the barriers set by the market and the financial policies of the U.S. government that inhibit the development of cooperatives owned and managed by workers.

2. Bonin et al. (1993: 1293) note, however, that many cooperatives exist in the Scandinavian countries.

3. Danny Lee (1994: vii) gives a total of fourteen hundred worker cooperatives in Britain employing between eight and nine thousand workers, and a total number in Western Europe of forty-five thousand cooperatives employing about seven hundred fifty thousand people. These figures apparently include production, consumer, and credit cooperatives combined. Lee also notes that Britain has a Co-op Party with fourteen members in parliament.

4. According to Government Order MS. 40/69 Ind. 4 February 1969, "the Central Society will buy raw materials in bulk and distribute to primary societies on credit [and] . . . will also extend credit to the primary societies for paying wages to the workers. . . . The Central Society will be the central marketing agency. The Central Society will also have its own inspectorate, a sales wing and public relations wing."

5. Initially, four government representatives were appointed to the director board of the central cooperative. But following changes in the cooperative laws in the state, the number of government nominees was reduced to two with five others to be elected.

6. At the end of the 1980s KDB and the Kerala State Forest Department experimented with a plantation of tendu leaves in an area of Kerala with degraded forest lands so that external reliance on tendu leaves might be reduced (KDBWCCS, *Ann. reports*, 1991: 6). The preliminary results are reportedly not encouraging.

7. The tax was cut from Rs 120 per thousand in 1994 to Rs 60 per thousand in 1995. In 1996 it was raised to Rs 75 per thousand. Beedi workers in Andhra Pradesh state northeast of Kerala appear to have suffered wage cuts and deterioration of working conditions when contractors there used the threat from small cigarettes to pressure them to the owners' advantage. The tax breaks to minicigarettes appear to be part of a government-supported plan to stimulate India's production of cigarettes for export in connection with structural adjustment programs of the World Bank (Srinivasulu 1997).

8. Details of the efficiency analysis and director board response to it are in chapter 6.

5. THE DYNAMICS OF SHOP FLOOR DEMOCRACY: EMPOWERMENT VERSUS SUPERVISION IN THE BEEDI PRIMARY COOPERATIVES

1. Franke ([1993] 1996) summarizes some of the literature in the context of Kerala and its social movements.

2. Zald and Ash (1966) call it the Weber-Michels approach. Rothschild and Whitt (1986) also use the term.

3. But see our discussion in chapter 6 where we note that the primary societies with high percentages of workers over forty-five do not seem to experience lower average output.

4. To get this figure, we computed the wages for an average beedi roller by assuming the average production of 921 beedis per day, as given on table 6.3. This gave a rolling wage of Rs 13.35 based on the rate in table 1.1 combined with the D.A. of Rs

18.90, also from table 1.1. This gives a daily wage of Rs 32.25. We then assumed the worker took the average of forty-six unpaid leave days, as explained in chapter 6. Multiplying by the remaining 319 days, which include all days worked and all paid Sundays and holidays, gives a figure of Rs 10,280. The annual bonus of 16.5 percent would raise the income to Rs 11,976.

5. KDB's salary egalitarianism compares favorably with the situation in advanced capitalist industry. A study by the Economic Policy Institute found that for 1989 the ratios of CEOs to production workers were 6.5 to one in Germany, 7.6 to one in Italy, 8.9 to one in France, 9.5 to one in Canada, 11.6 to one in Japan, 12.4 to one in the United Kingdom, and 17.5 to one in the United States (Corporations 1994: 4–5). When only the largest corporations are considered—that is, corporations in the same category as KDB within Kerala—U.S. CEOs earned 42 times what production workers earned in 1980. In 1992 that figure rose to 157. Comparable Japanese CEOs earned 32 times what production workers earned in 1992 (Sklar 1995: 8–9).

6. Gazetted officers are senior officials of the government whose appointments are announced in the gazette. Nongazetted officers are clerks, accountants, peons (messengers), and other lower-paid bureaucrats.

7. A similar dispute in somewhat different specific circumstances appears to have brought about the only strike in the Mondragón cooperatives (Kasmir 1996:110–13).

8. In extreme cases, a maistry may direct a worker to train with another, more skilled roller in order to come up to levels acceptable to the coop. Since workers are recruited through speed and quality competitions, this last stage of discipline is not frequent (Balakrishnan Int: 27 March 1993).

9. This is a minimum of 72 percent of the total of 154 primary society director board members. We have no reason to suspect that nonrespondents would be different from those who responded.

10. For some of the evidence on these issues for Kerala as a whole, see Franke and Chasin 1994, Franke 1996, and Jeffrey 1993.

11. Bayat (1991) discusses the transmission-belt role for unions in several countries.

12. During the heaviest monsoon days, work and income for rural laborers decline, along with the demand for "the poor man's smoke," as beedis are popularly known.

13. Nossiter (1982 and 1988) and Sathyamurthy (1985) describe the 1964 party split and detail much of the interparty rivalry between the CPM and CPI.

14. The Naxalites are named for an armed uprising that occurred in the Naxalbari area of northeastern India in 1967. Opposing what they viewed as too much compromise by the traditional Communist parties, Naxalites urged armed struggle and promoted a Maoist-type idea of creating liberated zones by military force. Banerjee (1984) gives an overview of the Naxalite movement in India.

6. EFFICIENCY AND PROFIT IN THE PRIMARY SOCIETIES: KDB'S MARKET DILEMMA

1. The 1995 output was 6.8 billion beedis.

2. As noted in chapter 4, the 1994 price went up to Rs 2.5 per bundle (or hank) of twenty-five, meaning a per-beedi cost of Rs 0.10, or ten paise (one hundred paise equals one rupee). This meant nearly a 10 percent price hike in about one year.

3. We computed the expenditure on raw materials from the primary society account sheets by adding the opening stock (raw materials) and the raw materials purchased. From this we subtracted the closing stock. The result is the expenditure on raw materials for the production year. We computed the labor cost as the sum of all

wages paid: regular wages, Sunday wages, holiday wages, and personal leave day wages for the combined wage cost. We also added the medical allowance of Rs 50 per worker per year as recorded on the balance sheets. The sum appears under the heading "Labor Costs" on table 6.1. We did not include the bonus or payments to welfare and provident funds. The bonus figure was a constant of 16.5 percent to all primary societies in 1992–93 and should not influence the analysis. It was paid out of central society profits, as noted earlier.

4. This method corresponds to that used in computing the "cash flow" profits of the Mondragón worker cooperatives in Spain, as detailed in Whyte and Whyte 1988:135–36. Because workers at Mondragón made dishwashers, thermostats, and other high-tech articles, labor costs were only 28 percent of sales, while materials were 59 percent and profits were 13 percent (1988: 136). The KDB profit figure includes gunnysack and other minor sales that represent less than 1 percent of the total.

5. Because we have a complete population instead of a sample, statistical significance tests on these coefficients are not relevant. For the multiple regression used later in the chapter, we can make use of significance tests by virtue of randomization tests.

6. We chose beedis per worker per day rather than total beedis per worker per year. The daily output is easier to understand, figures directly in wage calculations, and behaves in the same way in the correlations and regressions as does the yearly number. To construct the "Beedis per Day" column for table 6.3, we first divided the total number of beedis produced in each primary society for the year 1992–93 by the number of rollers in that primary society. This gave the number of beedis per roller for the year. We then divided by the average number of days that workers in each society attended. The attendance figure comes from primary society records; average attendance also becomes a possible efficiency factor.

7. We computed expected attendance as follows: from a calendar year of 365 days, subtract 52 Sundays, 14 holidays, and 15 personal leave days (1 per 20 days), leaving an expected work year of 284 days.

8. Daily output is given in actual type produced. For leaf outturn, no significant differences exist among the types, but for tobacco outturn, making the figures comparable among the primary societies is more complicated. Part of this problem is resolved by the fact that the total sales figures already take care of the different prices for the beedis sold to the central society. But tobacco outturn for Special and Rajadhani Beedis runs about eight hundred fewer per kilogram than for Medium Beedis, while that for Small Beedis runs almost a thousand fewer again. To make the figures comparable, we took the outturn for Medium Beedis for the twenty primary societies that produce any amount of them. Two primary societies—Thottada and Badagara—did not produce Medium Beedis in the last three to five years. To get figures for these two primary societies, we took their percentage of the average of Special Beedis manufactured by nineteen primary societies and multiplied this by the average figure for Medium Beedis for 1992–93 for the twenty primary societies producing Medium Beedis.

9. In 1995 the female proportion of the workers had risen to 60 percent.

10. A joke among some KDB board members is that women train in the north, then marry and move to the south.

11. A regression test with days worked and percentage of new workers together produced an R-square of 0.02. Putting days worked and percentage of new workers together with workers per work center and staff percentage, however, gave a combined R-square of 0.39, adjusted R-square of 0.25, and significance of $p \leq .06$.

12. Edgington (1980) provides a statistical justification and explanation for the randomization technique. We ran the randomization procedure in ANTHROPAC (Borgatti 1992) after testing several regression equations in SPSS.

7. KDB AND THE INTERNATIONAL MOVEMENT FOR WORKERS' COOPERATIVES

1. Bayat (1991) gives overviews of experiments in revolutionary Russia, China, and Cuba. Horvat (1982), Wachtel (1973), and Vanek (1971, 1977) describe the Yugoslavian cooperatives in detail. Bhaduri (1982) outlines the main features of agricultural cooperatives in Vietnam.

2. Rothschild and Whitt (1986: 1–2) *"define a collective or a cooperative as any enterprise in which control rests ultimately and overwhelmingly with the member-employees-owners, regardless of the particular legal framework through which this is achieved."*

3. Executive pay raises were not the only reason for the change, but they appear to have played a large role. Average CEO pay increased by a staggering 514 percent between 1980 and 1993, compared with worker increases of 68 percent versus consumer price increases of 75 percent (Sklar 1995: 8–9). More generally, the richest 1 percent of Americans experienced a 102 percent increase in after-tax incomes between 1977 and 1989. During the same period, the bottom 40 percent of Americans lost 10 percent (Sklar 1995: 7). See also Bok 1993: 63 and 95.

4. Through most of his book, Rawls separates liberty from income and wealth, but he recognizes that the overall concept treats them in similar fashion. For our purposes, the distinction is not necessary, since both political rights and wealth appear to be distributed similarly in worker-owned cooperatives.

5. Nozick (1974: 183–231) presents a detailed critique of Rawls aimed at restoring the conservative emphasis on entrepreneurs, whose rights Nozick feels have been abrogated by the call for equality.

6. The 16.5 percent bonus at KDB in 1993 compares favorably with that of European cooperatives. In recent years, bonuses in the U. K. averaged one week's wages (2 percent), in France two to eight weeks' (4 percent to 15 percent), and in Italy three to five weeks' (6 percent to 10 percent) (computed from Bonin et al. 1993: 1294). The 17 percent bonus in 1995 indicates continuing success on this measure.

7. Kasmir (1996: 158–64) presents evidence from a more recent period suggesting that workers feel less a part of one Mondragón cooperative than do managers. This may have to do with changed conditions in the cooperatives or with differences in research approaches between her and the Whytes.

8. In a questionnaire study, Rooney (1992) found greater job satisfaction among U.S. workers in producer coops than in either ESOPs or privately managed firms.

9. Bok argues that factors other than money are also important to happiness. His data show, however, that 21 percent of persons with incomes under $10,000 reported themselves as "not too happy," while only 5 percent of those with incomes over $75,000 felt that way (Bok 1993: 230).

10. Job security is one of the most important coop benefits at Mondragón also, but staying employed may require that workers be transferred to other branches or be appenticed at new jobs. (Greenwood et al. 1991: 101–2). Transfers appear to result in substantial worker disaffection despite their seeming advantage over unemployment (Greenwood et al. 1991: 114). At the same time, we recognize that Greenwood's study may not represent the statistical reality because of the problems in obtaining a representative sample. It is possible that the interviews inadvertently report the most extreme criticisms of a few workers who are the most interesting and vocal rather than the views of the majority, who might feel comfortable with the transfers.

11. Goleman (1993); Kaplan et al. (1994); Karasek and Theorell (1990).

12. An interesting related position on these issues was taken by the Austrian psychologist Wilhelm Reich, one of the first social scientists to attempt an analysis of the Nazi movement. Reich ([1933] 1970) argued that authoritarianism and mechanical,

routinized drudgery of the modern workplace robs workers of the opportunity to satisfy their creative, self-regulatory needs. When reinforced by certain forms of sexual repression that Reich believed also grew out of modern industrial capitalism, the authoritarianism of the workplace produces individuals whose potentially active, happy, cooperative selves mutate into passive, frustrated, and thus distorted individuals who easily become followers of authoritarian structures and believers in racial or other fantasies fed them by opportunistic leaders like Hitler. Reich argued that democracy at the workplace is essential to the survival of democratic institutions in all other sectors of life and society.

13. Greenwood et al. (1991: 40) also exemplify this view in their statement about Mondragón: "While the cooperatives attempt to treat members with dignity and to permit them to develop and express themselves fully, a reorganized working environment alone, no matter how successful, cannot restructure society at large."

14. Rothschild and Whitt (1986: 66) argue that the degree of democratic experience influences a cooperative's chances of success. KDB's development from a seasoned, determined, and activist union movement bears out this idea.

15. Herring (1983: 192–216) and Sathyamurthy (1985: 248–58) provide details of the dramatic interplay between parliamentary maneuvers and mobilization actions of peasants and workers in Kerala in 1969.

16. Possible explanations and references to contrasting views are offered in Franke and Chasin (1994) and Jeffrey (1993).

17. Zald and Ash (1966) emphasize this aspect of social movements.

18. Italics in the original. In her study of Mondragón, Kasmir (1996: 199) also concluded, "if workplace democracy is to be genuine, it seems that it must be premised on activism."

19. The formation of the cooperative was "an intensely political process" (Espinosa and Zimbalist 1978: 114), to borrow a phrase from a comparative experience during the Allende period in Chile (1970–73).

20. Heller (1996) argues that the CPM's labor policy since 1987 has emphasized mediation through Industrial Relations Committees rather than militancy, even in the private sector.

AFTERWORD: TOBACCO PRODUCTION AND
DIVERSIFICATION AT KDB

1. A Malayalam edition of the book will be published simultaneously with the English version. Kerala's active, participatory workers' culture—particularly strong in Malabar, where KDB is located—makes it certain that many of the participants in this study will be among its readers.

2. Horn (1968) summarizes Canadian and British studies with similar data.

3. The U.S. Department of Health and Human Services considers benzoapyrene to have an "established" causal link to cancer in laboratory animals and a "probable" link in humans. At least six other chemicals have established links in humans, while another thirty have established links in laboratory animals but have not yet been proved or disproved to have links in humans (computed from CDC 1989: 86–87). On 27 October 1996, the *New York Times*, sec. 4, p. 3, reported that scientists had used benzoapyrene in the laboratory to produce genetic mutations in lung cells identical to those found in the lung cells of cancer patients. This is the first clear proof of a causal connection between cigarette smoke and lung cancer.

4. Another 11 did not respond to the question, and 4 directors replied that they had "not thought about it." The total number in the survey was 143.

Bibliography

KERALA AND KERALA DINESH BEEDI

Aaron, Samuel C. 1974. *Jeevitha smaranakal [Life remembrances]*. Cannanore.

Abraham, Amrita. 1980. Beedi workers of Bombay. *Economic and Political Weekly* 15 (44): 1881–82.

All-India Convention of Beedi Workers. 1993. Draft report. Kannur, 3–5 December 1993.

Avachat, A. 1978. Beedi workers of Nippani. *Economic and Political Weekly* 13 (30): 1176–78 and 1203–5.

Aziz, B. K. Abdul. 1990. Beedi industry in Kerala—An economic analysis. Ph.D. diss., University of Calicut.

Balan, C. C. 1974. *Kerala Dinesh Beedi sahakarana sangham nettangalum kottangalum [KDB cooperative society—Strengths and weaknesses]*. Kannur: Kerala Dinesh Beedi Souvenir.

Balaraman, M. E. 1973. *Communist prasthanam adyanalukalil [The Communist movement in the early days]*. Trivandrum: Prabhat Book House.

Bala Subrahmanya, M. H. 1988. The beedi industry: How competition takes place. *Economic Times*, 30 May.

Banerjee, Sumanta. 1984. *India's simmering revolution: The Naxalite uprising*. London: Zed Books.

Basu, Timir. 1977. Beedi workers of Calcutta. *Economic and Political Weekly* 12 (4): 81–82.

Beedi workers of Sinnar. 1974. *Economic and Political Weekly* 9 (24): 945–46.

Beevi Imam, A. J. 1978. Impact of minimum wages legislation on cashew industry. M. Phil. diss., Centre for Development Studies (Jawaharlal Nehru University).

Bose, Ashish, Suresh Shanbhogue, and Mohan Sing Bist. 1994. *India's urban population: 1991 census data: States, districts, cities and towns*. New Delhi and Allahabad: Wheeler Publishing.

Chandran, Pookkadan. 1984. Adiantharavasthayile rakthasakshi [Martyrs of the Emergency]. In *Adyate twenty-five kollangal [The first twenty-five years]*. Calicut: Tellicherry Beedi Tozhilali Union.

Deshabhimani, 2 December 1991 (CPM daily newspaper).

Dharmalingam, A. 1993. Female beedi workers in a south Indian village. *Economic and Political Weekly* 28 (27–28): 1461–68.

Doshi, R. R. 1991. *Economics of tobacco production and marketing.* Poona: Vishwanil Publications.

Franke, Richard W. [1993] 1996. *Life is a little better: Redistribution as a development strategy in Nadur Village, Kerala.* Delhi: Promilla.

Franke, Richard W., and Barbara H. Chasin. 1994. *Kerala: Radical reform as development in an Indian state.* 2d ed. Oakland, Calif.: Institute for Food and Development Policy; Delhi: Promilla and Company, Publishers.

————. 1996. Female-supported households: A continuing agenda for Kerala Model? *Economic and Political Weekly* 31 (10): 625–30.

George, K. K. 1993. *Limits to Kerala Model of development: An analysis of fiscal crisis and its implications.* Trivandrum: Centre for Development Studies.

Giriappa, S. 1987. *Bidi-Rolling in rural development.* Delhi: Daya Publishing House.

Gopalan, A. K. 1962. *Kodungattinte maattoli [Echoes of the storm].* Trivandrum: Prabhat Book House.

Government of India. 1921. *Census of India 1921.* Vol. 13. Madras Province, Part II.

————. 1931. *Census of India 1931.* Vol. 14. Madras Province, Parts I, II, III.

————. 1961. *Census of India 1961.* Vol. 7. Kerala, Part IV and Part IV-B.

————. 1981a. *Census of India 1981.* Series 10, Kerala, Part-III, A and B (i), General Economic Tables, B-1 to B-17.

————. 1981b. *Report on working and living conditions of workers in bidi industry,* 1978. Chandigarh: Labour Bureau, Ministry of Labour Employment, and Rehabilitation.

————. 1988. *Shramshakti: Report of the National Commission on Self Employed Women and women in the informal sector.* New Delhi.

Government of Kerala. 1958. *Kerala Tripartite Committee for Beedi and Cigar Industries. Report for 1958.* Trivandrum: Government Press.

————. 1993. *Economic review, 1992.* Thiruvananthapuram: Kerala State Planning Board.

————. 1994. *Economic review, 1993.* Thiruvananthapuram: Kerala State Planning Board.

————. 1995. *Economic review, 1994.* Thiruvananthapuram: Kerala State Planning Board.

————. 1996a. *People's campaign for ninth plan: An approach paper.* Thiruvananthapuram: Kerala State Planning Board.

————. 1996b. *Power to the people: People's plan—ninth plan: A note on the training programme for resource persons.* Thiruvananthapuram: Kerala State Planning Board.

Government of Madras. 1947. *Report of court of enquiry into labour conditions in beedi, cigar, snuff, tobacco curing and tanning industries.* Madras: Government of Madras.

Hart, Henry H. 1950. *Sea road to the Indies: An account of the voyages and exploits of the Portuguese navigators, together with the life and times of Dom Vasco Da Gama, Capita-Mór, Viceroy of India and Count of Vidigueira.* Westport, Conn.: Greenwood Press.

Heller, Patrick. 1996. Social capital as a product of class mobilization and state intervention: Industrial workers in Kerala, India. *World Development* 24 (6): 1055–71.

Herring, Ronald J. 1983. *Land to the tiller: The political economy of agrarian reform in South Asia.* New Haven: Yale University Press.

Jeffrey, Robin. 1976. *Decline of Nayar dominance — Society and politics in Travancore 1847–1908.* New Delhi: Vikas Publishing House.

———. 1993. *Politics, women and well being: How Kerala became "a model."* Delhi: Oxford University Press.

———. 1997. Malayalam: "The day-to-day social life of the people." *Economic and Political Weekly* 32 (1–2): 18–21.

Jones, Vincent. 1978. *Sail the Indian Sea.* London: Gordon & Cremonesi.

Kannan, C. 1984. *Beedi vyavasayam Kannur jillayil [Beedi industry in Kannur district].* Smaranika [Remembrance]. Calicut: Tobacco Workers' Union (TWU).

Kannan, K. P. 1988. *Of rural proletarian struggles: Mobilisation and organisation of rural workers in South-West India.* Delhi: Oxford University Press.

Kannan, K. P., and K. Pushpangadan. 1988. Agricultural stagnation in Kerala: An exploratory analysis. *Economic and Political Weekly* 23 (39): A120–A128.

Karat, Prakash. 1976. Peasant movement in Malabar—1934–1940. *Social Scientist* 5 (2): 30–44.

KDBWCCS (Kerala Dinesh Beedi Workers' Cooperative Central Society). 1969. *Kerala Dinesh Beedi Kendra Sahakarana Sangathinte Niamavali [Kerala Dinesh Beedi Central Society Bylaws].* Cannanore: KDBWCCS.

———. 1975. Resolution of the Annual General Body Meeting of 31 October 1975 regarding excise duty on beedi. Mimeo. Kannur: KDBWCCS.

———. 1986–1993. Annual reports. Kannur: KDBWCCS.

———. 1988. Final audit [summary of defects], reply, and agenda notes. Annual general body meeting. 7 November, 1988. Kannur: KDBWCCS.

———. 1989. *Erupatham varshathe pulakojola sambava parambarakalude kala vivara pattika [A chronology of events of twenty great years].* Kannur: KDBWCCS.

———. 1994. Bye Laws of the Kerala Dinesh Beedi Workers' Cooperative. Kannur: KDBWCCS.

———. 1996. *A brief note highlighting the necessity to diversify the activities of Kerala Dinesh Beedi Workers' Central Co-op Society and its twenty-two primaries.* Kannur: KDBWCCS.

Kerala Sastra Sahitya Parishad (KSSP). 1991. *Lead kindly light: Operation Illiteracy Eradication. A report on the intensive campaign for eradication of illiteracy in Ernakulam.* Thiruvananthapuram: KSSP.

Krishnakumar, R. A Kerala initiative: The people's campaign for the ninth plan. *Frontline* 13 (16): 102–4.

Krishnan, R. Alathur. 1993. *Vizhumalayude Thazhavarayil Ninnu [From the Valley of Vizhumala]*. Thiruvananthapuram: Chintha Publishers.

Kumaran, M. P. 1984. 1940 September 15 talicheriyila beedi thozhilalikalum [September 15, 1940 and the Tellicherry beedi workers]. In *Adyathe erupathinanchu kollangal [The first twenty-five years]. Anpatham varshika souvenir [Fiftieth anniversary souvenir]*. Calicut: TBTU.

Kunhikannan, Velanti. 1984. Pazhaya ormakal [Memories of the past]. In *Anpatham varshika smaranika [Fiftieth anniversary collection of remembrances]*. Calicut: Tellicherry Beedi Tozhilali [Workers] Union (TBTU).

Kurien, John. 1995. The Kerala model: Its central tendency and the outlier. *Social Scientist* 23 (1–3): 70–90.

Mathew, George. 1991. Social background of Kerala district council members. *Economic and Political Weekly* 26 (21): 1320–21.

Mathrubhumi, May 1934–December 1969.

Menon, Dilip M. 1994. *Caste, nationalism, and communism in South India: Malabar, 1900–1948*. Cambridge: Cambridge University Press.

Miller, Roland E. 1976. *Mappila Muslims of Kerala: A study in Islamic trends*. Madras: Orient Longman.

Mohan, V. Nanda. 1994. Recent trends in the industrial growth of Kerala. In *Kerala's economy: Performance, problems, prospects*, edited by B. A. Prakash. New Delhi: Sage Publications.

Mohanan, N. 1982. A profile of beedi workers in Cannanore district of Kerala. Annexure B in Panikkar, G. K. 1982. *Thrilling story of Kerala Dinesh Beedi: A look back on working, various facets, problems, and achievements*. Cannanore: Kerala Dinesh Beedi.

———. 1983. Federal co-operatives: an overview and a case study. *Lok Lidyog (Monthly Journal of Public Enterprises)* 17 (4): 7–19.

———. 1984. *Industrial democracy in action: A study of beedi workers' cooperative in Kerala*. Cannanore: Kerala Dinesh Beedi.

Mohandas, M. 1980. Beedi workers in Kerala: Conditions of life and work. *Economic and Political Weekly* 15 (36): 1517–23.

Mohandas, M., and P. V. Praveen Kumar. 1992. Impact of co-operativisation on working conditions: Study of beedi industry in Kerala. *Economic and Political Weekly* 27 (26): 1333–38.

Mukherjee, Chandan, and T. M. Thomas Isaac. 1991. *Study of educated unemployed in Kerala: Report of the sample survey of restraints of employment exchange*. New Delhi: Planning Commission of India and Trivandrum, Centre for Development Studies.

Namboodiripad, E. M. S. 1984. *Communist Party Keralathil. I [The Communist Party in Kerala]*. Vol. 1. Trivandrum: Chintha Publishers.

———. 1990. *Kerala charitram Marxist veekshanathil [Kerala history: A Marxist perspective]*. Thiruvananthapuram: Chintha Publishers.

———. 1992. *Keralathinte vikasana prasanangal [Kerala's development problems]*. Thiruvananthapuram: Chinta Publishers.

Nanu, Punchayil. 1984. 1946'la panimudakinte ormakallil ninnu [Reminiscences of the 1946 strike]. Calicut: Tellicherry Beedi Tozhilali Union.

Narayanan, C. V. 1986. *Smaranakal charitrangal [Memoires and histories].* In *Smaranika* [Remembrance] Calicut: Payyanur Beedi Thozhilali Union.

Nossiter, T. J. 1982. *Communism in Kerala: A study in political adaptation.* Delhi: Oxford University Press.

———. 1988. *Marxist state governments in India.* London: Pinter Publishers.

Oommen, M. A. 1984. *Inter-State shifting of industries: A case study of selected industries in Kerala, Tamil Nadu, and Karnataka.* Trichur: Department of Economics, University of Calicut. Mimeo.

———. 1993. *Essays on Kerala economy.* New Delhi: Oxford and IBH Publishing Co.

Pandakal, Sreedharan. 1984. Chorapookal viranja Pandakapara [Panthakapara: Where red flowers bloomed]. In *Adyate twenty-five kollangal [The first twenty-five years].* Calicut: Tellicherry Beedi Tozhilali Union.

Panikkar, G. K. 1974. *The story of Kerala Dinesh Beedi: A thrilling experience.* Cannanore: Kerala Dinesh Beedi.

———. 1982. *Thrilling story of Kerala Dinesh Beedi: A look back on working, various facets, problems, and achievements.* Cannanore: Kerala Dinesh Beedi.

———. 1985. *Salient features of Kerala Dinesh Beedi.* Cannanore: Kerala Dinesh Beedi.

———. 1988. *Dinesh beedi sanghangalude valarchayila durgada gattangalum vidhi nirnaya sambhavangalum [Turning points and crises in the growth of Kerala dinesh cooperatives].* Kannur: KDBWCCS.

Panikkar, K. N. 1989. *Against lord and state: Religion and peasant uprisings in Malabar, 1836–1921.* Delhi: Oxford University Press.

Radhakrishnan, V., E. K. Thomas, and K. Jessy Thomas. 1994. Performance of rice crop in Kerala. In *Kerala's economy: Performance, problems, prospects,* edited by B. A. Prakash. New Delhi: Sage Publications.

Raghavan, Azhikodan. 1955. On P. Krishna Pillai. *Navayugam Krishna Pillai Special* 1955 [New Age Krishna Pillai Special].

Raghavan, Pyaralal. 1986. Organisation of production in beedi industry: A study of Cannanore district, 1920–1985. M. Phil. diss., Centre for Development Studies (Jawaharlal Nehru University).

———. 1995. Growth and performance of industrial cooperatives in India. D. Phil. diss., Centre for Development Studies (Jawaharlal Nehru University).

Raghaviah, Jai Prakash. 1989. *Mission industries in Malabar and South Kanara, 1834–1914.* New Delhi: Gian.

Rajagopalan, V. 1986. The handloom industry in North and South Kerala: A study of production and marketing structure. M. Phil. diss., Centre for Development Studies (Jawaharlal Nehru University).

Ramakrishnan, Kalathil. 1990. Dinesh Beedi makes coop history. *Indian Express,* 7 January.

Ramankutty. 1974. Dinesh Beedi captures a market. In *Kerala Dinesh Beedi souvenir 1974.* Calicut.

Ramunni, Murkoth. 1974. *Jeevitha smaranakal [Autobiographical memoirs].* Kottayam: National Book Stall.

Ranadive, B. T. 1943. *Report on production.* Bombay: People's Publishing House.

———. 1987. Introduction. In All-India Co-ordination Committee of Working Women. *Problems of working women and their participation in trade unions.* Delhi: Centre for Indian Trade Unions [CITU].

Ravi, K. 1979. Economics of beedi industry in Kerala. M. A. project report, University of Calicut.

Rutherford, T. G., ed. 1933. *Madras district gazeteers, Malabar district.* Vol. 2. Madras: Government of Madras.

Sathyamurthy, T. V. 1985. *India since independence: Studies in the development of the power of the state.* Vol. 1, *Centre-state relations, the case of Kerala.* Delhi: Ajanta.

Seetharam, S. P., and N. Mohanan. Workers' cooperative—An Indian experience. Annexure A in Panikkar, G. K. 1982. *Thrilling story of Kerala Dinesh Beedi: A look back on working, various facets, problems, and achievements.* Cannanore: Kerala Dinesh Beedi.

Sekhar, C. 1943. *Kshamam theerkan kuzhappam theerkan ulphadhanam vardipikkuka [Increase production to overcome scarcity and troubles.]* Calicut: All Kerala Trade Union Congress.

Sharma, Rama. 1917. *Coir spinning in Malabar—An economic study.* Calicut: Norman Printing Press.

Shenoi, N. Subramaniya. 1986. Ithu iver Payyanurinte charithra radhathinte chakrangalanu [Here are the wheels of the Payyanur chariot of history]. In *Fiftieth varshikam smaranika [Fiftieth anniversary souvenir].* Payyanur: Payyanur Beedi Thozhilali Union.

Sreedharan, Jayatella. 1984. Samoohya samskarika ranghathu beedi thozhilalikal nalkiya sambhavana [The contributions of beedi workers in social and cultural affairs]. In *Tellicherry Beedi Workers' Union anpatham varshikam smaranika [Tellicherry Beedi Workers' Union fiftieth anniversary memoirs].* Calicut: TBTU.

Srinivasulu, K. 1997. Impact of liberalization on beedi workers. *Economic and Political Weekly* 32(11): 515–17.

Subrahmanian, K. K. 1990. Development paradox in Kerala: Analysis of industrial stagnation. *Economic and Political Weekly* 35 (37): 2053–58.

Subramaniam, M. 1965. *Minimum Wages Committee for Beedi and Cigar Industry. Report for 1964.* Trivandrum: Government Press.

Sunny, K. P. 1988. Consumption behaviours in Kerala—A Study of national sample survey data 1965/66 to 1983. M. Phil. diss., Centre for Development Studies (Jawaharlal Nehru University).

Tellicherry Beedi Thozhilali Union (TBTU). 1984. *Anpatham varshika smaranika [Fiftieth Anniversary Collection of Remembrances].* Calicut: TBTU.

Thampy, M. M. 1994. Development of organised small-scale industries: Some issues. In *Kerala's economy: Performance, problems, prospects,* edited by B. A. Prakash. New Delhi: Sage Publications.

Tharakan, P. K. Michael. 1990. *The Ernakulam district total literacy programme: Report of the evaluation.* Trivandrum: Centre for Development Studies.

Thomas Isaac, T. M. 1984. Class struggle and industrial structure—A Study of coir weaving industry in Kerala, 1859–1980, D. Phil. diss., Centre for Development Studies (Jawaharlal Nehru University).

———. 1985. From caste consciousness to class consciousness: Alleppey coir workers during the interwar period. *Economic and Political Weekly* 20 (4): 5–18.

———. 1990. Evolution of organisation of production in coir yarn spinning in Kerala. Working paper no. 236. Thiruvananthapuram: Centre for Development Studies.

———. 1993. Economic consequences of the Gulf crisis: A study of India with special reference to Kerala. In *The Gulf crisis and South Asia: Studies on the economic impact,* edited by Piyasiri Wickramasekara. New Delhi: United Nations Development Programme and Asian Regional Team for Employment Promotion (ARTEP).

———. 1995. Kerala: Towards a new agenda. *Economic and Political Weekly* 30 (31–32): 1993–2004.

Thomas Isaac, T. M., and K. N. Harilal. 1996. Planning for empowerment: The people's campaign for decentralized planning in Kerala. Paper presented at the International Conference on Kerala's Development: National and International Dimensions. New Delhi: Institute of Social Sciences.

Thomas Isaac, T. M., and P. K. Michael Tharakan. 1986. Sree Narayana movement in Travancore 1888–1939—A study of social basis and ideological reproduction. Working paper no. 214. Thiruvananthapuram: Centre for Development Studies.

Thomas Isaac, T. M., P. A. Van Stuivenberg, and K. N. Nair. 1992. *Modernisation and employment: The coir industry in Kerala.* Indo-Dutch Studies on Development Alternatives, no. 10. New Delhi: Sage Publications.

Thomas Isaac, T. M., and S. Mohana Kumar. 1991. Kerala elections: Lessons and non lessons. *Economic and Political Weekly* 26 (47): 2691–2704.

Tobacco Workers' Union, Kannur (TWU). 1984. *Smaranakal [Souvenir — remembrances].* Kannur: TWU.

Törnquist, Olle (with P. K. Michael Tharakan). 1995. *The next left? Democratisation and attempts to renew the radical political development project: The case of Kerala.* Report series no. 24. Copenhagen: Nordic Institute of Asian Studies.

Velayudhan, P. S. 1978. *SNDP yoga charitram [History of the SNDP].* Quilon: SNDP Yogam.

Weiner, Myron. 1991. *The child and the state in India: Child labor and education policy in comparative perspective.* Princeton: Princeton University Press.

World Bank. 1995. *World development report* 1995: Workers in an integrating world. New York: Oxford University Press.

Zachariah, K. C. 1992. *Demographic transition in Kerala in the 1980s: Results of a survey in three districts.* Trivandrum: Centre for Development Studies, and Ahmedabad: Gujarat Institute of Area Planning.

Alchian, A., and H. Demsetz. 1972. Production, information costs, and economic organization. *American Economic Review* 62 (5): 777–95.

Aldrich, Howard, and Robert N. Stern. 1983. Resource mobilization and the creation of U.S. producers' cooperatives, 1835–1935. *Economic and Industrial Democracy* 4: 371–406.

Alleva, Ernest L., Jr. 1983. The justification of workers' self-management. Ph.D. diss. Columbia University.

Arrow, Kenneth. 1974. *The limits of organization*. New York: W. W. Norton.

Batstone, Eric. 1983. Organization and orientation: A life cycle model of French co-operatives. *Economic and Industrial Democracy* 4: 139–61.

Baviskar, B. S. 1971. Cooperatives and caste in Maharashtra: A case study. In *Two blades of grass: Rural cooperatives in agricultural modernization*, edited by Peter Worsley. Manchester: Manchester University Press.

Bayat, Assef. 1991. *Work, politics, and power: An international perspective on workers' control and self-management*. New York: Monthly Review Press.

Bellas, C. J. 1972. *Industrial Democracy and the worker-owned firm: A Study of twenty-one plywood companies in the Pacific Northwest*. New York: Praeger.

Bernstein, Paul. 1976. Necessary elements for effective worker participation in decision making. *Journal of Economic Issues* 10 (2): 490–522.

———. 1980. *Workplace democratization*. New Brunswick, N.J.: Transaction Books.

Bhaduri, Amit. 1982. Agricultural cooperatives and peasant participation in the Socialist Republic of Viet Nam. In *Studies in rural participation*, edited by Amit Bhaduri and M. D. Anisur Rahman. New Delhi: Oxford and IBH.

Blauner, Robert. 1964. *Alienation and freedom*. Chicago: University of Chicago Press.

Bok, Derek. 1993. *The cost of talent: How executives and professionals are paid and how it affects America*. New York: The Free Press.

Bonin, John P., Derek C. Jones, and Louis Putterman. 1993. Theoretical and empirical studies of producer cooperatives: Will ever the twain meet? *Journal of Economic Literature* 31 (3): 1290–1320.

Borgatti, Stephen P. 1992. ANTHROPAC 4.0. Columbia, S.C.: Analytic Technologies.

Braverman, Harry. 1974. *Labor and monopoly capital*. New York: Monthly Review Press.

Breman, Jan. 1978. Seasonal migration and cooperative capitalism: Crushing of sugarcane and of labour by sugar factories at Bardoli. *Economic and Political Weekly* 13 (32–33): 1317–60.

Burawoy, Michael. 1983. Between the labor process and the state: The changing face of factory regimes under advanced capitalism. *American Sociological Review* 48 (5): 587–605.

CDC (Centers for Disease Control). 1989. *Reducing the health consequences of smoking: A Report of the surgeon general.* Rockville, Md.: U.S. Department of Health and Human Services.

————. 1990. *The health benefits of smoking cessation: A report of the surgeon general.* Rockville, Md.: U.S. Department of Health and Human Services.

Chasin, Barbara H., and Gerald Chasin. 1974. *Power and ideology: A Marxist approach to political sociology.* Cambridge, Mass.: Schenkman.

Chiteleen, Ignatius. 1982. Sugar cooperatives in Maharashtra: A study of historical origin and trends in cane prices, 1974–81. M. Phil. diss., Centre for Development Studies (Jawaharlal Nehru University).

Clarke, Tom. 1977. Industrial democracy: The institutionalized suppression of industrial conflict? In *Trade unions under capitalism,* edited by Tom Clarke and Laurie Lements. Glasgow: Fontana/Collins.

Coates, Ken. 1976. *The new workers' co-operatives.* Nottingham: Spokesman Books.

Cornforth, Chris. 1983. Some factors affecting the success or failure of worker co-operatives: A review of empirical research in the United Kingdom. *Economic and Industrial Democracy* 4: 163–90.

Corporations. The short run. *Dollars and Sense.* 1994 195: 4–5.

Crossette, Barbara. 1990. Women in Delhi angered by smoking pitch. *New York Times,* 18 March sec. 1, p. 18.

Downie, N. M., and Robert W. Heath. 1983. *Basic Statistical Methods.* 5th ed. New York: Harper and Row.

Edgington, Eugene S. 1980. *Randomization tests.* New York: Marcel Dekker.

Egan, Daniel. 1990. Toward a Marxist theory of labor-managed firms: Breaking the degeneration thesis. *Review of Radical Political Economics* 22 (4): 67–86.

Espinosa, Juan Guillermo, and Andrew S. Zimbalist. 1978. *Economic democracy: Workers' participation in Chilean industry, 1970–73.* New York: Academic Press.

Estrin, Saul. 1981. Income dispersion in a self-managed economy. *Economica* 48: 181–94.

Estrin, Saul, Derek C. Jones, and Jan Svejnar. 1987. The productivity effects of worker participation: Producer cooperatives in Western economies. *Journal of Comparative Economics* 11 (1): 40–61.

Fanning, Connel, and Thomas McCarthy. 1983. Hypotheses concerning the nonviability of labour-directed firms in capitalist economies. *Economic Analysis and Workers' Management* 2 (17): 123–54.

Fanning, Connel, Thomas McCarthy, and David O'Mahoney. 1983. Economic theory of the worker co-operative: An exposition. *Economic and Industrial Democracy* 4: 225–41.

Fletcher, Richard. 1976. Worker co-ops and the co-operative movement. In *The new worker co-operatives,* edited by Ken Coates. Nottingham: Spokesman Books.

Fried, Morton. 1967. *The evolution of political society: An essay in political anthropology.* New York: Random House.

Fromm, Erich. [1941] 1965. *Escape from freedom*. New York: Avon.

———. 1973. *The anatomy of human destructiveness*. Greenwich, Conn.: Fawcett.

Goleman, Daniel. 1993. Stress and isolation tied to a reduced life span. *New York Times*, 7 December, sec. C5.

Gorz, Andre. 1973. *Socialism and revolution*. Garden City, N.Y.: Anchor.

Greenberg, Edward S. 1986. *Workplace democracy: The political effects of participation*. Ithaca, N.Y.: Cornell University Press.

Greenwood, Davydd J. et al. 1991. *Industrial democracy as process: Participatory action research in the Fagor Cooperative Group of Mondragón*. Assen/Maastricht, Netherlands: Van Gorcum.

Guérin, Daniel. 1970. *Anarchism: From theory to practice*. Translated by Mary Klopper. Introduction by Noam Chomsky. New York: Monthly Review Press.

Hammond, John L. 1988. *Building popular power: Workers' and neighborhood movements in the Portuguese revolution*. New York: Monthly Review Press.

Hilts, Philip J. 1994. Sharp rise seen in smokers' health care costs. *New York Times*, 8 July 1994, sec. A12.

Horn, Daniel. 1968. The health consequences of smoking. In *Smoking, health, and behavior*, edited by Edgar F. Borgatta and Robert R. Evans. Chicago: Aldine.

Horvat, Branko. 1982. *The political economy of socialism: A Marxist social theory*. Armonk, N.Y.: M. E. Sharpe.

Jensen, Michael C., and William H. Meckling. 1979. Rights and production functions: An application to labor-managed firms and codetermination. *Journal of Business* 52 (4): 469–506.

Jones, Derek C. 1976. British economic theory on associations of labourers, 1848–1973. *Annals of Public and Cooperative Economy* 47 (1): 5–36.

———. 1980. Producer co-operatives in industrialized Western economies. *British Journal of Industrial Relations* 18: 141–54.

Jones, Ernest. 1978a. A letter to the advocates of the co-operative principle and to the members of co-operative societies. In Marx, Karl, and Friedrich Engels. *Collected works*. Vol. 11. New York: International Publishers.

———. 1978b. Co-operation: What it is and what it ought to be. In Marx, Karl, and Friedrich Engels. *Collected works*. Vol. 11. New York: International Publishers.

Kanbargi, Ramesh. 1991. Introduction and overview. In *Child labour in the Indian subcontinent: Dimensions and implications*, edited by Ramesh Kanbargi. New Delhi: Sage Publications.

Kaplan, George A., Thomas W. Wilson, Richard D. Cohen, Ussi Kauhanen, Melien Wu, and Jukka T. Salonen. 1994. Social functioning and overall mortality: Prospective evidence from the Kuopio ischemic heart disease risk factor study. *Epidemiology* 5: 495–500.

Karasek, Robert, and Töres Theorell. 1990. *Healthy work: Stress, productivity, and the reconstruction of working life*. New York: Basic Books.

Kasmir, Sharryn. 1996. *The myth of Mondragón: Cooperatives, politics, and working-class life in a Basque town.* Albany: State University of New York Press.

Kerbo, Harold R. 1996. *Social stratification and inequality: Class conflict in historical and comparative perspective.* 3d ed. New York: McGraw-Hill.

Krimerman, Len, and Frank Lindenfeld, eds. 1992. *When workers decide: Workplace democracy takes root in North America.* Philadelphia: New Society.

Kumar, Rajesh. Controlling tobacco use. *Economic and Political Weekly* 29 (29): 1841.

Lee, Danny. 1994. Working together. *New Statesman and Society,* 17 June, p. vii.

Lenin, V. I. [1910] 1967a. Draft resolution on co-operative societies from the Russian Social-Democratic delegation at the Copenhagen congress. In *Collected works.* Vol. 16. Moscow: Progress Publishers.

———. [1910] 1967b. The question of co-operative societies at the International Socialist Congress in Copenhagen. In *Collected works.* Vol. 16. Moscow: Progress Publishers.

———. [1921] 1970a. Speech closing the discussion delivered at a meeting of the communist group of the congress of January 24. In *On trade unions: A collection of articles and speeches.* Moscow: Progress Publishers.

———. [1921] 1970b. Once again on the trade unions, the current situation and the mistakes of Trotsky and Bukharin. In *On trade unions: A collection of articles and speeches.* Moscow: Progress Publishers.

———. [1923] 1970c. Preliminary draft resolution of the tenth congress of the Russian Communist Party on the syndicalist and anarchist deviation in our party. In *On trade unions: A collection of articles and speeches.* Moscow: Progress Publishers.

———. [1922] 1970d. Draft theses on the role and functions of the trade unions under the new economic policy. In *On trade unions: A collection of articles and speeches.* Moscow: Progress Publishers.

Lenski, Gerhard. 1966. *Power and privilege.* New York: McGraw-Hill.

Levin, Henry M. 1984. Employment and productivity of producer cooperatives. In *Worker cooperatives in America,* edited by Robert Jackell and Henry M. Levin. Berkeley: University of California Press.

Luxemburg, Rosa. [1899, 1908] 1971. Social reform or revolution. In *Selected political writings of Rosa Luxemburg,* edited by Dick Howard. New York: Monthly Review Press.

Malyarov, O. V. 1983. *The role of the state in the socio-economic structure of India.* New Delhi: Vikas.

Marglin, Stephen A. 1974. What do bosses do? The origins and functions of hierarchy in capitalist production. *Review of Radical Political Economics* 6 (2): 33–60.

Marshall, Alfred. 1920. *Industry and trade.* 3d ed. London. Macmillan.

———. 1925. *Principles of economics.* 8th ed. London. Macmillan.

Marx, Karl [1864] 1972. Inaugural address of the Working Men's International Association. In *The Marx-Engels Reader,* edited by Robert C. Tucker. New York: Norton.

———. [1866] 1973. Instructions for the delegates of the Provisional General Council. In *The Karl Marx library,* edited and translated by Saul K. Padover. Vol. 3. New York: McGraw-Hill.

———. [1891] 1994. Critique of the Gotha Program. In *Karl Marx: Selected writings,* edited by Lawrence H. Simon. Indianapolis: Hacket.

Marx, Karl, and Friedrich Engels. [1848] 1972. *Manifesto of the Communist Party.* In *The Marx-Engels Reader,* edited by Robert C. Tucker. New York: Norton.

Mason, Ronald. 1982. *Participatory and workplace democracy: A theoretical development in critique of liberalism.* Carbondale and Edwardsville, Ill.: Southern Illinois University Press.

McClintock, Cynthia. 1981. *Peasant cooperatives and political change in Peru.* Princeton: Princeton University Press.

Michels, Robert. [1915] 1962. *Political parties: A sociological study of the oligarchical tendencies of modern democracy.* New York: The Free Press.

Mill, John Stuart. [1909] 1965. On the probable futurity of the labouring classes. In *Principles of political economy,* b. 4, chap. 7. Vol. 3 of *Collected works of John Stuart Mill.* Toronto: University of Toronto Press.

Nash, June, and Nicholas Hopkins. 1976. Anthropological approaches to the study of cooperatives, collectives, and self-management. In *Popular participation in social change,* edited by June Nash, J. Dandler, and N. Hopkins. The Hague and Paris: Mouton Publishers.

Nightingale, Donald V. 1982. *Workplace democracy: An inquiry into employee participation in Canadian work organizations.* Toronto: University of Toronto Press.

Nozick, Robert. 1974. *Anarchy, state, and utopia.* New York: Basic Books.

Oakeshott, Robert. 1978. *The case for workers' coops.* London: Routledge and Kegan Paul.

———. 1982. Spain: The Mondragón enterprises. In *The performance of labor-managed firms,* edited by Frank Stephen. New York: St. Martin's.

Pateman, Carole. 1970. *Participation and democratic theory.* Cambridge: Cambridge University Press.

Pencavel, John, and Ben Craig. 1994. The empirical performance of orthodox models of the firm: Conventional firms and worker cooperatives. *Journal of Political Economy* 102 (4): 718–44.

Poole, Michael. 1989. *The origins of economic democracy: Profit-sharing and employee-shareholding schemes.* London: Routledge.

Rawls, John. 1971. *A theory of justice.* Cambridge, Mass.: Belknap Press.

Reich, Wilhelm. [1933] 1970. *The mass psychology of Fascism.* Translated by Vincent R. Carfagno. New York: Farrar, Straus, and Giroux.

Richman, Barry M. 1969. *Industrial society in Communist China: A firsthand study of Chinese economic development and management—With significant comparisons with industry in India, the U.S.S.R., Japan, and the United States.* New York: Random House.

Rock, Charles P., and Mark A. Klinedinst. 1992. Worker-managed firms, democratic principles, and the evolution of financial relations. *Journal of Economic Issues* 26 (2): 605–13.

Rooney, Patrick Michael. 1992. ESOPS, producer co-ops, and traditional firms: Are they different? *Journal of Economic Issues* 26 (2): 593–603.

Rothschild, Joyce, and J. Allen Whitt. 1986. *The cooperative workplace: Potentials and dilemmas of organizational democracy and participation.* New York: Cambridge University Press.

Scurrah, Martin J. 1984. The sector and firm in self-management: 1. Institutional models. *Economic and Industrial Democracy* 5: 325–40.

Shenon, Philip. 1995. Asia's having one huge nicotine fit. *New York Times,* 15 May, sec. 4, pp. 1, 16.

Sklar, Holly. 1995. *Chaos or community? Seeking solutions, not scapegoats, for bad economics.* Boston: South End Press.

Srikantan, K. Sivaswamy. 1991. Demographic and social dimensions of child labor in India. In *Child labor in the Indian subcontinent: Dimensions and implications,* edited by Ramesh Kanbargi. New Delhi: Sage Publications.

Staber, Udo. 1993. Worker cooperatives and the business cycle: Are cooperatives the answer to unemployment? *American Journal of Economics and Sociology* 52 (2): 129–43.

Stephen, Frank. 1984. *The economic analysis of producers' cooperatives.* New York: St. Martin's.

Street, John. 1983. Socialist arguments for industrial democracy. *Economic and industrial democracy* 4: 519–39.

Thomas, Henk, and Chris Logan. 1982. The performance of the Mondragón cooperatives in Spain. In *Participatory and self-managed firms,* edited by D. C. Jones and J. Svejnar. Lexington, Mass.: Lexington Books.

Thornley, Jenny. 1983. Workers' co-operatives and trade unions: The Italian experience. *Economic and Industrial Democracy* 4: 321–44.

Vanek, Jaroslav. 1971. *The participatory economy: An evolutionary hypothesis and a strategy for development.* Ithaca, N.Y.: Cornell University Press.

———. 1977. *The labor-managed economy: Essays by Jaroslav Vanek.* Ithaca, N.Y.: Cornell University Press.

Wachtel, Howard M. 1973. *Workers' management and workers' wages in Yugoslavia: The theory and practice of participatory socialism.* Ithaca, N.Y.: Cornell University Press.

Ward, Colin. 1972. The anarchist contribution. In *The case for participatory democracy,* edited by C. George Benello. New York: Viking.

Warner, Malcolm, and Riccardo Peccei. 1978. Management decentralization and worker participation in a multinational company context. In *Workers' participation in an internationalized economy,* edited by Bernhard Wilpert, Ayse Kudat, and Yilmaz Özkan. Kent, Ohio: Kent State University Press.

Webb, Sidney, and Beatrice Webb. 1920. *A constitution for socialist commonwealth of Great Britain.* London: Longman Green.

Weber, Max. [1910] 1958. The meaning of discipline. In *From Max Weber: Es-*

says in sociology, edited by H. H. Gerth, C. Wright Mills. New York: Oxford University Press.

Whyte, William F., and Kathleen K. Whyte. 1988. *Making Mondragón: The growth and dynamics of the worker cooperative complex.* Report no. 14. Ithaca, N.Y.: Industrial and Labor Relations Press, Cornell University.

Worsley, Peter. 1971. Introduction. In *Two blades of grass: Rural cooperatives in agricultural modernization,* edited by Peter Worsley. Manchester: Manchester University Press.

Zald, Mayer N., and Roberta Ash. 1966. Social movement organizations: Growth, decay, and change. *Social Forces* 44 (3): 327–41.

INTERVIEWS

Note: Copies of the English transcriptions of these interviews are deposited at the Centre for Development Studies and the A. K. G. Centre for Research and Studies, both in Thiruvananthapuram. These interviews vary in length from about ten minutes (four pages) to two hours (forty-eight pages). Most are about thirty minutes (twelve pages).

1. Ambu, Kochi, Director Board Member, Payyanur Primary Society. 23 March 1993.

2. Anandan, C. K., Secretary, 1958 Workers' Cooperative. 9 July 1993.

3. Balakrishnan, K., Maistry, Neelishwar Primary Society. 27 March 1993.

4. Balan, C. C., Chief Foreman, Central Society. 9 June 1993.

5. Bharathan, Panniyan, Central Society Director Board Member, 1969–89. 9 June 1993.

6. Chandran, Pookkadan, Retired President, Chirakkal Primary Society and Retired Director Board Member, Central Society. 6 January 1993.

7. Chathukutty Nair, P., Secretary, Bediaduka Primary Society. 25 March 1993.

8. Damodaran, K. K., Director Board Member, Badagara Primary Society. 20 March 1993.

9. Ganapathy, P. C., Director Board Member, Neelishwar Primary Society. 13 March 1993.

10. Gopalakrishnan, N. P., First Secretary of the Central Society. 10 June 1993.

11. Govindan, M. N., Secretary, Chala Primary Society. 7 April 1993.

12. Haridasan, P. V., Secretary, Payyanur Primary Society. 5 January 1993.

13. Haridasan, P. V., Secretary, Payyanur Primary Society. 1 April 1993.

14. Kamalakshmi, T. V., Director Board Member, Payyanur Primary Society. 23 March 1993.

15. Kannan, C., President, Tobacco Workers' Union. 6 June 1993.

16. Kariangode Work Centre, Neelishwar Primary Society. Various workers. 5 January 1993.

17. Karivaloor Work Centre No. 2, Payyanur Primary Society. Various workers. 5 January 1993.

18. Karunakaran, K., Director Board Member, Neelishwar Primary Society. 12 March 1993.

19. Kumaran, T. C., Trade Union Activist. 10 June 1993.

20. Kunhambhu, T., Maistry, Kariangode Work Centre, Neelishwar Primary Society. 5 January 1993.

21. Kunhappan, P. V., Foreman, Payyanur Primary Society. 1 April 1993.

22. Kunhikannan, Nair, President, Neelishwar Primary Society. 12 March 1993.

23. Kunhikannan, Pannakada, First Chief Foreman of KDB. 10 June 1993.

24. Kunhikannan, V., Secretary, Neelishwar Primary Society. 13 March 1993.

25. Kunhiraman, K. C., Director of the 1958 Cooperative. 9 June 1993.

26. Mukundan, U., Director Board Member, Central Society. 20 October 1993.

27. Nanu, M. C., Director Board Member, Chala Primary Society. 2 April 1993.

28. Nanu, Punchayil, Trade Union Activist. 7 June 1993.

29. Narayanan, A. K., Director Board Member, Central Society. 13 October 1993.

30. Narayanan, K., President, Badagara Primary Society. 20 March 1993.

31. Narayanan, K. V., Maistry. Karivaloor Work Centre No. 1, Payyanur Primary Society. 5 January 1993.

32. Narayanan, M., Director Board Member, Payyanur Primary Society. 23 March 1993.

33. Panikkar, G. K., Chairman, Kerala Dinesh Beedi. 18 January 1993.

34. Panikkar, G. K., Chairman, Kerala Dinesh Beedi. 11 October 1993.

35. Panikkar, G. K., Chairman, Kerala Dinesh Beedi. 24 October 1993.

36. Pavithran, N., Director Board Member, Central Society. 20 October 1993.

37. Peringapurath, Narayanan, Director Board Member, Payyanur Primary Society. 23 March 1993.

38. Premrajan, U., Joint Secretary, Kannur Tobacco Workers' Union. 22 June 1994.

39. Raghavan, K., President, Payyanur Primary Society. 23 March 1993.

40. Raveendran, A. P., Office Manager, Central Society. 20 October 1993.

41. Raveendran, K., President, Chala Primary Society. 2 April 1993.

42. Ravindran, E. K., Director Board Member, Neelishwar Primary Society. 12 March 1993.

43. Sahadevan, K. P., Secretary, Tobacco Workers' Union. 9 June 1993.

44. Sankaran, V., Director Board Member, Payyanur Primary Society. 23 March 1993.

45. Sasidharan, Secretary, Badagara Primary Society. 16 March 1993.

46. Savithri, K., Director Board Member, Neelishwar Primary Society. 12 March 1993.

47. Vasu, Vadavathi, Vice President, Kannur District Council. 7 June 1993.

48. Vijayan, P., CITU District Committee. 7 June 1993.

The following interviews provided information used in this book but have not been transcribed and entered into the archives:

49. Central Society Director Board Members. 21 June 1994.

50. Gopalakrishnan, N. P., First Secretary, Central Society. 5 January 1993.

51. Gopalakrishnan, N. P., Retired First Secretary, Central Society. 20 October 1993.

52. Gopalakrishnan, N. P., Retired First Secretary, Central Society. 22 June 1994.

53. Kannan, C., President, Tobacco Workers' Union. 21 June, 1994.

54. Kannur Town Primary Society. Maistry and trade union activists. 5 January 1993.

55. Panikkar, G. K., Chairman, Kerala Dinesh Beedi. 18 October 1993.

56. Panikkar, G. K., Chairman, Kerala Dinesh Beedi. 8 June 1994.

57. Panikkar, G. K., Chairman, Kerala Dinesh Beedi. 20 June 1994.

58. Pavithran, N., Central Society Director Board Member. 21 June 1994.

59. Radha Madhavan, E., First Secretary, Central Society. 20 October 1993.

60. Radha Madhavan, E. First Secretary, Central Society. 22 June 1994.

Index

Abdulla, N., 200
Absenteeism: at KDB, 151–52, 166–67, 175, 193, 230nn6, 7
Accumulation debate, 87, 106, 116, 205, 213. *See also* Degeneration
Alienation, 189, 190–198. *See also* Working conditions
All-India Congress Committee, 43
All-India Coordination Committee of Working Women, 139
All-India Trade Union Congress (AITUC), 49, 63, 70, 143, 147, 148, 149
All-Kerala Conference of Beedi and Cigar Unions, 51, 58
All-Kerala Trade Union Congress, 44
Anarchism, 56, 207, 208
Anti-Jap melas, 43, 226n12
Antismoking campaign, 105, 117. *See also* Smoking; Tobacco
Ash, Roberta, 202, 232n17

Badagara, 160–61, 230n8
Balan, C. C., 70, 72, 113, 116
Banerjee, Sumanta, 229n14
Basel Evangelical Movement, 27
Bayat, Asset, 229n11, 231n1
Bediaduka, 113–14, 115, 148, 160, 203
Beedi and Cigar Industrial Premises Regulation Act, 51
Beedi and Cigar Labor Bill, 51
Beedi and Cigar Workers' Conditions of Employment Act, 10, 51, 52, 62, 63, 173
Beedi pillaers, 22
Beedis: counterfeit, 94, 101–2, 112; demand for, 6, 101–5, 117, 146–47, 219–20, 229n12; drying, 120 photo, 121; KDB output, 125, 140, 157–59,

165–66, 172, 177–78, 229n1, 230 nn6, 8; prices, 103, 157, 229n2; labeling, 98; marketing, 99–104; making, 6–9, 121; quality control, 131–32, 229n8; sales, 6, 75–76, 101–5, 110–11, 117, 159; taxes on, 102–3, 228n7
Beedi workers: absenteeism, 151–52, 166–67, 175, 193, 230nn6, 7; attitudes of, 152–54; conflicts with KDB management, 129–34, 144–45; democratic consciousness of, 22–23, 53, 55, 201–4; and independence movement, 33–36; as KDB directors, 134–40; as KDB staff, 127–28; statistics on, 47–48, 75–76; tortured or killed, 43, 46, 200; workday, 121. *See also* Women
Beedi Workers' Welfare Fund, 80
Beedi Workers' Welfare Fund Act, 10
Benefits: at KDB. *See* Wages; Working conditions
Benzoapyrene, 219, 232n3
Bernstein, Eduard, 209
Bernstein, Paul, 23, 53, 191
Besant, Annie, 33
Bhaduri, Amit, 231n1
Bharat Beedi, 48, 63
Bharathan, Panniyan, 61
Bharatiya Mazdoor Sangh, 143, 148
Bharat Seva Sangham, 54
Birth rates, 17, 173–75
BJP, 147–48
Blauner, Robert, 190–91, 194, 197–98
Bok, Derek, 231nn3, 9
Bonus: at KDB, 76, 79, 142, 188, 229n3; in European cooperatives, 231n6. *See also* Wages
British colonial rule, 5, 27
Burma (Mayanmar), 24, 44

Capitalism: and authoritarianism, 232n12; and caste, 26–27; and cooperatives, 86, 119, 183–84; and KDB, 180–81; and layoffs, 57; and workplace democracy, 188–90
Caste: and class, 32–33; reform movements, 26, 35; segregation, 25–26. *See also* Communalism
Casual leave wages: at KDB, 12–13, 79. *See also* Abstenteeism
C. C. Beedi, 103 table 4.1
Centre for Indian Trade Unions (CITU), 74, 139, 143, 146, 147, 148, 149, 150
Chala: dividends dispute, 114; labelers' dispute, 149
Chandran, Pookkadan, 74
Chandroth, Sardar, 32
Charka Beedi Company, 24, 31, 54
Chartists, 206
Chasin, Barbara, 119, 229n10
Chasin, Gerald, 119, 229n10
Chathopadhaya, Kamala Devi, 33
Chathukutty, 43
Chatta Beedi Company, 24
Cherumas, 25
Child labor, 9, 10, 25, 30–31, 37; and KDB, 81–83, 151
Child Labor Prohibition and Regulation Act, 83
China, 231n1
China Beedis, 103 table 4.1
Christian Socialists, 55, 207, 208
Civil Disobedience Action, 34–35
Coir industry, 26, 226n3
Commercialization of agriculture, 26–27
Commission system, 47, 226n15. *See also* Putting-out system
Communalism, 32, 226n9. *See also* Caste
Communist ministry of 1957, 18, 52, 58, 62, 227n20
Communist Party of India (CPI), 18, 58, 59, 70, 71, 143, 147, 148, 214, 229n13; banned, 46; and World War II, 41–45
Communist Party of India-Marxist (CPM), 66, 70, 71, 143, 155, 213, 214; and KDB elections, 72, 147, 148, 150, 229n13; and women, 139
Communist Party of Russia, 211
Congress Party. *See* Indian National Congress
Congress Socialist Party, 34–35, 38, 41
Contract system, 48. *See also* Putting-out system

Cooperative Act, 130, 158
Cooperative capitalism, 119
Cooperatives: and capitalism, 86, 119, 183–84; capital shortage, 86–87, 228n1; and economic development, 14; in Europe and North America, 55–57, 87, 183, 186, 199, 210–11, 228n3; in India, 14–15, 185; in Kerala, 15–17; Lenin on, 208–9; Marx on, 206–7; nineteenth century, 118; and popular mobilization, 22–23, 56–57, 119, 201–4, 228n2, 232nn14, 15, 18, 19; and trade unions, 56, 210–12
Corruption: and KDB, 97, 152, 196–97; in tobacco sales, 97
Cottage industries, 203. *See also* Traditional industries
Counterfeit beedis, 94, 101–2, 112
Counterfeit labels, 98
Cuba, 231n1

da Gama, Vasco, 5
Damodaran, K., 34–35, 41
Day care, 13, 179–81
Dearness allowance, 13, 145, 166, 173, 187, 220; debate over, 122–25; and leaf output, 177–78
Death benefit, 13, 79
Deductions, 10, 132. *See also* Wages
Deepak, 65
Degeneration: and KDB, 125, 127, 150–55, 165, 200–203, 204, 210, 214; theory of, 69, 118–21; Vanek's model of, 87–88, 106, 116, 205
Democracy, 184: and alienation, 191–92; and corruption, 196–97; and dictatorship, 197–200, 232n12; at KDB, 192–93; and KDB director boards, 71–72, 92–95, 134–41, 147–48, 221, 232n4; and mobility, 195–96; and Pension and Welfare Committee, 92, 95, 138; in worker cooperatives, 188
Democratic consciousness, 22–23, 53, 55, 84, 201–4
Development theorists, 14

Edgington, Eugene S., 230n12
Egalitarianism, 184–86; at KDB, 128–29, 134–40, 178–81, 186–88. *See also* Inequality
Employees' Retirement Benefit Scheme, 79
Ennakettu, 30, 37, 226n7

ESOPs, 183, 231n8
Ezhava (caste). *See* Tiyyas
Ezhava Social Reform Movement, 27–28

Fabian socialism, 206
Factories Act, 37, 38, 44, 46, 53. *See also*
New Factories Act
Federation of Beedi Trade Unions, 214
Foremen: at KDB, 127–29, 146, 164
Fromm, Erich, 197–98

Gandhi, Mahatma, 34, 36
Ganesh Beedi Company, 44, 47, 48, 63,
65, 72–73, 75, 103 table 4.1
General body: of KDB, 91–93, 108, 110,
114, 138, 221
Ghate, S. V., 33
Gherao, 62
Gift coupon scheme, 100
Goleman, Daniel, 231n11
Giriappa, S., 81
Goondas, 46, 226n14
Gopalakrishnan, N. P., 70, 71
Gopalan, A. K., 34–35, 38, 39, 51, 222
Gopalan, K. P., 35, 58
Gopalan, Susheela, 222
Gopalan Master, Pandiyala, 200
Gowri, K. R., 6 caption
Great Durbar Beedi Company, 43, 44, 48
Greenberg, Edward, 199
Greenwood, Davydd, 231n10, 232n13
Guntur, 96
Guru Kripa Beedi Company, 65

Handloom industry, 27
Haridas Beedi Company, 24
Herring, Ronald, 232n15
Hind Mazdoor Sabha (HMS), 49, 63, 143,
147
Hitler, Adolf, 232n12
Home Rule Movement, 33
Horn, Daniel, 232n2
Horvat, Branko, 231n1
Household production. *See* Putting-out
system

Independent Workers' Union (STU), 63,
143. *See also* Muslim League
India: beedis smoked, 6; beedi workers
in, 9–12; child labor in, 83, 227n9;
Cooperative Act, 158; cooperatives in,
14–15, 203–4; "emergency," 200;
independence movement in, 34–36

Indian Administrative Service, 129
Indian National Congress, 33, 39, 49, 70,
143, 147, 149. *See also* Congress
Socialist Party
Indian National Trade Union Congress
(INTUC), 49, 63, 143, 147, 149
Inequality, 118, 184–88, 229n5, 231n3. *See
also* Egalitarianism
Infant mortality, 17
Infrastructure: at KDB, 161–64
Iron Law of Oligarchy, 119, 150–55

Jaganath temple, 28–29
Janata Dal, 143, 147
Jan Sangh, 65
Jeffrey, Robin, 229n10, 232n16
Jensen, Michael C., 88
Job security, 194–95, 231n10. *See also*
Layoffs; Working conditions
Joint Action Council, 63, 64
Jones, Ernest, 206

Kannan, C., 35, 50, 51, 74, 84, 150–51
Kannan, M. C., 70
Kannur Beedi Workers' Industrial
Cooperative, 59
Kannur District Cooperative Bank, 68
Kaplan, George, 231n11
Karasek, Robert, 231n11
Kasmir, Sharryn, 231n7, 232n18
Kerala: birth rates in, 17, 174–75;
cooperatives in, 15–17; economic crisis
of, 18–19; land reform, 6 caption, 18,
202; leftist ministries, 18, 19–21, 52, 58,
62, 84, 140; literacy, 17, 20, 40–41, 71,
136, 169, 203; per capita income, 17,
194; political fragmentation in, 70–71,
213; state government and KDB, 68,
91, 93, 155, 228n5; trade unions in,
15–16; traditional industries in, 15–17;
unemployment in, 19; women, 140,
173–75
Kerala Beedi Thozhilali Union, 33
Kerala Desh Beedi, 101
Kerala Dinesh Beedi: absence of
corruption, 97, 152, 196-97;
absenteeism at, 151–52, 166–67, 175,
193, 230nn6, 7; benefits, 12–13, 76,
78–83, 152–53, 163, 229n3; and
degeneration theories, 87–88, 106, 116,
125, 127, 150–55, 165, 200–203, 204,
205, 210, 214; director boards, 71–72,
92–95, 134–41, 147–48, 221, 232n4;

Kerala Dinesh Beedi (*continued*)
diversification, 105, 117, 217–23;
egalitarianism, 128–29, 134–40,
178–81, 186–88; general body, 91–93,
108, 110, 114, 138, 221; and Kannur
community, 3–5, 154–55, 158; and
Kerala Model, 17, 21, 174, 202–4, 223;
and Kerala state, 68–69, 91, 93, 155,
203–4, 228n5; leaf outturn, 111, 125–26,
133, 141, 172, 176–79; management
staff, 16–17, 92–94, 127–34, 146, 162,
164–65; marketing, 73–75, 99–105,
219–20; output, 109–11, 125–27,
140–41, 157, 229n1, 230n6; Pension
and Welfare Committee, 92, 95, 138;
profits, 76, 77–78, 106, 157–59, 167,
176–77, 181; sales, 75–76, 101–5,
110–11, 117, 159; sales agents, 74–75,
99, 103; and social movements, 69–70,
84, 201–3, 214, 223, 232n19; tobacco
blending, 72, 97–98, 120 photo;
tobacco outturn, 111, 125–26, 166, 168;
trade unions and, 72, 141–50, 153–54,
160, 212–15; wages, 13–14, 76, 78–79,
121–25, 128–31, 194; women workers,
7, 13, 75–76, 114, 138–40, 168–73, 176,
178–81, 203, 223; workforce, 75–77,
81–83, 153–54, 158, 162–73; working
conditions, 12–13, 80–83, 112–15, 121,
131–34, 161–63, 166–67, 179, 193–95,
230n7
Kerala Model, 1, 2, 52; crisis of, 18–19;
and KDB, 17, 21, 174, 202–4, 223
Kerala Pradesh Congress Committee,
33, 42
Kerala People's Science Movement
(KSSP), 203
Kerala Swadesh Beedi, 101
Khader, K. P. Cheriya Abdul, 70
Khadi, 34
Knights of Labor, 210
Knights of Saint Crispin, 210
Krishnan, Kottiyah, 54
Kropotkin, Peter, 207
Kumaran, T. C., 60
Kunhiraman, K. C., 60–61
Kunjiraman, Sardar Chandroth, 32
Kutty, P. V., 69–70, 72

Labor costs, 159, 229n3, 230n4
Layoffs, 62–64, 66, 193. *See also* Job
security; Unemployment; Working
conditions

Leaf outturn, 111, 125–26, 141, 166–68,
172, 176, 177; Payyanur experiment,
133, 178; and women workers, 179
Lenin, V. I., 208–9, 211
Literacy: at KDB, 136, 169, 203; in
Kerala, 17, 20, 40–41, 71
Lung cancer, 218, 232n3
Luxemburg, Rosa, 209

Madan Beedi Company, 24
Madhavan, Potheri, 32–33, 38
Madhya Pradesh Marketing Federation,
96
Madras Labor Union, 28
Maha Laxmi Traders, 65
Maintenance of Internal Security Act,
200
Maistries: at KDB, 12, 92, 112, 113, 121,
127–34, 141, 146, 178, 187, 229n8
Malabar: description, 3–5, 225n1;
famine, 44–45
Malabar Reading Room Conference, 41
Malayan (caste), 25
Malayarov, O. V., 14
Management, 17, 183, 185, 188–92,
209–11; at KDB, 16–17, 92–94, 127–34,
146, 162, 164–65, 221–22
Mandel, Ernest, 208
Mangalam, 151
Mangalore Ganesh Beedi. *See* Ganesh
Beedi Company
Mappila (caste). *See* Muslims
Mappila rebellion, 34, 36, 226n10
Marketing, 73–75, 99–105, 219–20
Marx, Karl, 119, 206–9
Marxism, 56, 206
Maslow, Arthur, 23
Matchbox scheme, 100
Maternity Benefit Act, 47
Maternity benefits: at KDB, 13, 79,
173–75, 180
Medium Beedis, 110, 111, 147, 167–68,
230n8
Mercara, 63, 66
Meckling, William H., 88
Michels, Robert, 119, 202, 228n2
Mill, John Stuart, 189, 198
Minimum Wages Act, 59
Minimum Wages Committee, 48, 50, 79,
123, 141, 212
Mobilization: and KDB, 69–70, 84, 201–3,
214, 223, 232n19. *See also* Strikes
Mohanan, N., 152

Mondragón, 186, 190, 211, 212, 229n7, 230n4, 231n10, 232nn13, 18
Morazha, 42–43
Murkothu family, 27
Muslim League, 70, 143, 147, 150
Muslims, 5, 25, 27, 31, 34, 42, 49, 65, 80; and early beedi industry, 23–24. *See also* Mappila rebellion

Nair (caste), 25–26, 32
Nair, M. P. Narayanan, 36
Namboodiripad, E. M. S., 33, 34, 41, 42, 71, 213
Nanu, Punchayil, 74
Narayana Guru, Sree, 27–28, 32
National Labor Organization, 143
Naxalites, 149, 229n14
Nayanar, V. R., 54
Nazi regime, 198, 231n12
New Democratic Initiatives, 19–21
New Durbar Beedi Company, 40
New Durbar Factory, 38–39
New Factories Act, 47
New Lanark, 55, 206
New Left, 56, 208
Nippani, 10, 96
Nossiter, T. J., 229n13
Nozick, Robert, 231n5

Orissa Forest Development Corporation, 96, 97
Output: at KDB, 125, 140, 157–59, 165–66, 172, 177–78, 229n1, 230nn6, 8
Outturn. *See* Leaf outturn; Tobacco: outturn
Outwork. *See* Putting-out system
Owen, Robert, 55, 56, 184, 206

Panikkar, G. K., 69–70, 73, 80–81, 100, 109, 124, 132–33, 152, 155, 165, 215, 221
Paris Commune, 56
Pavithran, N., 94, 101
Pavithran, P. T., 70
Payment of Wages Act, 47
Payyanur (primary society): leaf outturn experiment, 133, 178
Payyanur (town), 34
Peccei, Riccardo, 192
Pension and Welfare Committee, 72, 92, 95, 138, 148, 212
Pensions, 6 caption, 12, 13, 79
People's Campaign for the Ninth Plan, 20–21, 223

People's Resource Mapping Programme, 20
Personal days. *See* Absenteeism; Casual leave wages
Piece-rate system. *See* Wages
Pillai, P. Krishna, 34–35, 36, 41, 55, 57
Poduval, Chinta, 46
Politics of development action, 71
Prabhatham, 41
Prabhu, C. L., 40
Price enhancements debate, 106–9
Prizes, 132–33, 141, 194
Production policy, 43
Productivity. *See* Leaf outturn; Output; Tobacco: outturn
Profits: at KDB, 76, 77–78, 106, 157–59, 167, 176–77, 181; in private sector, 101–2, 188. *See also* Marketing; Sales
Proudhon, Pierre, 207
Provident fund, 13
Proximity hypothesis, 198–200
Putting-out system, 9–11, 48, 50, 64, 66, 77. *See also* Wages
P. V. S. Beedi, 44, 48

Quit India Struggle, 43

Ragavan, Kolangaroth, 200
Raghavan, Azhikodan, 57–58
Rajadhani Beedis, 100, 167–68, 230n8
Rajan, A. T., 200
Rashtriya Swayam Sevak Sangh, 65, 66, 200
Raveendran, K., 108
Rawls, John, 185–86, 231nn4, 5
Rebates. *See* Price enhancements debate
Reich, Wilhelm, 231n12
Retrenchment. *See* Layoffs
Revolutionary Socialist Party, 143
Rochdale pioneers, 55
Rooney, Patrick, 231n8
Rothschild, Joyce, 23, 52–53, 202, 231n1, 232n14
Russia, 231n1
RSS. *See* Rashtriya Swayam Sevak Sangh

Sadhoo Beedi Company, 47, 48, 103 table 4.1
Sahadevan, K. P., 70
Sale-purchase system, 11–12. *See also* Putting-out system

Sales: of beedis, 6; of KDB, 75–76, 101–5, 110–11, 117, 159. *See also* Marketing
Sangham Saranam, 29, 226n5
Sathyamurthy, T. V., 229n13, 232n15
Sattar Beedi Factory, 36
Satyagraha, 31, 34, 50, 226n8
Secretaries: at KDB, 92, 127–31
Sexual harassment, 10
Shekhar, N. C., 41
Shelter organization, 87, 109
Shlyapnikov, A. G., 211
Sinnar (Maharashtra), 10–11
Sivaprasad, Sadhu, 28, 226n4
Small Beedis, 100, 167–68, 230n8
Small cigarettes, 104–5
Smoking, 24; and health, 217–19
Socialist Party, 70
Society Beedi, 59
Soviet Union, 41, 42, 43
Special Beedis, 100, 110, 111, 147, 160–61, 167–68, 230n8
Spillover hypothesis, 198–200
Sree Narayana Beedi Thozhilali Sangham, 28–29, 30, 40, 54
Sree Narayana Dharma Paripalana Yogam, 28
Sri Gnanodaya Yogam, 28
Standing orders dispute, 131
State intervention: and cooperatives, 14–17, 184–85; and KDB, 66–73, 155, 203–5
Stress, 195
Strikes, 55, 207, 209; in 1934, 31; in 1937, 36–40; in 1946, 45–47; in 1960s, 50; in Bombay, 11; by KDB staff, 130
Structural adjustment, 97
Struggle Solidarity Committees, 65, 74
St. Thomas, 4
STU, 63, 143. *See also* Muslim League
Sunday wage. *See* Wages
Swatantra Beedi Thozhilali Union, 49

Tellicherry: police station attack, 65
Tellicherry Beach killings, 43
Tellicherry Beedi Thozhilali Union, 49
Tellicherry Beedi Workers' Cooperative, 60–61
Tendu (leaf), 7 photo, 8, 68, 96, 97, 111, 121, 125, 228n6. *See also* Leaf outturn
Theorell, Töres, 231n11
Thomas, T. V., 68
Thornley, Jenny, 213

Thottada, 230n8
Thozhilali Beedi Factory, 54
Thrift fund, 12, 13, 105–6, 135
Tiyyas, 25–26, 32, 195, 226n1. *See also* Ezhava Social Reform Movement
Tobacco: blending, 72, 97–98, 120 photo; diversification from, 219–23; health dangers of, 9, 217–19; outturn, 111, 125–26, 166, 168
Tobacco Trade Group, 70
Tobacco Workers' Union, 49, 50–51, 74, 150
Total Literacy Campaign, 203
Trade unions: and birth of KDB, 61–66; and child labor, 31, 81–82; and cooperatives, 56, 210–12; in early beedi industry, 28, 31–33, 35–41, 44–47, 49–53; at KDB, 141–47, 153–54, 212–15; in Kerala, 15–18; names of, 143; and Pension and Welfare Committee, 72, 92, 95, 148, 212; rivalries, 147–50, 160, 213
Traditional industries, 15–17, 19, 26–27, 203, 214
Tripartite Committee for the Beedi and Cigar Industry, 58–59
Trotsky, Leon, 211
Tuberculosis, 30–31

Unemployment: in Kerala, 19; stress and, 195. *See also* Layoffs
Unions. *See* Trade unions
United Trade Union Centre, 143
Utopian socialists, 208

Vaccination rates, 17
Vanek, Yaroslav, 87–88, 106, 116, 205, 231n1
Vietnam, 231n1
Vijayan, P., 74
Vimal Beedi, 103 table 4.1

Wachtel, Howard M., 231n1
Wages: CEOs to workers, 229n5, 231n3; dearness allowance debate, 122–25, 141; in early beedi industry, 25, 29, 38, 44, 47–48, 50, 59; health, happiness, and, 194, 231n9; in Kannur, 194; of KDB management staff, 128–31; of KDB workers, 13, 76, 78–80, 121–22, 133, 142, 153–54, 182, 184–88, 194; in private sector, 10, 132, 153–54, 228n7; prize system, 132, 141